taste of home

$HOP SMART
eat great

taste of home
B O O K S

REIMAN MEDIA GROUP, LLC • GREENDALE, WI

taste of home Reader's Digest

A TASTE OF HOME/READER'S DIGEST BOOK

Editor-in-Chief: **Catherine Cassidy**
Vice President, Executive Editor/Books: **Heidi Reuter Lloyd**
Creative Director: **Howard Greenberg**
North American Chief Marketing Officer: **Lisa Karpinski**
Food Director: **Diane Werner, RD**
Senior Editor/Retail Books: **Faithann Stoner**
Editors: **Sara Rae Lancaster, Janet Briggs**
Associate Creative Director: **Edwin Robles Jr.**
Project Art Director: **Holly Patch**
Content Production Manager: **Julie Wagner**
Layout Designer: **Kathy Crawford**
Copy Chief: **Deb Warlaumont Mulvey**
Copy Editor: **Barbara Schuetz**
Recipe Asset System Manager: **Coleen Martin**
Recipe Testing & Editing: **Taste of Home Test Kitchen**
Food Photography: **Taste of Home Photo Studio**
Administrative Assistant: **Barb Czysz**

The Reader's Digest Association, Inc.
President and Chief Executive Officer: **Robert E. Guth**
President, North America: **Dan Lagani**
President/Publisher, Trade Publishing: **Harold Clarke**
Associate Publisher: **Rosanne McManus**
Vice President, Sales & Marketing: **Stacey Ashton**

Pictured on front cover: Slow-Cooked Pork Tacos (p. 51)
International Standard Book Number (10): 0-89821-965-5
International Standard Book Number (13): 978-0-89821-965-4
Library of Congress Control Number: 2011943076

For other Taste of Home books and products, visit tasteofhome.com
For more Reader's Digest products and information,
visit rd.com (in the United States)
rd.ca (in Canada)

The content of this book was published previously under the title *Taste of Home Dinner on a Dime*.

Printed in China
1 3 5 7 9 10 8 6 4 2

TABLE OF **Contents**

Shop Smart, Eat Great

It's true! You can keep a **frugal grocery list** and still **serve fantastic meals**! Just ask the editors of *Taste of Home* magazine. They've collected **hundreds of enticing yet low-cost recipes** and created **Shop Smart, Eat Great**...the ultimate source for comfort foods that **won't break your budget**.

Now it's easier than ever to **surprise your family** with a **sensational yet affordable dinner**. You won't be accused of penny pinching when you set any of these **403 dishes** on the table. Favorites such as Chuck Roast Dinner (p. 28), Plum-Glazed Country Ribs (p. 59) and Turkey Tetrazzini (p. 82) come together easily without expensive ingredients. Let **Shop Smart, Eat Great** show you how.

Thrifty Grocery Shopping Tips

It used to be that only certain items at the grocery store hit your pocketbook hard. But now prices are increasing across the board. Here are some hints to help keep your food bills in line with your budget.

USE IT OR LOSE IT.

Most people's pantries, refrigerators and freezers are brimming with an abundance of items they've stocked up on. Before another shopping trip, try to use as many items as you can. One way to do this, is to plan a few meals around what is in the pantry. This prevents having to throw out food that has become spoiled. Then, restock as items go on sale.

LEARN TO LOVE LEFTOVERS.

Instead of pushing those extra entrees to the back of the fridge (and then discovering them weeks later), eat them up within a few days. In fact, you can turn leftovers into a whole different dish or two. (For inspiration, turn to the Planned Overs chapter beginning on page 97.)

PLAN MENUS AROUND ADS.

One of the most economical ways to stay within your grocery budget is to create menus based on what's on sale at the store. This is especially true of meats. If it's not on sale, don't buy it. You can also ask if your store will honor prices in competitor ads.

WHEN A SALE IS NOT A SALE.

If it's on sale, but your family doesn't particularly like the product...it's not a sale for you. If it's more than you can use before it goes bad...it's not a sale. If two or more items are packaged together and sold at a "budget" price, but you can buy the items individually for less...it's not a sale. If you just don't need it...it's just not a sale.

MAKE A LIST...AND STICK TO IT.

It's a proven fact that shoppers buy (and spend) less when they stick to a list. Resist the urge to work off a mental list, and write it down instead.

DON'T HEAD OUT WHEN HUNGRY.

If you shop on an empty stomach, the sights and smells at the store will likely have you throwing your grocery list—not to mention your budget—out the window.

SHOP WITH A SAVER'S CARD.

If your grocery store offers a saver's card, use it! Many times, the deals at the store are available only to card members. Plus, you may get some extra discounts and money-saving coupons.

CHANGE STORES.

You can generally buy household cleaning products, paper goods and storage products for less at variety stores rather than supermarkets. Also, check out the local supersavers; they may have the items you routinely purchase for less.

STAY ON BUDGET.

Set a dollar amount of what you will spend at the store. To avoid going over the amount, consider paying in cash instead of with a debit or credit card or with a check. If you're not sure how to set a budget, track how much you spend on groceries over a two-month period, then divide by the number of weeks and that's what you spend. Then review your receipts to see if you can eliminate any nonessential items and reduce your spending.

USE COUPONS.

They can provide some savings—but only if the item is something your family really needs. Take advantage of in-store coupon displays as well as online coupon offers. Save even more by shopping on double-discount days or by using both in-store and manufacturer coupons on a single item.

THINK ABOUT WHERE YOU SHOP.

One store has a sale on milk. One has better prices on produce. Another is discounting their bakery items. It's tempting to travel to different stores to take advantage of each sale. But keep in mind the soaring gas prices... not to mention the value of your time. If possible, choose one or two nearby stores that will give you the most for your money.

PLAN YOUR TRIPS.

If a store across town carries a product you always use at a bargain price, don't make a special trip there. Instead, the next time you need to be in that area for another purpose, plan to stop at that store and stock up. This way you'll save gas and time.

BUY GENERIC.

Store brands are almost always cheaper than name brands—frequently even if you have a coupon for the name brand—and the quality is often similar. If you're unsure about the taste, buy only one item to try at home before stocking up.

COMPARISON SHOP.

Determine the true value of a product by reading the cost per unit, not just the package price. The cost per unit is listed on a sticker located on the shelf. Since not all cost-per-unit measurements use the same unit (ounces vs. pounds), carry a calculator to do the math. Just because a box is bigger doesn't mean it's cheaper.

BUY IN BULK.

There are pros and cons to buying in bulk. If you have a big family, are planning a party or have a large freezer, purchasing perishable items in bulk may be economical. Household items like paper towels, toilet paper and soap purchased in bulk are usually a good buy even for a small household. But if the bulk items won't be used within a reasonable time, they aren't a deal.

AVOID CONVENIENCE FOODS.

Convenience comes with a price. A package of cut-up chicken costs more than a whole chicken. Bagged lettuce is more expensive than a head of lettuce. Shredded cheese is more expensive than a block of cheese. Of course, when you buy convenience, you're saving on your time. You'll need to consider the cost of the convenience item vs. the value of your time.

BUY IN SEASON.

Fresh fruits and vegetables are more affordable during peak months. If the item is suitable for freezing, buy extra and freeze for a later use. Rely on frozen or canned products when they are out of season.

BEWARE OF MARKETING PLOYS.

Higher-priced items (like name-brand products) and impulse products are usually placed on shelves at eye level, on island displays, at end caps and at checkouts. Avoid the temptation to grab what you see first.

REMEMBER RAIN CHECKS AND REBATES.

If the store is out of a sale item, take the time to get a rain check. Rebate checks are another great way to get some cash back.

SKIP SNACKS.

Snack foods are overpriced when compared to the nutritional value they provide. If you do purchase them, do so only when they're on sale or with a coupon.

STAY AWAY FROM BOTTLED WATER.

Sure, bottled water is convenient, but it's also costly...to both your budget and the environment. Instead, turn on your tap. If you need filtered water, buy an inexpensive system you can keep in your refrigerator. Fill reusable plastic bottles when heading out.

Grocery Shopping Guidelines—Aisle by Aisle

PRODUCE

- Buy fresh fruit and vegetables only when on sale and when in season.
- Beware of "Buy One/Get One Free" offers. It's a good deal only if you can use it before it spoils.
- Before buying bags of apples, oranges, onions or potatoes, make sure none of the items is bruised or spoiled.
- Instead of purchasing expensive bagged salad greens, buy in bulk.
- Baby carrots can break the bank. Instead, buy whole carrots and cut them yourself.

MEATS & SEAFOOD

- Meats are one of the most expensive items at the store, so plan your menus to use smaller portions.
- Never buy full-price meats and seafood. Stock up when on sale and freeze what you don't need.
- It's more economical to buy "whole" meats (like pork roasts, large beef cuts, a package of ground beef and whole chickens) than it is to buy "convenient" cuts (like pork chops, steak for stir-frys, hamburger patties and boneless, skinless chicken breasts).
- Look for inexpensive beef cuts and help tenderize them by marinating or slow cooking them.
- Walk past cuts of meat that have already been marinated, stuffed or seasoned. They are generally more expensive. Do the seasoning at home.
- Turn to other sources of protein such as canned tuna, salmon and beans.

CANNED GOODS

- Buy generic brands and stock up when on sale.

FROZEN FOODS

- Turn to frozen fruits and vegetables when fresh varieties are not in season and are more expensive.
- Don't buy veggies with sauces. They're more expensive (and not as healthy).
- Skip buying frozen pancakes, French toast and waffles and make your own. Freeze leftovers for fast breakfasts in the future.

BREADS, CEREALS AND PASTA

- Day-old breads are cheaper and are great for toast, bread crumbs and stuffing.
- Bulk hot cereals cost less than the individual packets.
- Bigger boxes of cold cereal are more economical than individual boxes.
- Plain pasta and rice are more affordable than kits or mixes with sauces.

DAIRY

- Need shredded cheese? Buy a block and shred it at home.
- Check the milk prices at your local gas station mini mart. Milk is often less expensive there than in the supermarket.

Cost-Effective Pantry

Did you know that a well-organized pantry can save you money? Think about it. Have you ever bought a duplicate item because you couldn't remember if you already had one at home? Have you ever picked up a can from your shelves only to see that the expiration date has come and gone? Do you continue to buy canned goods even though you have plenty to use at home?

It's time to stop needlessly stocking your pantry by getting organized. These tips can help.

1 Empty everything out of the pantry and put it on a counter or table.

2 Wipe down shelves and dry thoroughly.

3 Decide to save or discard each item. If you know you'll never use the item (and if it's not past the expiration date), donate it to a local food pantry.

4 Group like items together:

- Baking items (mixes, frosting, decorating items)
- Beverages and drink mixes
- Canned fruits and vegetables
- Canned soups
- Cereals and breakfast items
- Paper goods like plates, napkins and utensils
- Pasta and rice
- Sauces and condiments
- Snacks

5 Think about storage items that would make your pantry more useful, such as:

- Airtight containers for flour and sugar
- Baskets
- Hooks
- Lighting
- Pull-out drawers
- Racks for soup or soda cans
- Small plastic containers for little items like mixes
- A spice jar organizer
- Stepstool to reach items on high shelves
- Tiered shelves

6 Restock your shelves, keeping the following in mind:

- Don't put heavy, bulky items up too high. Place heavy items like soda and juice bottles on bottom shelves.
- Turn items so you can easily read labels.
- Place frequently used items at eye level.
- Label the shelves so anyone in the family can easily put the items away in the correct place.
- Rotate items as you restock so that the first in is the first out.

7 Make two lists as you work: one for items to add to your grocery list and one for an inventory of items in the pantry. Mount the pantry inventory list inside the pantry along with a pen or pencil.

8 Clean out the pantry every six months.

Stocking Up and Storage Guidelines

Stocking your pantry, refrigerator and freezer with the ingredients and foods you use most often can simplify menu planning and dinner preparation. Having a variety of meat, poultry and seafood in the freezer makes it easy to select a main dish. And keeping your refrigerator and pantry stocked with the fresh foods and packaged products called for in your favorite recipes means there's no need to make a last-minute shopping trip.

Plus, it's helpful to know you have these items stocked in your kitchen should you want to serve an impromptu meal to unexpected guests.

Stocking up can trim your grocery bill in the long run, too, because you can take advantage of weekly sales and more economical bulk pricing. But you won't save money if the items you buy spoil or lose their flavor before you use them up. Carefully choose the size of packages to be sure you'll finish them before the use-by dates listed. If you know you won't be using an item within a day or two and it's suitable for freezer storage, freeze it immediately using the guidelines that follow.

PANTRY STORAGE

Check the sell-by or use-by dates on pantry items. Discard items that are past those dates. In the pantry, store opened items tightly closed and place in a cool, dry place. Times given in the chart that follows are for pantry storage of opened items.

REFRIGERATED FOODS

The use-by date on refrigerated items is only for the unopened item. Use the times given in the chart for opened foods. Keep the refrigerator temperature between 34°-40°. In the refrigerator, store leftovers in covered refrigerator containers or wrap them in plastic wrap or foil. Resealable plastic bags also are great for storage.

FROZEN FOODS

For the best quality, foods should be frozen in a freezer that maintains 0° and is at least two-thirds full. Cool cooked food quickly before freezing. Store food in containers that are moisture-proof and vapor-proof, such as foil, freezer bags, freezer wrap and plastic freezer containers. Remove as much air as possible when packaging the food. Label and date packages before freezing. Spread out the packages for quicker freezing, and then stack them after they are solidly frozen.

Defrost foods in the refrigerator, microwave oven or cold water. Generally, small items will defrost overnight in the refrigerator. Most items take 1 or 2 days. Bulky, large items will take even longer to thaw. To defrost in a microwave oven, follow the manufacturer's directions. To defrost in cold water, place food in a watertight plastic storage bag. Place the bag in cold water. Change the water every 30 minutes until the food is thawed.

Food Item	Opened Item Pantry Storage	Opened Item Refrigerator Temperature 34°-40°	Freezer Temperature 0°
DAIRY			
Butter		1 to 3 months	6 to 9 months
CHEESE			
Brie		1 week	6 months
Cottage/ricotta cheese		1 week	not suitable
Cream cheese		2 weeks	not suitable
Cheddar, brick, Monterey Jack, Swiss		3 to 4 weeks	6 months
Mozzarella		1 week	6 months
Parmesan/Romano, grated		2 months	6 months
CREAM			
Ultrapasteurized		1 month	not suitable
Whipping, half-and-half		3 days	2 to 4 months
EGGS			
Whole (in the shell)		4 to 5 weeks	not suitable
Whites, uncooked		2 to 4 days	12 months
Yolks, uncooked		2 to 4 days	12 months

Food Item	Opened Item Pantry Storage	Opened Item Refrigerator Temperature 34°-40°	Freezer Temperature 0°
MILK			
Milk		7 days	3 months
Buttermilk		7 to 14 days	3 months
Evaporated		4 to 5 days	
Sweetened condensed		4 to 5 days	
Margarine		4 to 5 months	12 months
Sour Cream		7 to 21 days	not suitable
Yogurt		7 to 14 days	1 to 2 months
MEATS: BEEF, PORK, LAMB			
Fresh			
Chops		3 to 5 days	4 to 6 months
Ground Meat or Stew Meat		1 to 2 days	3 to 4 months
Roasts		3 to 5 days	4 to 12 months
Sausage, fresh		1 to 2 days	1 to 2 months
Steaks		3 to 5 days	6 to 12 months
Leftover cooked meats/ casseroles		1 to 4 days	2 to 3 months
Process Meats			
Bacon		7 days	1 month
Ham		3 to 5 days	1 to 2 months
Hot Dogs		1 week	1 to 2 months
Luncheon meat		3 to 5 days	1 to 2 months
POULTRY			
Chicken/Turkey			
Whole		1 to 2 days	1 year
Parts		1 to 2 days	9 months
Leftover, cooked		1 to 4 days	1 to 4 months
FISH & SEAFOOD			
Lean Fish (Fillets/Steaks)			
Cod, Sole, Halibut, Orange Roughy, Flounder		1 to 2 days	1 year
Fatty Fish (Fillets/Steaks)			
Catfish, Perch, Salmon, Whitefish		1 to 2 days	2 to 3 months
Crab, Cooked		1 to 2 days	3 months
Scallops/Shrimp			
Uncooked		1 to 2 days	3 to 6 months
Cooked		3 to 4 days	3 months
Leftover, cooked seafood		3 to 4 days	3 to 6 months
FRUITS			
Apples, fresh		1 to 3 weeks	
Berries, fresh		1 to 2 days	12 months
Citrus fruits, fresh		3 to 5 days	not suitable
Cherries, fresh		1 to 2 days	12 months
Juice concentrates			
Frozen			12 months
Reconstituted		6 days	
Melons, fresh		1 week	not suitable
Peaches, fresh		3 to 5 days	12 months
Pears, fresh		3 to 5 days	12 months
VEGETABLES			
Asparagus		3 to 4 days	8 to 12 months
Broccoli		3 to 5 days	8 to 12 months
Carrots		1 to 2 weeks	8 to 12 months
Cauliflower		3 to 5 days	8 to 12 months

Food Item	Opened Item Pantry Storage	Opened Item Refrigerator Temperature 34°-40°	Freezer Temperature 0°
Celery		1 to 2 weeks	not suitable
Cucumbers		3 to 5 days	not suitable
Mushrooms		2 to 3 days	not suitable
Onions			
Yellow, red	2 to 3 weeks		
Green		1 to 2 weeks	
Peppers		3 to 5 days	8 to 12 months
Potatoes	1 to 2 months	not suitable	not suitable
Salad Greens			
Head lettuce		5 to 7 days	not suitable
Loose		1 to 2 days	not suitable
Spinach		3 to 5 days	not suitable
Tomatoes	until ripened	2 to 3 days	not suitable
Vegetables, other fresh		1 to 2 days	8 to 12 months
STAPLES			
Baking Powder	18 months		
Baking Soda	18 months		
CANNED GOODS			
Fish & seafood		2 days	
Fruit		1 week	
Pasta sauces		5 days	
Vegetables		2 to 3 days	
CEREAL			
Cook before eating	6 months		
Ready to eat	2 to 3 months		
Cornmeal	12 months		
Cornstarch	18 months		
FLOUR			
All-purpose	15 months		
Whole wheat		6 months	
HERBS/SPICES			
Herbs	6 months		
Ground spices	6 months		
Whole spices	1 to 2 years		
Jams & Jelly		12 months	
Ketchup/Chili Sauce		4 to 6 months	
Mayonnaise		2 months	
Mustard		6 to 12 months	
Nuts	3 to 6 months	3 to 6 months	6 to 12 months
OILS			
Canola, corn oils	6 months		
Olive oil	4 months		
PIES			
Custard		2 to 3 days	not suitable
Fruit, unbaked			8 months
Fruit, baked		4 to 5 days	1 to 2 months
Pumpkin		4 to 5 days	2 months
RICE			
Brown	1 month	6 months	
White	2 years		
Salad Dressings		3 months	
Shortening	8 months		
Soy Sauce		12 months	
SUGAR			
Brown	4 months		
Granulated	2 years		
Worcestershire sauce	12 months		

Breakfast
& Brunch

Vegetable Ham Quiche

This easy egg dish is filled with zucchini, bell pepper, ham and cheese. With our garden produce, it's even more economical.

—Betty Albee, Buhl, Idaho

- 1 egg, lightly beaten
- 3 cups frozen shredded hash brown potatoes, thawed
- 1/4 cup grated Parmesan cheese

FILLING:

- 1-1/2 cups thinly sliced zucchini
- 1 small sweet red pepper, chopped
- 1 tablespoon butter
- 1/2 cup diced fully cooked ham
- 1 tablespoon minced fresh basil
- 1/4 teaspoon salt
- 1/4 teaspoon pepper
- 2 eggs
- 1/4 cup milk
- 3/4 cup shredded Colby-Monterey Jack cheese

1 In a large bowl, combine the egg, hash browns and Parmesan cheese. Press onto the bottom and up the sides of a greased 9-in. pie plate. Bake at 400° for 15 minutes or until crust is set and edges begin to brown.

2 Meanwhile, in a large skillet, saute zucchini and red pepper in butter for 5 minutes or until crisp-tender. Stir in the ham, basil, salt and pepper. Remove from the heat; cool slightly.

3 In a large bowl, beat eggs and milk; add zucchini mixture. Stir in cheese. Pour into crust. Bake for 15-20 minutes or until a knife inserted near the center comes out clean. Let stand for 5 minutes before cutting. **Yield:** 4 servings.

Orange Slush

I make this refreshing orange drink as a cool snack for my family, but it's also a delightful addition to breakfast or brunch.

—Amy Voights, Brodhead, Wisconsin

- 1 cup water
- 1 can (6 ounces) frozen orange juice concentrate
- 1 carton (6 ounces) vanilla yogurt
- 1/2 cup sugar
- 1/2 cup cold milk
- 1/2 teaspoon vanilla extract
- 10 to 12 ice cubes

1 In a blender, combine the water, orange juice concentrate, yogurt, sugar, milk and vanilla; cover and process until smooth. While processing, add a few ice cubes at a time until mixture achieves desired thickness. Pour into chilled glasses; serve immediately. **Yield:** 4 servings.

Tomato and Cheese Strata

This is a great make-ahead dish for brunch. It's delicious! People are always asking for the recipe.

—Molly Seidel, Edgewood, New Mexico

- 10 slices white bread
- 4 medium tomatoes, sliced 1/2 inch thick
- 1 cup (4 ounces) shredded cheddar cheese
- 4 green onions, thinly sliced
- 4 eggs
- 2 cups milk
- 1/2 teaspoon salt

1 Line a greased 8-in. square baking dish with four bread slices. Layer with half of the tomatoes, cheese and onions. Top with remaining bread (slices will overlap). Layer with remaining tomatoes, cheese and onions.

2 In a small bowl, whisk the eggs, milk and salt. Pour over the top. Cover and refrigerate overnight.

3 Remove from the refrigerator 30 minutes before baking. Bake, uncovered, at 350° for 45-50 minutes or until a knife inserted near the center comes out clean. Let stand for 5 minutes before cutting. **Yield:** 4-6 servings.

Sausage Pancakes

The batter for these fluffy pancakes features savory pork sausage. It's an easy, inexpensive way to fill up kids before school...and adults before work.

—Barbara Downey, Preston, Iowa

- 2 cups all-purpose flour
- 2 teaspoons baking powder
- 1 teaspoon salt
- 1/2 teaspoon baking soda
- 2 eggs
- 2 cups buttermilk
- 2 tablespoons vegetable oil
- 1 pound bulk pork sausage, cooked and drained
- 1-1/2 cups pancake syrup

1 In a large bowl, combine the flour, baking powder, salt and baking soda. In another bowl, beat the eggs, buttermilk and oil. Stir into dry ingredients just until moistened. Fold in sausage.

2 Pour batter by 1/4 cupfuls onto a lightly greased hot griddle; turn when bubbles form on top. Cook until second side is golden brown. Serve with syrup. **Yield:** 6 servings.

Hot Fruit and Sausage

Pineapple, brown sugar and cinnamon make plain pork sausage links extra tasty. It's a hearty dish sure to wake up taste buds.

—Marian Peterson, Wisconsin Rapids, Wisconsin

- 1 package (12 ounces) uncooked pork sausage links
- 3/4 cup pineapple tidbits
- 2 tablespoons brown sugar

Pinch ground cinnamon

- 1 medium firm banana, sliced

1 In a large skillet, cook sausage according to package directions; drain. Add pineapple, brown sugar and cinnamon; heat through. Stir in banana just before serving. **Yield:** 6 servings.

Peanut Butter Banana Oatmeal

The classic flavors of peanut butter and bananas come together in this kid- and adult-friendly oatmeal. We have eaten it many mornings.

—Deborah Purdue, Westland, Michigan

- 3 cups milk *or* water
- 1/4 teaspoon salt
- 1-1/2 cups quick-cooking oats
- 2 large bananas, sliced
- 2 tablespoons peanut butter
- 1/2 teaspoon vanilla extract

1 In a large saucepan, bring milk and salt to a boil. Stir in oats; cook for 1-2 minutes or until thickened, stirring occasionally. Remove from the heat. Stir in the bananas, peanut butter and vanilla. **Yield:** 4 servings.

Toasted Granola

I serve my family this granola with milk for cereal. We also like to use it as a topping for yogurt and ice cream...or to eat right from the container!

—Susan Lajeunesse, Colchester, Vermont

- 1 cup packed brown sugar
- 1/3 cup water
- 4 cups old-fashioned oats
- 2 cups bran flakes
- 1 jar (12 ounces) toasted wheat germ
- 2 tablespoons all-purpose flour
- 3/4 teaspoon salt
- 1/3 cup vegetable oil
- 2 teaspoons vanilla extract

1 In a large saucepan, bring brown sugar and water to a boil. Cook and stir until sugar is dissolved. Remove from the heat; set aside. In a large bowl, combine the oats, bran flakes, wheat germ, flour and salt. Stir oil and vanilla into sugar mixture; pour over oat mixture and toss to coat.

2 Transfer to two 15-in. x 10-in. x 1-in. baking pans coated with cooking spray. Bake at 250° for 1-1/4 to 1-1/2 hours or until dry and lightly browned, stirring every 15 minutes. Cool completely on wire racks. Store in an airtight container. **Yield:** 10-1/2 cups.

Chive-Ham Brunch Bake

Canned ham and biscuit mix get this brunch dish ready quickly. To lighten up the casserole a bit, try using fat-free milk and a reduced-fat biscuit/baking mix.

—Edie DeSpain, Logan, Utah

- 1/2 cup chopped onion
- 1 tablespoon butter
- 1 can (5 ounces) chunk ham, drained
- 1 medium tomato, chopped
- 2 cups biscuit/baking mix
- 1/2 cup water
- 1 cup (4 ounces) shredded Swiss *or* cheddar cheese
- 2 eggs
- 1/4 cup milk
- 1/4 teaspoon dill weed
- 1/4 teaspoon salt
- 1/8 teaspoon pepper
- 3 tablespoons minced chives

1 In a small skillet, saute onion in butter until tender. Stir in ham and tomato; set aside.

2 In a small bowl, combine biscuit mix and water; mix well. Press onto the bottom and 1/2 in. up the sides of a greased 13-in. x 9-in. x 2-in. baking dish. Spread ham mixture over the crust; sprinkle with cheese. In a bowl, beat the eggs, milk, dill, salt and pepper; pour over cheese. Sprinkle with the chives.

3 Bake, uncovered, at 350° for 25-30 minutes or until a knife inserted near the center comes out clean. Let stand for 5 minutes before cutting. **Yield: 8 servings.**

Asian Oven Omelet

A great source of low-cost protein, eggs are an ideal way to liven up any meal on a budget. If you enjoy egg foo yong, you're sure to like this recipe.

—Edna Hoffman, Hebron, Indiana

- 2 packages (3 ounces *each*) ramen noodles
- 1/2 cup thinly sliced celery
- 2 teaspoons vegetable oil
- 1 package (8 ounces) sliced fresh mushrooms
- 4 tablespoons green onions, thinly sliced, *divided*
- 2 tablespoons minced fresh gingerroot
- 3 eggs
- 6 egg whites
- 1 teaspoon sesame oil
- 1/2 teaspoon sugar
- 1/2 teaspoon salt
- 2 tablespoons reduced-sodium soy sauce

1 Discard seasoning packet from ramen noodles or save for another use. Cook noodles according to package directions. Drain and rinse in cold water; transfer to a bowl and set aside.

2 Meanwhile, in a large nonstick, ovenproof skillet over medium heat, cook celery in vegetable oil for 1 minute. Stir in the mushrooms, 2 tablespoons green onions and ginger; cook and stir for 7 minutes or until the mushrooms are lightly browned. Stir into noodles.

3 Whisk the eggs, egg whites, sesame oil, sugar and salt. Stir into noodle mixture; spread into an even layer in the skillet. Cook on medium for 2 minutes.

4 Bake, uncovered, at 350° for 10-12 minutes or until set. Cut into wedges. Sprinkle with remaining green onions. Drizzle with soy sauce. **Yield:** 6 servings.

TIP . . . .

Learn About Gingerroot

Fresh gingerroot is available in your grocer's produce section. It should have a smooth skin.

When stored in a heavy-duty resealable plastic bag, unpeeled gingerroot can be frozen for up to 1 year. When needed, simply peel and grate.

Garlic Zucchini Frittata

This flavorful egg dish can be made in minutes and is easily doubled. Sometimes I use leftover taco meat or chopped ham instead of bacon.

—Michelle Krzmarzick
Redondo Beach, California

- 1   tablespoon butter
- 1   tablespoon finely chopped onion
- 4   garlic cloves, minced
- 1   medium zucchini, shredded
- 6   eggs
- 1/4   teaspoon ground mustard
- 4   bacon strips, cooked and crumbled
- 1/4   teaspoon salt
- 1/8   teaspoon pepper
- 1/4   cup shredded Swiss cheese
- 1/4   cup sliced green onions

1 In a 10-in. ovenproof skillet, melt butter over medium-high heat. Add the onion and garlic; saute for 1 minute. Add the zucchini; cook for 3 minutes or until tender.

2 In a large bowl, beat eggs and mustard. Pour into skillet. Sprinkle with bacon, salt and pepper. As eggs set, lift edges, letting uncooked portion flow underneath. Cook until eggs are nearly set, about 7 minutes. Meanwhile, preheat broiler.

3 Place skillet under the broiler, 6 in. from the heat, for 30-60 seconds or until the eggs are completely set. Sprinkle with cheese and green onions. Broil 30 seconds longer or until cheese is melted. Cut into wedges. **Yield:** 4 servings.

French Toast Fingers

Why buy French toast sticks when you can make your own at home for less? These are great for a buffet...and kids love them.

—Mavis Diment, Marcus, Iowa

- 2   eggs
- 1/4   cup milk
- 1/4   teaspoon salt
- 1/2   cup strawberry preserves
- 8   slices day-old white bread

Confectioners' sugar, optional

1 In a small bowl, whisk the eggs, milk and salt; set aside. Spread preserves on four slices of bread; top with the remaining bread. Trim crusts; cut each sandwich into three strips.

2 Dip both sides in egg mixture. Cook on a lightly greased hot griddle for 2 minutes on each side or until golden brown. Dust with confectioners' sugar if desired. **Yield:** 4 servings.

Baked Southern Grits

I turn a southern favorite into a tasty, low-fat dish. Jalepeno peppers add a welcome kick while reduced-fat cheese creates a rich texture.

—Karen Mau, Jacksboro, Tennessee

- 4 cups water
- 1 cup quick-cooking grits
- 4 egg whites
- 2 eggs
- 1-1/2 cups (6 ounces) shredded reduced-fat cheddar cheese
- 1/2 cup fat-free milk
- 1 to 2 jalapeno peppers, seeded and chopped
- 1/2 teaspoon garlic salt
- 1/4 teaspoon white pepper
- 4 green onions, chopped, *divided*

1 In a large saucepan, bring water to a boil. Add grits; cook and stir over medium heat for 5 minutes or until thickened. Remove from the heat.

2 In a small bowl, whisk egg whites and eggs. Stir a small amount of hot grits into eggs; return all to the pan, stirring constantly. Stir in the cheese, milk, jalapenos, garlic salt, pepper and half of the onions.

3 Transfer to a 2-qt. baking dish coated with cooking spray. Bake, uncovered, at 350° for 30-35 minutes or until golden brown. Sprinkle with remaining onions. **Yield:** 8 servings.

EDITOR'S NOTE: When cutting hot peppers, disposable gloves are recommended. Avoid touching your face.

TIP

Separating an Egg

Place an egg separator over a custard cup or a measuring cup; crack egg into the separator. As each egg is separated, place yolk in another bowl and empty egg whites into a mixing bowl. It's easier to separate eggs when they are cold.

Yogurt Breakfast Drink

Sleepyheads will savor this dreamy smoothie. Simply blend yogurt, milk and orange juice concentrate for a fresh start to your day.

—Renee Gastineau, Seattle, Washington

- 2 cups (16 ounces) reduced-fat vanilla yogurt
- 2 cups (16 ounces) reduced-fat peach yogurt
- 1/2 cup frozen orange juice concentrate
- 1/2 cup fat-free milk
- 2 cups ice cubes

1 In a blender, combine the first four ingredients; cover and process until smooth. Add ice cubes; cover and process until smooth. Pour into glasses; serve immediately. **Yield:** 6 servings.

Lightly Scrambled Eggs

This fluffy entree is enhanced with sour cream, green onions and cheese.

—Patricia Kaliska, Phillips, Wisconsin

- 9 egg whites
- 3 eggs
- 1/2 cup reduced-fat sour cream
- 1/4 cup fat-free milk
- 2 green onions, thinly sliced
- 1/4 teaspoon salt
- 1/8 teaspoon pepper
- 6 drops yellow food coloring, optional
- 3/4 cup shredded reduced-fat cheddar cheese

1 In a large bowl, whisk the egg whites and eggs. Add the sour cream, milk, onions, salt, pepper and food coloring if desired.

2 Pour into a large nonstick skillet coated with cooking spray; cook and gently stir over medium heat until eggs are completely set. Remove from the heat. Sprinkle with cheese; cover and let stand for 5 minutes to allow cheese to melt. **Yield:** 6 servings.

Baked Omelet Roll

This interesting omelet bakes in the oven, so you don't have to keep a constant eye on it like eggs you cook on the stovetop.

—Susan Hudon, Fort Wayne, Indiana

- 6 eggs
- 1 cup milk
- 1/2 cup all-purpose flour
- 1/2 teaspoon salt
- 1/4 teaspoon pepper
- 1 cup (4 ounces) shredded cheddar cheese

1 Place eggs and milk in a blender. Add the flour, salt and pepper; cover and process until smooth. Pour into a greased 13-in. x 9-in. x 2-in. baking pan. Bake at 450° for 20 minutes or until eggs are set.

2 Sprinkle with cheese. Roll up omelet in pan, starting with a short side. Place with seam side down on a serving platter. Cut into 3/4-in. slices. **Yield:** 6 servings.

After-Holiday Ham on Biscuits

When my children were young, they loved to color lots of Easter eggs, so this recipe was a great way to use them up.

—Billie George, Saskatoon, Saskatchewan

- 1 cup all-purpose flour
- 2 teaspoons baking powder
- 1/4 teaspoon salt
- 3 tablespoons cold butter
- 1/2 cup milk

CREAM SAUCE:

- 1 cup cubed fully cooked ham
- 1/4 cup chopped onion
- 3 tablespoons butter
- 1/2 teaspoon chicken bouillon granules
- 1/2 teaspoon Worcestershire sauce
- 1/8 teaspoon pepper
- 3 tablespoons all-purpose flour
- 1-3/4 cups milk
- 3 hard-cooked eggs, chopped
- 1 tablespoon minced fresh parsley

1 In a large bowl, combine the flour, baking powder and salt. Cut in butter until mixture resembles coarse crumbs. Stir in the milk just until moistened. Turn onto a lightly floured surface; knead 8-10 times.

2 Pat or roll out to 1/2-in. thickness; cut with a floured 2-1/2-in. biscuit cutter. Place 2 in. apart on a greased baking sheet. Bake at 425° for 10-12 minutes or until golden brown.

3 Meanwhile, in a large skillet, saute ham and onion in butter for 3-4 minutes or until onion is crisp-tender. Stir in the bouillon, Worcestershire sauce and pepper. Combine flour and milk until smooth; gradually stir into pan. Bring to a boil; cook and stir for 2 minutes or until thickened. Gently stir in eggs and parsley.

4 Split warm biscuits in half horizontally; top with ham mixture. **Yield:** 4 servings.

Cinnamon Breakfast Bites

These early-morning treats with a sweet, crispy coating are baked in the oven instead of deep-fried.

—Ruth Hastings, Louisville, Illinois

- 1-1/3   cups all-purpose flour
- 1   cup crisp rice cereal, coarsely crushed
- 2   tablespoons plus 1/2 cup sugar, *divided*
- 3   teaspoons baking powder
- 1/2   teaspoon salt
- 1/4   cup butter-flavored shortening
- 1/2   cup milk
- 1   teaspoon ground cinnamon
- 1/4   cup butter, melted

1 In a large bowl, combine the flour, cereal, 2 tablespoons sugar, baking powder and salt; cut in shortening until mixture resembles coarse crumbs. Stir in milk just until moistened. Shape into 1-in. balls.

2 In a shallow bowl, combine cinnamon and remaining sugar. Dip balls in butter, then roll in cinnamon-sugar.

3 Arrange in a single layer in an 8-in. round baking pan. Bake at 425° for 15-18 minutes or until toothpick comes out clean. **Yield:** 6 servings (2-1/2 dozen).

Old-Fashioned Doughnuts

These finger-licking good delicacies are so light and luscious, my family has always referred to them as "Angel Food Doughnuts!" They're lovely at Christmas with a dusting of confectioners' sugar.

—Darlene Brenden, Salem, Oregon

- 1/2   cup sour cream
- 1/2   cup buttermilk
- 1   cup sugar
- 3   eggs
- 1   teaspoon vanilla extract
- 4   cups all-purpose flour
- 2   teaspoons baking powder
- 1/2   teaspoon baking soda
- 1/4   teaspoon salt
- Oil for deep-fat frying
- Confectioners' sugar

1 In a large bowl, beat sour cream and buttermilk until smooth. Beat in sugar until smooth. Beat in eggs and vanilla just until combined. Combine the flour, baking powder, baking soda and salt. Gradually add flour mixture to buttermilk mixture just until combined (dough will be sticky). Cover and refrigerate for 2-3 hours.

2 Turn dough onto a well-floured surface; knead for 2-3 minutes or until smooth. Roll out to 1/2-in. thickness. Cut with a floured 2-1/2-in. doughnut cutter.

3 In an electric skillet or deep-fat fryer, heat oil to 375°. Fry doughnuts, a few at a time, for 3 minutes or until golden brown on each side. Drain oil on paper towels. Dust with confectioners' sugar if desired. **Yield:** about 1-1/2 dozen doughnuts plus doughnut holes.

Ham Mushroom Pie

This hearty brunch recipe was given to me by my grandmother, who loved making fast and delicious meals. Even the most finicky eaters enjoy it.

—Howie Wiener, Spring Hill, Florida

- 1 boneless ham steak (about 1 pound)
- 1 pastry shell (9 inches), baked
- 2/3 cup condensed cream of mushroom soup, undiluted
- 2/3 cup sour cream
- 3 eggs, lightly beaten
- 2 tablespoons minced chives

Dash pepper

1 Cut ham to fit the bottom of pastry shell; place in shell. In a large bowl, combine the remaining ingredients. Pour over ham. Cover edges loosely with foil.

2 Bake at 425° for 35-40 minutes or until a knife inserted near the center comes out clean. **Yield:** 6 servings.

Zucchini Pancakes

These are a tasty change of pace from ordinary potato pancakes. Paired with any entree, they're a budget-conscious way to round out a brunch.

—Charlotte Goldberg, Honey Grove, Pennsylvania

- 1-1/2 cups shredded zucchini
- 1 egg, lightly beaten
- 2 tablespoons biscuit/baking mix
- 3 tablespoons grated Parmesan cheese

Dash pepper

- 1 tablespoon vegetable oil

1 In a large bowl, combine the zucchini, egg, baking mix, cheese and pepper. In a large skillet, heat oil over medium heat; drop 1/4 cupfuls of batter into skillet. Fry for 2 minutes on each side or until golden brown. **Yield:** 4 servings.

Beef

Roast Beef and Gravy

This is by far the simplest way to make roast beef and gravy. On busy days, I can put this main dish in the slow cooker and forget about it. My family likes it with mashed potatoes and fruit salad.

—Abby Metzger, Larchwood, Iowa

- 1 boneless beef chuck roast (3 pounds)
- 2 cans (10-3/4 ounces *each*) condensed cream of mushroom soup, undiluted
- 1/3 cup sherry *or* beef broth
- 1 envelope onion soup mix

1 Cut roast in half; place in a 3-qt. slow cooker. In a large bowl, combine the remaining ingredients; pour over roast. Cover and cook on low for 8-9 hours or until meat is tender. **Yield:** 8-10 servings.

Beef Cabbage Hash

As a busy working mother of two, I often rely on this comforting all-in-one skillet recipe when we need a quick meal. It's simple and satisfying.

—Penny Wolverton, Parsons, Kansas

- 1 pound ground beef
- 4 medium baking potatoes, peeled and julienned
- 4 cups shredded cabbage
- 1 large onion, sliced and quartered
- 3/4 cup water
- 1 teaspoon salt
- 1/2 teaspoon pepper

1 In a large skillet, cook beef over medium heat until no longer pink; drain. Add all the remaining ingredients. Cover and cook over medium-high heat for 10 minutes or until potatoes are tender. **Yield:** 4 servings.

Braised Beef and Mushrooms

Our home economists came up with this flavorful treatment for beef. Bits of vegetables in a hearty wine-flavored sauce make the meat delicious.

—**Taste of Home Test Kitchen**

1-1/2	pounds boneless beef chuck roast, cut into 3/4-inch cubes
1	tablespoon olive oil
1	cup finely chopped turnips
1/2	finely chopped onion
3	cups sliced fresh mushrooms
6	garlic cloves, minced
1-3/4	cups red wine vinegar *or* reduced-sodium beef broth
1-1/4	cups water
1/4	cup tomato paste
3	teaspoons sodium-free beef bouillon granules
2	teaspoons prepared horseradish
1-1/2	teaspoons dried tarragon
1/4	teaspoon pepper
4	teaspoons cornstarch
2	tablespoons cold water

Hot cooked noodles, optional

1 In a large nonstick saucepan, brown meat in oil; drain. Remove meat from pan; set aside. In same pan, cook turnip and onion for 3 minutes or until lightly browned. Stir in mushrooms and garlic; cook and stir for 3-4 minutes or until turnips are tender.

2 In a small bowl, combine the wine or broth, water, tomato paste, bouillon granules, horseradish, tarragon and pepper until smooth. Gradually stir into skillet. Return meat to pan. Bring to a boil. Reduce the heat; cover and simmer for about 1-1/4 hours or until meat is tender. Uncover; simmer 15 minutes longer.

3 In a small bowl, combine cornstarch and cold water until smooth. Gradually stir into pan. Bring to a boil; cook and stir for 2 minutes or until thickened. Serve with noodles if desired. **Yield:** 4 servings.

Barbecued Beef Sandwiches

The great thing about this recipe—especially for non-cabbage lovers!—is that you can't taste the cabbage in the meat. Yet, at the same time, it adds a nice heartiness and moistness to it.

—**Denise Marshall, Bagley, Wisconsin**

2	pounds beef stew meat
2	cups water
4	cups shredded cabbage
1/2	cup bottled barbecue sauce
1/2	cup ketchup
1/3	cup Worcestershire sauce
1	tablespoon prepared horseradish
1	tablespoon prepared mustard
10	hamburger *or* other sandwich buns, split

1 In a covered Dutch oven or saucepan, simmer beef in water for 1-1/2 hours or until tender. Drain cooking liquid, reserving 3/4 cup.

2 Cool beef; shred and return to the Dutch oven. Add cabbage, barbecue sauce, ketchup, Worcestershire sauce, horseradish, mustard and the reserved cooking liquid. Cover and simmer for 1 hour. Serve warm in buns. **Yield:** 10 servings.

1. In a large skillet, saute the beef, green pepper and onion in butter until meat is no longer pink. Stir in the tomato sauce, mushrooms, salt, basil and pepper. Bring to a boil. Reduce heat; cover and simmer for 20-25 minutes or until meat is tender.

2. Cook fettuccine according to package directions; drain. Serve with beef mixture; sprinkle with Parmesan cheese. **Yield:** 6 servings.

Beef Shish Kabobs

These kabobs can be assembled ahead, so they're ideal for family get-togethers. They're a delicious alternative to hot dogs and hamburgers.

—**Gerri Layo, Massena, New York**

- 1 cup soy sauce
- 1/2 cup red wine vinegar
- 1/2 cup water
- 1/2 cup vegetable oil
- 1 teaspoon dried oregano
- 1/2 teaspoon onion powder
- 1 to 2 garlic cloves, minced
- 1 pound beef stew meat, cut into 1-1/2-inch cubes
- 1 pound sliced bacon, halved widthwise
- 1 can (8 ounces) sliced water chestnuts, drained
- 1 can (8 ounces) pineapple chunks, drained

1. In a large resealable plastic bag, combine the first seven ingredients. Reserve 1/3 cup for basting; cover and refrigerate. Add beef to bag; seal and turn to coat. Refrigerate overnight. In a large skillet, over medium heat, partially cook bacon. Wrap each piece around a water chestnut slice.

2. Drain and discard marinade from beef. On four metal or soaked wooden skewers, alternately thread bacon-wrapped water chestnuts, pineapple and beef.

3. Cover and grill over medium heat for 10-15 minutes or until meat reaches desired doneness, basting frequently with reserved marinade. **Yield:** 4 servings.

Pepper Steak Fettuccine

My husband is a pasta lover, so I created this tangy dish for him. Strips of round steak, green pepper and onion make it hearty—and it's economical, too.

—**Crystal West, New Straitsville, Ohio**

- 1-1/4 pounds boneless beef round steak (1/2 inch thick), cut into thin strips
- 1 medium green pepper, julienned
- 1 medium onion, julienned
- 2 tablespoons butter
- 2 cans (15 ounces *each*) tomato sauce
- 1 can (4 ounces) mushroom stems and pieces, drained
- 1-1/2 teaspoons salt
- 1 teaspoon dried basil
- 1/4 teaspoon pepper
- 1 package (16 ounces) fettuccine
- 1/3 cup shredded Parmesan cheese

Country-Fried Steak

This down-home main course is simple to make and so delicious!

—Betty Claycomb, Alverton, Pennsylvania

- 3/4 cup buttermilk
- 1 cup crushed saltines
- 1/2 cup all-purpose flour
- 1/2 teaspoon salt
- 1/2 teaspoon pepper
- 4 beef cube steaks (1 pound)
- 3 tablespoons vegetable oil
- 1 can (10-3/4 ounces) condensed cream of mushroom soup, undiluted
- 1 cup milk

1 Place buttermilk and saltine crumbs in separate shallow bowls. In another shallow bowl, combine flour, salt and pepper. Coat cube steaks with flour mixture, then dip in milk and roll in saltine crumbs.

2 In a large skillet, heat oil over medium-high heat. Cook steaks in oil for 2-3 minutes on each side or until golden and no longer pink. Remove and keep warm. Add soup and milk to skillet; bring to a boil, stirring to loosen browned bits from pan. Serve gravy with steaks. **Yield:** 4 servings.

Oven Beef Hash

With just the two of us, we usually have leftovers of some sort, so hash is a regular menu item at our house. It's nice to have a hash dish that I can pop in the oven.

—Dorothy Pritchett, Wills Point, Texas

- 3 cups diced cooked potatoes
- 1-1/2 cups cubed cooked roast beef
- 1 can (5 ounces) evaporated milk
- 1/4 cup minced fresh parsley
- 1/4 cup finely chopped onion
- 2 teaspoons Worcestershire sauce
- 1/2 teaspoon salt
- 1/8 teaspoon pepper
- 1/3 cup crushed saltines
- 1 tablespoon butter, melted

1 In a large bowl, combine the first eight ingredients. Spoon into a greased 1-1/2-qt. baking dish. Combine saltines and butter; sprinkle over top. Bake, uncovered, at 350° for 30 minutes or until heated through. **Yield:** 4 servings.

Chuck Roast Dinner

A tasty tomato sauce nicely coats this comforting combination of beef, potatoes and carrots. My father gave me the recipe.

—Cindy Miller, Estes Park, Colorado

- 1 boneless beef chuck roast (3 pounds), cut into serving-size pieces
- 3 medium potatoes, peeled and cut into chunks
- 4 medium carrots, cut into chunks
- 2 cans (11-1/2 ounces *each*) tomato juice
- 1/4 cup Worcestershire sauce
- 3 tablespoons quick-cooking tapioca

1 In a 5-qt. slow cooker, combine all ingredients. Cover and cook on high for 6-8 hours or until meat is tender. **Yield:** 8-10 servings.

Baked Salisbury Steak

I bake ground beef patties in a mushroom soup gravy to make this mild, moist entree. The recipe is easy to prepare and always brings compliments.

—Elsie Epp, Newton, Kansas

- 1 cup quick-cooking oats
- 2 eggs, lightly beaten
- 1/2 cup *each* chopped green pepper, celery and onion
- 1/2 teaspoon salt
- 2 pounds ground beef
- 1 can (10-3/4 ounces) condensed golden mushroom *or* cream of mushroom soup, undiluted
- 3/4 cup water
- 1/4 teaspoon pepper

1. In a large bowl, combine the oats, eggs, green pepper, celery, onion and salt. Crumble beef over mixture and mix well. Shape into eight oval patties. In a large skillet, brown patties on both sides; drain.

2. Place patties in an ungreased 13-in. x 9-in. x 2-in. baking dish. Combine the soup, water and pepper; pour over beef. Cover and bake at 350° for 30-35 minutes or until the meat is no longer pink. **Yield:** 8 servings.

Italian Beef Sandwiches

With a little kick and plenty of tender meat and juices, these hearty sandwiches eat like a meal! If you'd like, add a slice of provolone for a real treat.

—Troy Parkos, Verona, Wisconsin

- 1 boneless beef chuck roast (3 pounds)
- 1 teaspoon Italian seasoning
- 1/4 teaspoon cayenne pepper
- 1/4 teaspoon pepper
- 1/4 cup water
- 1 jar (16 ounces) sliced pepperoncinis, undrained
- 1 medium sweet red pepper, julienned
- 1 medium green pepper, julienned
- 1 garlic clove, minced
- 1 envelope reduced-sodium onion soup mix
- 2 tablespoons Worcestershire sauce
- 2 loaves (1 pound each) Italian bread, halved lengthwise

1. Cut roast in half; place in a 5-qt. slow cooker. Sprinkle with the Italian seasoning, cayenne and pepper. Add water. Cover and cook on high for 4 hours or until meat is tender.

2. Remove roast; shred meat with two forks and return to the slow cooker. In a large bowl, combine the pepperoncinis, peppers, garlic, soup mix and Worcestershire sauce; pour over meat. Cover and cook on high for 1 hour longer or until peppers are tender.

3. Spoon beef mixture over the bottom halves of bread; replace bread tops. Cut each loaf into six sandwiches. **Yield:** 12 servings.

Spanish Rice Dinner

This recipe has been a family favorite since I discovered it in our church cookbook. I always have the ingredients on hand, and it reheats very well in the microwave.

—Jeri Dobrowski, Beach, North Dakota

- 1 pound ground beef
- 1-1/2 cups cooked long grain rice
- 1 can (14-1/2 ounces) stewed tomatoes
- 1 can (14-1/2 ounces) cut green beans, drained
- 1 tablespoon dried minced onion
- 1 tablespoon sugar
- 1 teaspoon salt
- 1 teaspoon Worcestershire sauce
- 1/2 teaspoon ground mustard
- 1/4 teaspoon garlic powder
- 1/8 teaspoon pepper
- 1/8 teaspoon hot pepper sauce

1. In a large skillet, cook beef over medium heat until no longer pink; drain. Stir in the remaining ingredients. Bring to a boil. Reduce heat; cover and simmer for 5-10 minutes or until heated through. **Yield:** 4 servings.

1 In a large skillet, cook the beef, celery and onion over medium heat, until meat is no longer pink; drain. Stir in the flour, salt, oregano and pepper until blended. Add tomato sauce and peas; simmer for 5 minutes.

2 Transfer to a greased 13-in. x 9-in. x 2-in. baking dish. Separate biscuits; arrange over beef mixture. Sprinkle with cheese. Bake, uncovered, at 350° for 20 minutes or until biscuits are golden brown and cheese is melted. **Yield:** 6 servings.

TIP

Tips for Biscuit-Topped Casseroles

Biscuits baked on top of casseroles can become doughy on the bottom. For better heat circulation, use a shallow baking dish and arrange biscuits so they're not touching each other. Also, the casserole ingredients should be warm before the biscuits are placed on top.

Ground Beef 'n' Biscuits

This recipe was given to me by a good friend when I got married, and I have used it many times since. The saucy meal is both family- and budget-pleasing.

—Lois Hill, Trinity, North Carolina

1-1/2	pounds ground beef
1/2	cup chopped celery
1/2	cup chopped onion
2	tablespoons all-purpose flour
1	teaspoon salt
1/4	teaspoon dried oregano
1/8	teaspoon pepper
2	cans (8 ounces *each*) tomato sauce
1	package (10 ounces) frozen peas
1	tube (7-1/2 ounces) refrigerated buttermilk biscuits
1	cup (4 ounces) shredded cheddar cheese

Stuffed Cube Steaks

A vegetable stuffing turns an inexpensive cut of meat into a satisfying main dish. Complete the meal with an easy side dish.

—Mary Reynolds, Gardner, Massachusetts

8	beef cube steaks (2 pounds)
1-1/4	teaspoons salt, *divided*
1/4	teaspoon pepper
1/2	cup French salad dressing
1	cup shredded carrots
3/4	cup finely chopped onion
3/4	cup finely chopped celery
1/2	cup finely chopped green pepper
1/4	cup beef broth
2	tablespoons vegetable oil
1	tablespoon cornstarch
1/4	teaspoon browning sauce, optional

1. Pound steaks to 1/4-in. thickness. Sprinkle with 1 teaspoon salt and pepper. Place in a greased 13-in. x 9-in. x 2-in. baking dish. Spoon salad dressing over steaks. Cover and chill for 1 hour.

2. In a large saucepan, combine the vegetables, broth and remaining salt. Cover and cook over medium heat for 6-8 minutes or until tender. Drain, reserving liquid.

3. Spoon 1/4 cup vegetable mixture onto each steak; roll up and secure with toothpicks. In a large nonstick skillet, brown meat rolls in oil on all sides. Cover and simmer for 35-40 minutes or until meat is tender. Remove with a slotted spoon; keep warm.

4. Combine cornstarch and reserved cooking liquid until smooth; stir into pan drippings. Bring to a boil; cook and stir for 2 minutes or until thickened. Add browning sauce if desired. Remove toothpicks. Serve with steak rolls. **Yield:** 8 servings.

Slow Cooker Beef Au Jus

It's easy to fix this roast, which has lots of onion flavor. Sometimes I also add cubed potatoes and baby carrots to the slow cooker to make a terrific meal plus leftovers.

—**Carol Hille, Grand Junction, Colorado**

    1   boneless beef rump roast (3 pounds)
    1   large onion, sliced
  3/4   cup reduced-sodium beef broth
    1   envelope (1 ounce) au jus gravy mix
    2   garlic cloves, halved
  1/4   teaspoon pepper

1. Cut roast in half. In a large nonstick skillet coated with cooking spray, brown meat on all sides over medium-high heat.

2. Place onion in a 5-qt. slow cooker. Top with meat. Combine the broth, gravy mix, garlic and pepper; pour over the meat. Cover and cook on low for 6-7 hours or until meat and onion are tender.

3. Remove meat to a cutting board. Let stand for 10 minutes. Thinly slice meat and return to the slow cooker; serve with pan juices and onion. **Yield:** 10 servings.

Family-Pleasing Sloppy Joes

Feeding a family doesn't have to break your budget. These simple-to-prepare sandwiches satisfy hearty appetites.

—**Patricia Ringle, Edgar, Wisconsin**

    2   pounds ground beef
    1   large onion, chopped
 1-1/4 cups ketchup
  1/2   cup water
    1   tablespoon brown sugar
    1   tablespoon white vinegar
  1/2   teaspoon salt
  1/2   teaspoon ground mustard
  1/2   teaspoon chili powder
  1/4   teaspoon ground allspice
    8   sandwich buns, split

1. In a Dutch oven, cook beef and onion over medium heat until meat is no longer pink; drain. Stir in the ketchup, water, brown sugar, vinegar, salt, mustard, chili powder and allspice. Bring to a boil. Reduce heat; simmer, uncovered, for 35-40 minutes or until heated through. Spoon about 1/2 cup meat mixture onto each bun. **Yield:** 8 servings.

Pineapple Beef Stir-Fry

Chock-full of veggies, seasonings and pineapple chunks, this stir-fry makes a colorful presentation when I serve it to relatives and friends.

—Helen Vail, Glenside, Pennsylvania

1	can (20 ounces) pineapple chunks
1/2	cup minced fresh cilantro
1/4	cup soy sauce
1	tablespoon ground ginger
1	pound boneless beef round steak, thinly sliced
1	teaspoon cornstarch
2	teaspoons vegetable oil
1	medium sweet red pepper, thinly sliced
1/2	cup cut fresh green beans
1	tablespoon chopped green chilies
2	garlic cloves, minced
2	green onions, sliced

Hot cooked rice

1 Drain the pineapple, reserving 1 cup pineapple and 3/4 cup juice. (Cover and refrigerate remaining pineapple for another use.) In a small bowl, combine the cilantro, soy sauce, ginger and reserved pineapple juice. Remove 3/4 cup; cover and refrigerate.

2 In a large resealable plastic bag, combine the beef and remaining marinade. Seal bag and turn to coat; refrigerate for 30 minutes.

3 Drain and discard marinade. Combine cornstarch and reserved juice mixture until smooth. In a skillet, stir-fry beef in oil for 5-6 minutes. Remove beef with a slotted spoon and keep warm. Add the red pepper, beans, chilies and garlic in skillet; stir-fry for 5 minutes.

4 Stir the juice mixture; stir into the skillet. Bring to a boil; cook and stir for 1 minute or until slightly thickened. Add the onions, beef and the reserved pineapple; heat through. Serve with rice. **Yield:** 4 servings.

Garlic Swiss Steak

Cooking round steak slowly in a tangy tomato sauce makes the meat turn out tender every time. My family loves this beefy budget-stretcher.

—Patricia Craft, Greenville, Texas

1-1/2	pounds bone-in round steak
1/3	cup all-purpose flour
1	teaspoon salt
1/2	teaspoon pepper
2	tablespoons vegetable oil
1	can (14-1/2 ounces) stewed tomatoes
1	small onion, chopped
1/2	medium green pepper, chopped
2	garlic cloves, minced

1 Cut steak into serving-size pieces; discard bone. Combine flour, salt and pepper; pound to 1/4-in. thickness. In a large skillet over medium heat, brown steak on both sides in oil.

2 Transfer to a greased 13-in. x 9-in. x 2-in. baking dish. Combine the tomatoes, onion, green pepper and garlic; pour over steak. Cover and bake at 350° for 1-1/2 hours or until tender. **Yield:** 6 servings.

Mushroom Swiss Burgers

These skillet burgers are perfect cold-weather food. Heaping with mushrooms and the wonderful flavor of Swiss cheese, these burgers really deliver.

—James Bowles, Ironton, Ohio

1-1/2	pounds ground beef
1	pound sliced fresh mushrooms
1	can (10-3/4 ounces) condensed cream of mushroom soup, undiluted
1	cup water
6	slices Swiss cheese
6	hamburger buns, split

1 Shape beef into six patties. In a large skillet, cook the patties over medium-high heat for 5-7 minutes on each side or until meat is no longer pink. Remove to paper towels; drain, reserving 2 tablespoons drippings. Saute mushrooms in drippings until tender.

2 Meanwhile, in a microwave-safe bowl, combine soup and water. Cover and microwave on high for 2-1/2 to 3-1/2 minutes or until heated through. Return patties to the skillet. Stir in soup. Bring to a boil. Reduce heat; simmer, uncovered, for 3 minutes.

3 Top each patty with a slice of cheese. Remove from the heat; cover and let stand until cheese is melted. Serve on buns topped with mushrooms. **Yield:** 6 servings.

TIP . . . .
Preparing Mushrooms
Just before using mushrooms, gently remove any dirt by rubbing the mushrooms with a vegetable brush or by wiping them with a damp paper towel. You can also quickly rinse them under cold water, drain and pat dry with paper towels. Trim stems.

Round Steak Roll-Ups

Since I'm a working mom, I like to assemble these tasty steak rolls the night before and pop them in the slow cooker the next morning before we're all out the door.

—**Kimberly Alonge, Westfield, New York**

2	pounds boneless beef round steak
1/2	cup grated carrot
1/3	cup chopped zucchini
1/4	cup chopped sweet red pepper
1/4	cup chopped green pepper
1/4	cup sliced green onions
2	tablespoons grated Parmesan cheese
1	tablespoon minced fresh parsley *or* 1 teaspoon dried parsley flakes
1	garlic clove, minced
1/4	teaspoon salt
1/4	teaspoon pepper
2	tablespoons vegetable oil
1	jar (14 ounces) meatless spaghetti sauce

Hot cooked spaghetti
Additional Parmesan cheese, optional

1 Cut meat into six serving-size pieces; pound to 1/4-in. thickness. Combine the vegetables, Parmesan cheese and seasonings; place 1/3 cup in the center of each piece. Roll meat up around filling; secure with toothpicks.

2 In a large skillet, brown roll-ups in oil over medium-high heat. Transfer to a 5-qt. slow cooker; top with spaghetti sauce. Cover and cook on low for 6 hours or until meat is tender. Discard toothpicks. Serve roll-ups and sauce with spaghetti. Sprinkle with additional Parmesan cheese if desired. **Yield:** 6 servings.

Herbed Sirloin Tip

I count on this recipe for family feasts as well as company suppers. It's simple to prepare and delicious every time.

—**Janice Connelley, Spring Creek, Nevada**

2	teaspoons salt
1/2	teaspoon garlic salt
1/2	teaspoon celery salt
1/2	teaspoon dried rosemary, crushed
1/4	teaspoon onion powder
1/4	teaspoon paprika
1/4	teaspoon pepper
1/8	teaspoon dill weed
1/8	teaspoon rubbed sage
1	sirloin tip roast (about 2 pounds)

1 Combine seasonings; rub over entire roast. Cover and refrigerate for at least 2 hours.

2 Place roast on a rack in a large shallow roasting pan. Bake, uncovered, at 425° for 40-60 minutes or until meat reaches desired doneness (for medium-rare, a meat thermometer should read 145°; medium, 160°; well-done, 170°). Let stand for 10-15 minutes before slicing. **Yield:** 6-8 servings.

Chili Spaghetti

My husband often asked his grandmother to make this hearty pasta casserole. With a combination of chili ingredients and spaghetti, it's always a winner.

—Pam Thompson, Girard, Illinois

- 1 pound ground beef
- 1/2 cup chopped onion
- 2 garlic cloves, minced
- 3 cups tomato juice
- 1 can (16 ounces) kidney beans, rinsed and drained
- 6 ounces spaghetti, broken into 3-inch pieces
- 1 tablespoon Worcestershire sauce
- 2 to 3 teaspoons chili powder
- 1 teaspoon salt
- 1/2 teaspoon pepper

1 In a large skillet, cook the beef, onion and garlic over medium heat until meat is no longer pink; drain. Transfer to a greased 2-1/2-qt. baking dish; stir in the remaining ingredients.

2 Cover and bake at 350° for 65-70 minutes or until the spaghetti is just tender. Let stand, covered, for 10 minutes. **Yield:** 6 servings.

Savory Beef Stew

You'll be surprised at the unique flavor in this stew. The secret ingredient is cranberry juice.

—Kay Fortier, Wildrose, North Dakota

- 1 cup all-purpose flour
- 2 teaspoons salt, optional
- 2 pounds lean beef stew meat, cut into 1-inch cubes
- 4 bacon strips, cut into 1-inch pieces, optional
- 10 small onions
- 2 cups cranberry juice, *divided*
- 1 can (14-1/2 ounces) beef broth
- 4 whole cloves
- 1 bay leaf
- 1/2 teaspoon pepper
- 1/2 teaspoon dried marjoram
- 1/4 teaspoon dried thyme
- 1/4 teaspoon garlic powder
- 5 medium carrots, cut into chunks
- 5 medium potatoes, peeled and cubed
- 2 cups frozen peas, thawed

1 In a small bowl, combine flour and salt if desired. Place half of the flour mixture in large resealable plastic bag. Add beef, a few pieces at a time, and shake to coat. Reserve remaining flour mixture; set aside.

2 Place beef in a Dutch oven. Add bacon if desired. Bake, uncovered, at 400° for 30 minutes.

3 Add onions, 1-1/2 cups cranberry juice, broth and seasonings. Cover and bake at 350° for 1 hour.

4 Add carrots and potatoes; bake 1 hour longer or until meat and vegetables are tender.

5 Combine reserved flour mixture and remaining cranberry juice until smooth; stir into stew. Cover and bake 30 minutes longer. Remove bay leaf. Add peas; return to the oven for 5 minutes or until heated through. **Yield:** 10 servings.

Meatball Skillet Meal

With colorful vegetables and nicely seasoned meatballs, this tasty meal-in-one offers a lot of flavor for a little cash.

—Donna Smith, Victor, New York

- 1/2 cup finely chopped fresh mushrooms
- 1/3 cup quick-cooking oats
- 2 tablespoons finely chopped green pepper
- 2 tablespoons finely chopped onion
- 2 tablespoon dried parsley flakes
- 1 teaspoon dried basil
- 1 teaspoon dried oregano
- 1/2 teaspoon dried thyme
- 1/2 teaspoon salt
- 1/4 teaspoon pepper
- 1 pound ground beef
- 4 medium carrots, sliced
- 1 small zucchini, sliced
- 1 can (14-1/2 ounces) diced tomatoes, undrained
- 4 cups hot cooked rice

1 In a large bowl, combine the first 10 ingredients. Crumble beef over mixture and mix well. Shape into 1-1/4-in. balls.

2 In a large skillet, cook meatballs over medium heat until no longer pink; drain. Add carrots and zucchini; cook, uncovered, for 5 minutes or until tender. Stir in tomatoes; heat through. Serve with rice. **Yield:** 6 servings.

Brisket for a Bunch

This makes tender slices of beef in a delicious au jus. To easily get very thin slices, chill the brisket before slicing and reheat in the juices.

—**Dawn Fagerstrom, Warren, Minnesota**

- 1 fresh beef brisket (2-1/2 pounds), cut in half
- 1 tablespoon vegetable oil
- 1/2 cup chopped celery
- 1/2 cup chopped onion
- 3/4 cup beef broth
- 1/2 cup tomato sauce
- 1/4 cup water
- 1/4 cup sugar
- 2 tablespoons onion soup mix
- 1 tablespoon cider vinegar
- 12 hamburger buns, split

1 In a large skillet, brown brisket in oil on both sides; transfer to a 3-qt. slow cooker. In the same skillet, saute celery and onion for 1 minute. Gradually add the broth, tomato sauce and water; stir to loosen the browned bits from pan. Add the sugar, soup mix and vinegar; bring to a boil. Pour over brisket.

2 Cover and cook on low for 7-8 hours or until meat is tender. Let stand for 5 minutes before slicing. Skim fat from cooking juices. Serve meat in buns with cooking juices. **Yield:** 10 servings.

EDITOR'S NOTE: This is a fresh beef brisket, not corned beef.

Hamburger Hot Dish

You won't mind when your family asks for seconds of this comforting casserole, because the satisfying supper dish is so economical.

—**Dee Eastman, Fairfield Glade, Tennessee**

- 2 cups uncooked elbow macaroni
- 2 pounds ground beef
- 1 can (28 ounces) whole tomatoes, undrained and quartered
- 1 can (15 ounces) tomato sauce
- 1 jar (12 ounces) beef gravy
- 1/2 cup chopped onion
- 1 teaspoon garlic powder

1 Cook macaroni according to package directions. Meanwhile, in a large skillet, cook beef over medium heat until no longer pink; drain. Stir in the tomatoes, tomato sauce, gravy, onion and garlic powder. Drain macaroni; add to beef mixture.

2 Transfer to a greased shallow 3-qt. baking dish. Bake, uncovered, at 350° for 25-30 minutes or until heated through. **Yield:** 8 servings.

Apricot Round Steak

Looking for a fun alternative to traditional steak sauce? Serve tender slices of round steak with a sweet apricot sauce. The broiled entree is a snap to prepare and easy on the pocketbook, too.

—Bernadine Dirmeyer, Harpster, Ohio

1-3/4	pounds boneless top round steak (3/4 inch thick)
3/4	cup apricot preserves
1	tablespoon lemon juice
1/2	teaspoon salt
1/8	teaspoon hot pepper sauce

1 Place steak on broiler pan rack; broil for 6-8 minutes on each side. Meanwhile, in a saucepan or microwave-safe bowl, combine remaining ingredients. Cook until preserves are melted. Set aside 1/2 cup; brush remaining sauce over steak.

2 Broil 2-3 minutes longer or until meat reaches desired doneness (for medium-rare, a meat thermometer should read 145°; medium, 160°; well-done, 170°). Slice meat on the diagonal; serve with reserved apricot sauce. **Yield:** 8 servings.

1 In a large nonstick skillet, cook beef and jalapeno over medium heat until meat is no longer pink; drain. Stir in the corn, tomatoes, milk, cornmeal, chilies, olives, egg whites and taco seasoning until blended.

2 Transfer to a 13-in. x 9-in. x 2-in. baking dish coated with cooking spray. Bake, uncovered, at 350° for 40 minutes. Sprinkle with cheese. Bake 5 minutes longer or until cheese is melted. Let stand for 10 minutes before cutting. Serve with salsa. **Yield:** 8 servings.

EDITOR'S NOTE: When cutting hot peppers, disposable gloves are recommended. Avoid touching your face.

Tamale Casserole

This casserole really heats up dinnertime. It's a family-pleasing main course guaranteed to put a little kick in your menu.

—Kathleen Reid, Petaluma, California

1	pound lean ground beef
1	jalapeno pepper, seeded and diced
2	cups frozen corn, thawed
1	can (28 ounces) diced tomatoes, undrained
1-1/2	cups fat-free milk
1	cup cornmeal
1	can (4 ounces) chopped green chilies, drained
1	can (2-1/2 ounces) sliced ripe olives, drained
2	egg whites, lightly beaten
1	envelope reduced-sodium taco seasoning
1	cup (4 ounces) shredded reduced-fat cheddar cheese
1	cup salsa

Corned Beef 'n' Cabbage

Apple juice gives this recipe a tasty twist and a mellow flavor. The long, slow cooking assures that the meat will be tender.

—Jo Ann Honey, Longmont, Colorado

1	large onion, cut into wedges
1	cup apple juice
1	bay leaf
1	corned beef brisket with spice packet (2-1/2 to 3 pounds), cut in half
1	small head cabbage, cut into wedges

1 Place the onion in a 5-qt. slow cooker. Combine the apple juice, bay leaf and contents of spice packet; pour over onion. Top with brisket and cabbage. Cover and cook on low for 8-10 hours or until meat and vegetables are tender. Discard bay leaf before serving. **Yield:** 6 servings.

Vegetable Beef Stew

Tasty vegetable chunks add color to this satisfying stew. I serve it with corn bread and a tossed salad for a delicious meal in no time.

—Bobbie Jo Yokley, Franklin, Kentucky

- 1-1/2 pounds beef bottom round roast, cut into 1/2-inch cubes
- 2 tablespoons vegetable oil
- 4-1/3 cups water, *divided*
- 1 medium onion, diced
- 3 celery ribs, cut into 1-inch chunks
- 3 small carrots, cut into 1-inch chunks
- 3 medium potatoes, peeled and cubed
- 2 tablespoons beef bouillon granules
- 1 cup frozen peas
- 3 tablespoons all-purpose flour

1 In a Dutch oven, brown beef on all sides in oil; drain. Add 4 cups water, onion, celery, carrots, potatoes and bouillon. Bring to a boil. Reduce heat; cover and simmer for 25-30 minutes or until vegetables are tender.

2 Stir in peas. Bring to a boil. Combine flour and remaining water until smooth; add to beef mixture. Cook and stir for 2 minutes or until thickened and bubbly. **Yield:** 6 servings.

Polynesian Roast Beef

This delicious recipe came from my sister and has been a family favorite for years. Pineapple and peppers add color and taste.

—Annette Mosbarger, Peyton, Colorado

- 1 boneless beef top round roast (3-1/4 pounds)
- 2 tablespoons browning sauce, optional
- 1/4 cup all-purpose flour
- 1 teaspoon salt
- 1/4 teaspoon pepper
- 1 medium onion, sliced
- 1 can (8 ounces) unsweetened sliced pineapple
- 1/4 cup packed brown sugar
- 2 tablespoons cornstarch
- 1/4 teaspoon ground ginger
- 1/2 cup beef broth
- 1/4 cup soy sauce
- 1/2 teaspoon minced garlic
- 1 medium green pepper, sliced

1 Cut roast in half; brush with browning sauce if desired. Combine the flour, salt and pepper; rub over meat. Place onion in a 3-qt. slow cooker; top with roast.

2 Drain pineapple, reserving juice; refrigerate the pineapple. In a small bowl, combine the brown sugar, cornstarch and ginger; whisk in the broth, soy sauce, garlic and reserved pineapple juice until smooth. Pour over meat. Cover and cook on low for 7-8 hours.

3 Add pineapple and green pepper. Cook 1 hour longer or until meat and green pepper are tender. **Yield:** 10-11 servings.

Curried Beef with Dumplings

I like making this hearty pot roast in winter and serving leftovers the next day. It's not only easy to prepare, but the aroma is just wonderful while it's cooking.

—Janell Schmidt, Athelstane, Wisconsin

1	boneless beef rump roast (3 pounds)
2	tablespoons olive oil
6	medium carrots, cut into chunks
1	can (14-1/2 ounces) diced tomatoes, undrained
1	medium onion, sliced
2	teaspoons curry powder
1	teaspoon sugar
2	teaspoons salt, *divided*
1	teaspoon Worcestershire sauce
1	cup hot water
1-2/3	cups all-purpose flour
3	teaspoons baking powder
2	tablespoons cold butter
3/4	cup milk
2	tablespoons minced fresh parsley
2	tablespoons chopped pimientos

1 In a Dutch oven, brown roast in oil on all sides; drain. Combine the carrots, tomatoes, onion, curry powder, sugar, 1 teaspoon salt and Worcestershire sauce; pour over roast. Bring to a boil. Reduce heat to low; cover and cook for 2-1/2 hours or until meat and carrots are tender.

2 Remove roast and carrots; keep warm. Add hot water to pan; bring to a boil. For dumplings, combine the flour, baking powder and remaining salt in a large bowl. Cut in butter until mixture resembles fine crumbs. Stir in the milk, parsley and pimientos just until moistened.

3 Drop by tablespoonfuls onto simmering liquid. Cover and cook for 15 minutes or until a toothpick inserted in a dumpling comes out clean (do not lift cover while simmering). Remove dumplings. Strain cooking juices; serve with roast, dumplings and carrots. **Yield:** 8 servings.

Swiss Pot Roast

Pot roast has been a family-pleaser for generations. With potatoes and carrots, it's a mouthwatering meal in one.

—Darlene Brenden, Salem, Oregon

1	boneless beef chuck roast (3 pounds)
1	tablespoon vegetable oil
8	medium potatoes, peeled and quartered
8	medium carrots, cut into chunks
1	medium onion, sliced
3	tablespoons all-purpose flour
1	cup water
1	can (8 ounces) tomato sauce
1	teaspoon beef bouillon granules
1/2	teaspoon salt
1/2	teaspoon pepper

1 In a Dutch oven, brown roast on all sides in oil; drain. Add the potatoes, carrots and onion. In a large bowl, combine the flour, water, tomato sauce, bouillon, salt and pepper until smooth. Pour over the roast and vegetables.

2 Cover and bake at 325° for 2-1/2 to 3 hours or until the meat is tender. **Yield:** 8 servings.

Flavorful Onion Burgers

Cheddar cheese and Thousand Island dressing make this moist and juicy burger a real family treat. The amount of flavor this burger packs with just a few simple ingredients will really surprise you.

—Dave Bremson, Plantation, Florida

- 1 large onion
- 1 to 2 tablespoons olive oil

Salt and pepper to taste, optional

- 1/2 cup chopped green pepper
- 1/2 cup shredded cheddar cheese
- 2 tablespoons minced fresh parsley
- 1 tablespoon Worcestershire sauce
- 1-1/2 pounds ground beef
- 6 whole wheat hamburger buns, split
- 6 tablespoons prepared Thousand Island salad dressing
- 6 lettuce leaves
- 6 slices tomato

1 Slice onion into 1/2-in.-thick rings; thread onto metal or soaked wooden skewers. Brush with oil. Season with salt and pepper if desired. Grill, covered, over medium-hot heat for 8-10 minutes on each side.

2 Meanwhile, in a large bowl, combine the green pepper, cheese, parsley and Worcestershire sauce. Crumble beef over mixture and mix well. Shape into six patties.

3 Move onion to indirect heat. Place burgers over direct heat. Grill, covered, for 5-7 minutes on each side or until meat is no longer pink. Cook onion 10 minutes longer or until tender.

4 Spread bun bottoms with dressing; top each with lettuce, tomato, onion and a burger. Replace bun tops. **Yield:** 6 servings.

Cajun Macaroni

When I prepare my favorite meat loaf, I usually end up with an extra half pound of ground beef. I created this Cajun-flavored dish as a way to use it up.

—June Ellis, Erie, Illinois

- 1/2 pound ground beef
- 1/3 cup chopped onion
- 1/3 cup chopped green pepper
- 1/3 cup chopped celery
- 1 can (14-1/2 ounces) diced tomatoes, undrained
- 1-1/2 teaspoons Cajun seasoning
- 1 package (7-1/4 ounces) macaroni and cheese dinner mix
- 2 tablespoons milk
- 1 tablespoon butter

1 In a large saucepan, cook the beef, onion, green pepper and celery over medium heat until meat is no longer pink; drain. Add the tomatoes and Cajun seasoning. Cook, uncovered, for 15-20 minutes, stirring occasionally.

2 Meanwhile, prepare the macaroni and cheese, using 2 tablespoons milk and 1 tablespoon butter. Stir in beef mixture; cook for 2-3 minutes or until heated through. **Yield:** 4 servings.

Roast Beef Chimichangas

Your family is sure to enjoy this fabulous homemade version of a restaurant favorite—and it's a terrific way to use up leftover roast beef.

—Delia Kennedy, Deer Park, Washington

- 1/2 cup chopped onion
- 1/2 teaspoon minced garlic
- 1 tablespoon vegetable oil
- 1-1/2 cups shredded cooked roast beef
- 1 can (2-1/4 ounces) sliced ripe olives, drained
- 1/2 cup salsa
- 1/4 teaspoon ground cumin
- 1/2 cup shredded cheddar cheese
- 6 flour tortillas (10 inches), warmed

Oil for deep-fat frying

1 In a large skillet, saute onion and garlic in oil for 1-2 minutes or until tender. Add the roast beef, olives, salsa and cumin. Cook and stir over medium heat for 4-6 minutes or until heated through. Stir in cheese. Remove from the heat.

2 Spoon about 1/3 cup meat mixture off-center on each tortilla. Fold sides and ends over filling and roll up; secure with a toothpick. Repeat.

3 In an electric skillet or deep-fat fryer, heat oil to 375°. Fry chimichangas for 2-3 minutes on each side or until lightly browned. Drain on paper towels. Discard toothpicks. **Yield:** 6 servings.

TIP
Shredding Beef

To easily shred leftover roast beef, or any cooked roast for that matter, set two forks in opposite ends of the meat. Pull the forks away from one another, shredding the meat as you go.

Ranchero Supper

This hearty dish is quick and easy to fix after a busy workday. We like to use hickory and bacon baked beans. For a complete meal, serve it with fruit or a green salad.

—Karen Roberts, Lawrence, Kansas

- 1-1/2 pounds ground beef
- 1 can (28 ounces) baked beans
- 1 can (11 ounces) whole kernel corn, drained
- 1/4 cup barbecue sauce
- 2 tablespoons ketchup
- 1 tablespoon prepared mustard
- 3/4 cup shredded cheddar cheese

Sliced green onions and sour cream, optional
- 7 cups tortilla chips

1 In a large skillet, cook beef over medium heat until no longer pink; drain. Stir in the baked beans, corn, barbecue sauce, ketchup and mustard; heat through. Sprinkle with cheese; cook until melted. Serve with onions and sour cream, if desired. Serve with tortilla chips. **Yield:** 7 servings.

Beer-Braised Beef

I modified the ingredients in this main dish to suit my family. It's quick to put together in the morning, and at the end of the day, all we do is cook the noodles and eat!

—Geri Faustich, Appleton, Wisconsin

- 3 bacon strips, diced
- 2 pounds beef stew meat, cut into 1-inch cubes
- 1/2 teaspoon pepper
- 1/4 teaspoon salt
- 1 teaspoon vegetable oil
- 1 medium onion, cut into wedges
- 1 teaspoon minced garlic
- 1 bay leaf
- 1 can (12 ounces) beer *or* nonalcoholic beer
- 1 tablespoon soy sauce
- 1 tablespoon Worcestershire sauce
- 1 teaspoon dried thyme
- 2 tablespoons all-purpose flour
- 1/4 cup cold water

Hot cooked noodles

1 In a large skillet, cook bacon over medium heat until crisp. Remove to paper towels; drain, discarding drippings. Sprinkle beef with pepper and salt. In the same skillet, brown beef on all sides in oil; drain.

2 Transfer to a 5-qt. slow cooker. Add the bacon, onion, garlic and bay leaf. In a small bowl, combine the beer, soy sauce, Worcestershire sauce and thyme. Pour over beef mixture.

3 Cover and cook on low for 5-1/2 to 6 hours or until meat is tender.

4 In a small bowl, combine flour and water until smooth. Gradually stir into slow cooker. Cover and cook on high for 30 minutes longer or until thickened. Discard bay leaf. Serve beef with noodles. **Yield:** 8 servings.

Traditional Meat Loaf

Topped with a sweet sauce, this meat loaf tastes so good that you might want to double the recipe so everyone can have seconds. It also freezes well.

—Gail Graham, Maple Ridge, British Columbia

1	egg, lightly beaten
2/3	cup milk
3	slices bread, crumbled
1	cup (4 ounces) shredded cheddar cheese
1	medium onion, chopped
1/2	cup finely shredded carrot
1	teaspoon salt
1/4	teaspoon pepper
1-1/2	pounds ground beef
1/4	cup packed brown sugar
1/4	cup ketchup
1	tablespoon prepared mustard

1 In a large bowl, combine the first eight ingredients. Crumble beef over mixture and mix well. Shape into a loaf. Place in a greased 9-in. x 5-in. x 3-in. loaf pan.

2 In a small bowl, combine the brown sugar, ketchup and mustard; spread over loaf. Bake at 350° for 60-75 minutes or until no pink remains and a meat thermometer reads 160°. Drain. Let stand for 10 minutes before slicing. **Yield:** 6 servings.

Peppery Roast Beef

With its spicy coating and creamy horseradish sauce, this tender roast is sure to be the star of any meal, whether it's a sit-down dinner or serve-yourself potluck.

—Maureen Brand, Somers, Iowa

1	tablespoon olive oil
1	tablespoon seasoned pepper
2	garlic cloves, minced
1/2	teaspoon dried thyme
1/4	teaspoon salt
1	boneless beef eye round roast (4 to 5 pounds)

HORSERADISH SAUCE:

1	cup (8 ounces) sour cream
2	tablespoons lemon juice
2	tablespoons milk
2	tablespoons prepared horseradish
1	tablespoon Dijon mustard
1/4	teaspoon salt
1/8	teaspoon pepper

1 In a small bowl, combine the oil, seasoned pepper, garlic, thyme and salt; rub over roast. Place fat side up on a rack in a shallow roasting pan.

2 Bake, uncovered, at 325° for 2-1/2 to 3 hours or until meat reaches desired doneness (for medium-rare, a meat thermometer should read 145°; medium, 160°; well-done, 170°). Let stand for 10 minutes before slicing.

3 In a small bowl, combine the sauce ingredients. Serve with roast. **Yield:** 10-12 servings.

Flavorful Meat Loaf

Since I can't have much salt, I've come up with a recipe for meat loaf that is really tasty without it.

—Lillian Wittler, Wayne, Nebraska

2	egg whites
1/2	cup 1% milk
3	slices whole wheat bread, torn into pieces
1/4	cup finely chopped onion
1	teaspoon Worcestershire sauce
1/4	teaspoon onion powder
1/4	teaspoon garlic powder
1/4	teaspoon ground mustard
1/4	teaspoon rubbed sage
1/4	teaspoon pepper
1	pound lean ground beef
3	tablespoons ketchup

1 In a large bowl, beat egg whites. Add milk and bread; let stand for 5 minutes. Stir in the onion, Worcestershire sauce and seasonings. Crumble beef over mixture and mix well.

2 Shape into a loaf in an 11-in. x 7-in. x 2-in. baking pan coated with cooking spray. Bake, uncovered, at 350° for 35 minutes; drain.

3 Spoon ketchup over loaf. Bake 10-20 minutes longer or until a meat thermometer reads 160°. Let stand for 10 minutes before slicing. **Yield:** 5 servings.

Steak over Potatoes

I enjoy preparing this dish since it is one of the heartiest meals I serve...it's so tasty, too. The chicken gumbo soup adds a unique flavor to the rest of the ingredients.

—Dennis Robinson, Laurel, Montana

2-1/2	pounds beef round steak
1	can (10-3/4 ounces) condensed cream of onion soup, undiluted
1	can (10-1/2 ounces) condensed chicken gumbo soup, undiluted
1/4	teaspoon pepper
8	baking potatoes

1 Cut steak into 3-in. x 1/4-in. strips; place in a bowl. Stir in soups and pepper. Transfer to a greased 2-1/2-qt. baking dish. Cover and bake at 350° for 30 minutes.

2 Place potatoes on a baking pan. Bake potatoes and steak mixture for 1-1/2 hours or until meat and potatoes are tender. Serve steak over the potatoes. **Yield:** 8 servings.

TIP

Ground Beef Basics

Ground beef is often labeled using the cut of meat that it is ground from, such as ground chuck or ground round. (Ground beef comes from a combination of beef cuts.)

Ground beef can also be labeled according to the fat content of the ground mixture or the percentage of lean meat to fat, such as 85% or 90% lean. The higher the percentage, the leaner the meat.

Mile-High Shredded Beef

This tender beef has become a tasty tradition when I cook for our harvest crews and for neighboring ranchers who come to help us sort our cattle. Those hungry folks have been a good testing ground for recipes.

—Betty Sitzman, Wray, Colorado

- 1 boneless beef chuck roast (3 pounds)
- 1 can (14-1/2 ounces) beef broth
- 1 medium onion, chopped
- 1 celery rib, chopped
- 3/4 cup ketchup
- 1/4 cup packed brown sugar
- 2 tablespoons white vinegar
- 1 teaspoon salt
- 1 teaspoon ground mustard
- 1 teaspoon Worcestershire sauce
- 1 garlic clove, minced
- 1 bay leaf
- 1/4 teaspoon garlic powder
- 1/4 teaspoon paprika
- 3 drops hot pepper sauce
- 12 to 15 hoagie buns, split

1 Place the roast in a Dutch oven; add broth, onion and celery. Bring to a boil. Reduce heat; cover and simmer for 2-1/2 to 3 hours or until the meat is tender.

2 Remove roast and cool slightly; shred the meat with two forks. Strain vegetables and set aside. Skim fat from cooking liquid and reserve 1-1/2 cups. Return the meat, vegetables and reserved cooking liquid to the pan.

3 Stir in the ketchup, brown sugar, vinegar, salt, mustard, Worcestershire sauce, garlic, bay leaf, garlic powder, paprika and hot pepper sauce. Bring to a boil. Reduce heat; cover and simmer for 30 minutes. Discard bay leaf. Serve beef on buns. **Yield:** 12-15 servings.

Veggie Beef Bundles

These individual foil packets of meat and veggies were a mainstay for my husband and me when we were building a log home. The meal-in-one bundles make cleanup a snap. Feel free to experiment with whatever vegetables your family likes.

—Carolyn Dixon, Wilmar, Arkansas

- 2 cups julienned uncooked potatoes
- 1 pound lean ground beef
- 1 envelope onion soup mix
- 1/4 cup water
- 1 cup sliced fresh mushrooms
- 1 package (9 ounces) frozen cut green beans, thawed

1 Coat four pieces of heavy-duty foil (about 12 in. square) with cooking spray. Place 1/2 cup potatoes on each square. Shape beef into four patties; place over potatoes. Combine soup mix and water; spoon half over patties. Top with mushrooms, green beans and remaining soup mixture. Fold foil around meat and vegetables and seal tightly.

2 Place on a baking sheet. Bake at 375° for 25-30 minutes or until meat is no longer pink and potatoes are tender. **Yield:** 4 servings.

Cajun-Style Pot Roast

I often make this zippy roast when expecting dinner guests. It gives me time to visit and everyone always enjoys it—even my friend who's a chef.

—**Ginger Menzies, Oak Creek, Colorado**

- 1 boneless beef chuck roast (2 to 3 pounds)
- 2 tablespoons Cajun seasoning
- 1 tablespoon olive oil
- 2 cans (10 ounces *each*) diced tomatoes and green chilies
- 1 medium sweet red pepper, chopped
- 1-1/2 cups chopped celery
- 3/4 cup chopped onion
- 1/4 cup quick-cooking tapioca
- 1-1/2 teaspoons minced garlic
- 1 teaspoon salt

Hot cooked rice

1 Cut roast in half; sprinkle with Cajun seasoning. In a large skillet, brown roast in oil on all sides; drain. Transfer to a 5-qt. slow cooker.

2 Combine the tomatoes, red pepper, celery, onion, tapioca, garlic and salt; pour over roast. Cover and cook on low for 6-8 hours or until meat is tender. Slice and serve with rice. **Yield:** 6 servings.

TIP.............................
Cajun Seasoning Secret

Look for Cajun seasoning in the spice section of your grocery store. You can also make your own blend by experimenting with different seasonings. A typical mix includes salt, onion powder, garlic powder, cayenne pepper, ground mustard, celery seed and pepper.

Pork

Chinese New Year Skillet

This main dish was inspired by a recipe on the back of a rice package in 1957. If you like pork, I guarantee you'll love this recipe.

—Sherilyn West, Lubbock, Texas

1	pound boneless pork butt roast, cut into 1/2-inch cubes
1	tablespoon vegetable oil
1	can (20 ounces) unsweetened pineapple tidbits
2	tablespoons white wine vinegar
1	tablespoon sugar
3/4	teaspoon salt
1/4	teaspoon garlic powder
1	cup uncooked long grain rice
1	tablespoon cornstarch
2	tablespoons cold water
1/2	cup coarsely chopped green pepper
1	medium tomato, cut into wedges
2	tablespoons Worcestershire sauce

1 In a large skillet, cook pork in oil over medium heat on all sides until pork is lightly browned; drain. Drain pineapple, reserving juice in a 2-cup measuring cup; set pineapple aside.

2 Add enough water to the juice to measure 1-1/4 cups; stir into pork. Add the vinegar, sugar, salt and garlic powder. Bring to a boil, stirring constantly. Reduce heat; cover and simmer for 20 minutes or until meat is tender. Meanwhile, cook rice according to package directions.

3 In a small bowl, combine cornstarch and water until smooth; stir into pork mixture. Bring to a boil; cook and stir for 2 minutes or until thickened. Stir in the green pepper, tomato, Worcestershire sauce and reserved pineapple; heat through. Serve with rice. **Yield:** 4 servings.

Slow-Cooked Pork Tacos

Sometimes I'll substitute Bibb lettuce leaves for the tortillas to make crunchy lettuce wraps. I find that leftovers are perfect for burritos.

—Kathleen Wolf, Naperville, Illinois

1	boneless pork sirloin roast (2 pounds), cut into 1-inch pieces
1-1/2	cups salsa verde
1	medium sweet red pepper, chopped
1	medium onion, chopped
1/4	cup chopped dried apricots
2	tablespoons lime juice
2	garlic cloves, minced
1	teaspoon ground cumin
1/2	teaspoon salt
1/4	teaspoon white pepper

Dash hot pepper sauce

10	flour tortillas (8 inches), warmed

Reduced-fat sour cream, thinly sliced green onions, cubed avocado, shredded reduced-fat cheddar cheese and chopped tomato, optional

1 In a 3-qt. slow cooker, combine the first 11 ingredients. Cover and cook on high for 4-5 hours or until meat is very tender.

2 Shred pork with two forks. Place about 1/2 cup pork mixture down the center of each tortilla. Serve with toppings if desired. **Yield:** 10 tacos.

Pork Potpie

The first time I put this tasty potpie on the table, my family said the recipe was a hands-down keeper.

—Linda Flor, Marmarth, North Dakota

CRUST:

3	cups all-purpose flour
1/2	teaspoon salt
1	cup shortening
5	to 6 tablespoons cold water
1	egg
1	tablespoon vinegar

FILLING:

1-1/2	cups cubed peeled potatoes
1/2	cup thinly sliced carrots
1/4	cup thinly sliced celery
1/4	cup chopped onion
1	cup water
2	cups diced cooked pork
3/4	cup pork gravy
1/2	teaspoon dried rosemary, crushed, optional
1/4	teaspoon salt
1/8	teaspoon pepper

Half-and-half cream, optional

1 In a bowl, combine flour and salt; cut in shortening until the mixture resembles coarse crumbs. Combine 5 tablespoons water, egg and vinegar; sprinkle over dry ingredients, 1 tablespoon at a time. Toss lightly with a fork until dough forms a ball; add additional water if necessary. Divide into two balls; chill while preparing filling.

2 In a saucepan, cook potatoes, carrots, celery and onion in water for 10 minutes or until crisp-tender; drain well. Add pork, gravy, rosemary if desired, salt and pepper; set aside.

3 On a floured surface, roll one ball of dough to fit a 9-in. pie plate. Fill with meat mixture. Roll remaining pastry to fit top of pie. Cut slits in top crust and place over filling; seal and flute edges. Brush pastry with cream if desired. Bake at 375° for 50-55 minutes or until golden brown. **Yield:** 6 servings.

2 In a Dutch oven, brown roast in oil on all sides; drain. Drain and rinse beans, discarding liquid; stir parsley into beans. Place beans around roast. Stir in broth.

3 Cover and simmer for 2 hours or until a meat thermometer reads 150°.

4 Place apples and onions on top of beans; cover and simmer 30 minutes longer or until a meat thermometer reads 160°. Let stand 10-15 minutes before slicing. **Yield:** 12 servings.

Shredded Italian Pork Sandwiches

To keep kitchens cool in summer, our home economists prepare a pork shoulder roast on the grill, then shred it for satisfying sandwiches.

—**Taste of Home Test Kitchen**

- 1/4 cup minced garlic
- 1 tablespoon olive oil
- 2 teaspoons dried basil
- 1 teaspoon salt
- 1 teaspoon dried oregano
- 1 teaspoon dried rosemary, crushed
- 1 teaspoon pepper
- 1 boneless pork shoulder roast (3 pounds)
- 2 cups soaked wood chips, optional
- 8 kaiser rolls, split

Roasted sweet red pepper halves, fresh basil leaves and balsamic vinaigrette, optional

1 In a small bowl, combine the garlic, oil, basil, salt, oregano, rosemary and pepper. Open roast; place fat side down so it lies flat. Spread garlic mixture evenly over the meat. Close roast; tie several times with kitchen string. Cover and chill overnight.

2 Prepare grill for indirect heat, using a drip pan with 1 in. of water. Add 1 cup of soaked wood chips to grill if desired. Grill roast, covered, over medium-low heat for 2 hours, adding remaining wood chips after 1 hour.

3 Wrap roast in a double thickness of aluminum foil. Return to grill over indirect medium heat. Cover and grill for 1 to 1-1/2 hours or until meat is fork-tender. Carefully open the foil. When cool enough to handle, shred meat. Serve on rolls with roasted peppers, basil and vinaigrette if desired. **Yield:** 8 servings.

Oktoberfest Roast Pork

We especially enjoy this roast at our family's own Oktoberfest dinner, but it can be served any time of year.

—**Carol Stevens, Basye, Virginia**

- 1 pound dried navy beans
- 1 teaspoon rubbed sage
- 1 teaspoon salt, optional
- 1/2 teaspoon pepper
- 1/8 teaspoon ground allspice

Dash cayenne pepper

- 1 boneless pork sirloin roast (3 pounds)
- 2 tablespoons vegetable oil
- 2 tablespoons chopped fresh parsley
- 1/2 cup chicken broth
- 2 medium tart apples, cut into wedges
- 1 large red onion, cut into wedges

1 Sort beans and rinse with cold water. Place beans in a Dutch oven; add water to cover by 2 in. Bring to a boil; boil for 2 minutes. Remove from the heat; cover and let stand for 1 to 4 hours or until beans are softened. Meanwhile, combine the sage, salt if desired, pepper, allspice and cayenne; rub over roast.

Sausage with Apple Sauerkraut

Dress up sauerkraut with apple and fennel, and serve it with Polish sausage or bratwurst. Top with your favorite mustard or relish.

—Carolyn Schmeling, Brookfield, Wisconsin

- 1 medium sweet onion, sliced
- 3 tablespoons butter
- 2 medium apples, peeled and shredded
- 1 tablespoon lemon juice
- 1 can (8 ounces) sauerkraut, rinsed and well drained
- 1/2 cup unsweetened apple juice
- 1 teaspoon caraway seeds
- 1/2 teaspoon fennel seed, crushed
- 1 package (16 ounces) smoked Polish sausage

1 In a large skillet, saute the onion in butter for 15 minutes or until lightly browned.

2 In a large bowl, toss apples with lemon juice. Add the apples, sauerkraut, apple juice, caraway and fennel to the onion. Bring to a boil. Reduce heat; cover and simmer for 15 minutes. Meanwhile, heat sausage according to package directions; cut into slices. Serve with sauerkraut. **Yield:** 4 servings.

Teriyaki Pork Roast

This is the only kind of meat my two young kids will eat and enjoy—other than hot dogs! It's also incredibly easy to make and simply delicious.

—Debbie Dunaway, Kettering, Ohio

- 1 boneless pork shoulder roast (3 to 4 pounds), trimmed
- 1 cup packed brown sugar
- 1/3 cup unsweetened apple juice
- 1/3 cup soy sauce
- 1/2 teaspoon salt
- 1/4 teaspoon pepper
- 2 tablespoons cornstarch
- 3 tablespoons cold water

1 Cut roast in half; rub with brown sugar. Place in a 5-qt. slow cooker. Pour apple juice and soy sauce over roast. Sprinkle with salt and pepper. Cover and cook on low for 6 to 6-1/2 hours or until meat is tender.

2 Remove roast; cover and let stand for 15 minutes. Meanwhile, strain cooking juices and return to slow cooker. Combine cornstarch and cold water until smooth; gradually stir into juices. Cover and cook on high for 15 minutes or until thickened. Slice pork; serve with gravy. **Yield:** 6-8 servings.

TIP
Pork Shoulder Roasts

A pork shoulder roast (also referred to as a Boston blade roast or Boston-style butt) is an economical cut that, when cooked properly, is very flavorful and tender. It is available with the bone in (about 6 to 9 pounds) or boneless (about 3 to 7 pounds). The boneless roast, which has the blade bone removed, is usually tied with string or placed in netting to hold the roast together.

Pork Chop Potato Dinner

Tender chops cook on a bed of creamy potatoes in this all-in-one meal. It's a snap to assemble, thanks to frozen hash browns, canned soup, shredded cheese and french-fried onions.

—Dawn Huizinga, Owatonna, Minnesota

- 6 bone-in pork chops (1/2 inch thick)
- 1 tablespoon vegetable oil
- 1 package (30 ounces) frozen shredded hash brown potatoes, thawed
- 1-1/2 cups (6 ounces) shredded cheddar cheese, *divided*
- 1 can (10-3/4 ounces) condensed cream of celery soup, undiluted
- 1/2 cup milk
- 1/2 cup sour cream
- 1/2 teaspoon seasoned salt
- 1/8 teaspoon pepper
- 1 can (2.8 ounces) french-fried onions, *divided*

1 In a large skillet, brown chops in oil on both sides; set aside and keep warm. In a large bowl, combine the potatoes, 1 cup cheese, soup, milk, sour cream, seasoned salt and pepper. Stir in half of the onions.

2 Transfer to a greased 5-qt. slow cooker; top with pork chops. Cover and cook on high for 2-1/2 to 3 hours or until meat juices run clear. Sprinkle with remaining cheese and onions. Cover and cook 10 minutes longer or until cheese is melted. **Yield:** 6 servings.

Italian Sausage Stew

One day when I was preparing Italian sausages, I decided to do something different. After browning them, I put the sausages in a pot and added other ingredients, ending up with this stew, which my husband and I like very much.

—Ann Erney, Middlebury Center, Pennsylvania

1-1/2	pounds Italian sausage links, cut into 1-inch pieces
3	cups water
4	medium potatoes, peeled and cut into chunks
2	medium carrots, cut into chunks
2	celery ribs, cut into chunks
2	small onions, cut into wedges
1/4	cup Worcestershire sauce
1	teaspoon dried oregano
1/2	teaspoon *each* dried basil, thyme and rosemary, crushed
1	bay leaf

Salt and pepper to taste

3/4	cup ketchup
1/2	large green *or* sweet red pepper, cut into chunks
1	tablespoon minced fresh parsley
1	tablespoon cornstarch
1	tablespoon cold water

1 In a Dutch oven over medium heat, brown sausage; drain. Add the water, potatoes, carrots, celery, onions, Worcestershire sauce and seasonings. Bring to a boil. Reduce heat; cover and cook over low heat for 1 hour or until sausage is no longer pink and vegetables are tender.

2 Add the ketchup, green pepper and parsley; cook 12-15 minutes longer or until pepper is tender. Discard bay leaf.

3 Combine cornstarch and cold water until smooth; stir into the stew. Bring to a boil; cook and stir for 2 minutes or until thickened. **Yield:** 6 servings.

Pork Pasta Bake

Less expensive cuts of pork become tender and tasty in this creamy casserole.

—Bernice Morris, Marshfield, Missouri

2	cups uncooked egg noodles
2	pounds boneless pork, cut into 3/4-inch cubes
2	medium onions, chopped
2	cans (15-1/4 ounces *each*) whole kernel corn, drained
2	cans (10-3/4 ounces *each*) condensed cream of mushroom soup, undiluted
1/2	teaspoon salt
1/2	teaspoon pepper

1 Cook noodles according to package directions. In a large skillet, cook pork and onions over medium heat until meat is no longer pink. Drain noodles. Stir the noodles, corn, soup, salt and pepper into the pork mixture.

2 Transfer to a greased 3-qt. baking dish. Cover and bake at 350° for 30 minutes. Uncover; bake 15 minutes longer. **Yield:** 8 servings.

Barbecue Italian Sausages

The tangy barbecue sauce found in this recipe from our home economists is fast, flavorful and extremely versatile. It's fantastic on sausages as well as ribs and pulled pork.

—Taste of Home Test Kitchen

- 4 uncooked Italian sausage links
- 1/2 cup chopped green pepper
- 1/4 cup chopped onion
- 1 tablespoon olive oil
- 1/3 cup dry red wine *or* beef broth
- 1/2 cup ketchup
- 1 tablespoon cider vinegar
- 1 tablespoon soy sauce
- 1 teaspoon brown sugar
- 1/4 teaspoon ground cumin
- 1/4 teaspoon chili powder
- 1/8 teaspoon Liquid Smoke, optional
- 4 hot dog buns, split

1 Grill the sausages, covered, over medium heat for 5-8 minutes on each side or until no longer pink. Meanwhile, in a large skillet, saute green pepper and onion in oil for 3-4 minutes or until tender. Stir in wine or broth. Bring to a boil; cook for 2 minutes or until liquid is evaporated.

2 Stir in the ketchup, vinegar, soy sauce, brown sugar, cumin, chili powder and Liquid Smoke if desired. Bring to a boil. Reduce heat; simmer for 2-3 minutes or until thickened. Place sausages in buns; serve with sauce. **Yield:** 4 servings.

Hay and Straw

This dish is not only quick and easy to prepare, but it's colorful too. Start cooking the ham about 5 minutes before the linguine is done. That way, all the ingredients will be ready at the same time.

—Priscilla Weaver, Hagerstown, Maryland

- 1 package (16 ounces) linguine
- 2 cups julienned fully cooked ham
- 1 tablespoon butter
- 3 cups frozen peas
- 1-1/2 cups (6 ounces *each*) shredded Parmesan cheese
- 1/3 cup heavy whipping cream

1 Cook linguine according to package directions. Meanwhile, in a large skillet, saute ham in butter for 3 minutes. Add peas; heat through. Drain linguine; toss with the ham mixture, Parmesan cheese and cream. Serve immediately. **Yield:** 8 servings.

TIP
Freezing Peppers

Stock up on peppers when they're on sale. Chop them and pack into resealable plastic freezer bags; freeze for 3-6 months.

Use them directly from the freezer in a variety of recipes.

Sausage Macaroni Bake

Everyone's bound to want seconds of this satisfying Italian-style bake. Oregano seasons the pork sausage, macaroni and tomato sauce mixture that's topped with a sprinkling of Parmesan cheese.

—Kelli Bucy, Massena, Iowa

- 1/2 cup uncooked elbow macaroni
- 1/2 pound bulk pork sausage
- 1/4 cup chopped green pepper
- 2 tablespoons chopped onion
- 1/4 teaspoon dried oregano
- 1/8 teaspoon pepper
- 1 can (8 ounces) tomato sauce
- 1/2 cup water
- 4 tablespoons grated Parmesan cheese, *divided*

1 Cook macaroni according to package directions; drain and set aside. In a large skillet, cook sausage over medium heat until no longer pink; drain. Add the green pepper, onion, oregano and pepper. Stir in tomato sauce and water. Bring to a boil. Reduce heat; simmer, uncovered, for 5 minutes.

2 Stir in macaroni and 2 tablespoons Parmesan cheese. Transfer to an ungreased 1-qt. baking dish. Sprinkle with the remaining Parmesan cheese. Bake, uncovered, at 350° for 20-25 minutes or until bubbly. **Yield:** 2 servings.

Pizza from Scratch

Why pay for takeout or throw a frozen pizza in the oven? You can make this homemade version with hardly any fuss. Mix and match toppings to suit your family's tastes.

—Audra Dee Collins, Hobbs, New Mexico

- 1 package (1/4 ounce) active dry yeast
- 1 cup warm water (110° to 115°)
- 2 tablespoons vegetable oil
- 1 teaspoon salt
- 1 teaspoon sugar
- 2-3/4 to 3-1/4 cups all-purpose flour

SAUCE:
- 1 can (15 ounces) tomato sauce
- 1/2 cup chopped onion
- 3/4 teaspoon Italian seasoning
- 1/4 teaspoon garlic powder
- 1/4 teaspoon salt
- 1/8 teaspoon pepper

TOPPING:
- 1/2 pound bulk Italian sausage, cooked and drained
- 1 can (4 ounces) mushroom stems and pieces, drained
- 1 medium green pepper, sliced
- 1-1/2 cups (6 ounces) shredded part-skim mozzarella cheese

1 In a large bowl, dissolve yeast in water. Add oil, salt, sugar and 2 cups flour. Beat on medium speed for 3 minutes. Stir in enough remaining flour to form a soft dough.

2 Turn onto a floured surface; knead until smooth and elastic, about 6-8 minutes. Place in a greased bowl, turning once to grease top. Cover and let rest in a warm place for 10 minutes.

3 Meanwhile, combine sauce ingredients; set aside. Divide dough in half. On a floured surface, roll each portion into a 13-in. circle. Transfer to greased 12-in. pizza pans; build up edges slightly. Prick dough thoroughly with a fork.

4 Bake at 375° for 15 minutes or until lightly browned. Spread sauce over hot crusts to within 2-in. of edges; sprinkle with the sausage, mushrooms, green pepper and cheese. Bake 20 minutes longer or until cheese is melted. **Yield:** 2 pizzas (8 servings each).

Plum-Glazed Country Ribs

When planning to make ribs one day, I remembered that a friend had given me homemade plum jelly. I stirred some into the sauce for a pleasant fruity accent.

—Ila Mae Alderman, Galax, Virginia

- 4 to 4-1/2 pounds bone-in country-style pork ribs
- 1 bottle (12 ounces) chili sauce
- 1 jar (12 to 13 ounces) plum preserves *or* preserves of your choice
- 1/4 cup soy sauce
- 1/4 teaspoon hot pepper sauce

1 Place the ribs in two ungreased 13-in. x 9-in. x 2-in. baking dishes. Bake, uncovered, at 350° for 45 minutes; drain.

2 In a small saucepan, combine the remaining ingredients. Bring to a boil, stirring occasionally. Remove from the heat. Set aside 3/4 cup sauce for serving.

3 Brush ribs with some of the remaining sauce. Bake, uncovered, for 30-45 minutes or until ribs are tender, turning and basting frequently with remaining sauce. Serve with reserved sauce. **Yield:** 8 servings.

Barbecued Ham 'n' Peaches

These individual foil packets are both sweet and savory in every bite. You can substitute canned ham if you wish.

—Cornelia Whiteway, Chilliwack, British Columbia

- 1/4 cup ketchup
- 1 tablespoon brown sugar
- 1 tablespoon cider vinegar
- 2 teaspoons Worcestershire sauce
- 1 teaspoon vegetable oil
- 1/4 teaspoon pepper
- 4 boneless fully cooked ham slices (4 ounces *each*)
- 1 can (8-1/2 ounces) sliced peaches, drained

1 In a small bowl, combine the ketchup, brown sugar, vinegar, Worcestershire sauce, oil and pepper; brush some of the mixture over ham slices. Place each slice on a greased 12-in. square of heavy-duty foil. Top with peaches; drizzle with remaining ketchup mixture.

2 Fold foil over ham and peaches and seal tightly. Grill, covered, over medium heat for 5-6 minutes on each side or until heated through. **Yield:** 4 servings.

Harvest Stew

To make this tasty stew extra eye-appealing, our home economists topped it with easy-to-cut leaf biscuits, and flavored it with savory pieces of pork plus vegetables and herbs.

—Taste of Home Test Kitchen

HERBED BISCUITS:

2	cups cake flour
1	tablespoon sugar
2	teaspoons baking powder
2	teaspoons minced fresh basil or 3/4 teaspoon dried basil
1	teaspoon minced fresh rosemary or 1/4 teaspoon dried rosemary, crushed
1/2	teaspoon baking soda
1/2	teaspoon salt
6	cups cold butter, cubed
2/3	cup buttermilk

STEW:

1-1/2	pounds boneless pork, cut into 1-inch cubes
2	tablespoons vegetable oil
2	cups chicken broth
1-1/2	cups chopped onion
2	garlic cloves, minced
2	teaspoons each minced fresh basil and rosemary or 3/4 teaspoon each dried basil and rosemary, crushed
1/2	teaspoon salt
1/4	teaspoon pepper
1	medium rutabaga (1-1/4 pounds), cut into 1/2-inch cubes
2	large carrots, cut into 1/2-inch slices
3/4	pound fresh green beans, cut into 1-1/2-inch pieces
3	tablespoons cornstarch
3	tablespoons cold water

1 In a large bowl, combine the first seven ingredients. Cut in butter until mixture resembles coarse crumbs. Stir in buttermilk just until moistened (dough will be slightly sticky).

2 Turn onto a lightly floured surface; knead 8-10 times. Roll out to 1/4-in. thickness; cut with a floured 2-1/2-in. maple leaf or round cutter. Cover and refrigerate.

3 In a Dutch oven, brown pork in oil over medium heat. Stir in the broth, onion, garlic, basil, rosemary, salt and pepper; cover and simmer for 1 hour.

4 Add rutabaga and carrots; cover and simmer for 30 minutes or until vegetables are crisp-tender. Add beans; cook for 10 minutes longer or until beans are crisp-tender. Combine cornstarch and water; stir into stew. Bring to a boil; cook and stir for 2 minutes or until thickened.

5 Pour into an ungreased shallow 2-1/2- to 3-qt. baking dish. Immediately top with 12 biscuits. Bake, uncovered, at 400° for 15 minutes or until biscuits are golden brown. Bake remaining biscuits on an ungreased baking sheet for 10-12 minutes. **Yield:** 6-8 servings.

TIP.............
Rutabaga Basics
Store rutabagas in the refrigerator crisper drawer for up to 2 weeks. Before using, trim the top and bottom. Cut in half, peel and rinse with cold water.

Pineapple Ham Loaf

This loaf is nice enough for the holidays. But we have it often for everyday meals, too, since it's easy to prepare and easy on the pocketbook.

—Linda Manley, Morgantown, West Virginia

- 2 eggs
- 1 cup milk
- 1 cup crushed saltines (about 30 crackers)
- 1/2 teaspoon salt
- 1/8 teaspoon pepper
- 1-1/2 pounds ground fully cooked ham
- 1/2 pound ground pork
- 1/4 cup packed brown sugar
- 2 tablespoons cider vinegar
- 1 teaspoon ground mustard
- 1 can (8 ounces) sliced pineapple, drained, *divided*

1 In a large bowl, combine the first five ingredients. Crumble ham and pork over mixture and mix well. Set aside.

2 In a small bowl, combine the brown sugar, vinegar and mustard; pour into an ungreased 9-in. x 5-in. x 3-in. loaf pan. Arrange three pineapple slices in pan (refrigerate remaining pineapple for another use). Pat meat mixture into pan.

3 Cover and bake at 325° for 1-1/2 hours. Uncover; bake 30 minutes longer or until a meat thermometer reads 160°. Let stand for 15 minutes. Invert onto a serving platter. **Yield:** 8 servings.

Spaghetti Squash Supper

Here's a deliciously different way to serve "spaghetti." This meal is loaded with vegetables and flavor. I sometimes season the meat mixture with cumin instead of Italian seasoning.

—Joyce Hunsberger, Quakertown, Pennsylvania

- 1 medium spaghetti squash (3 to 3-1/2 pounds)
- 1/2 cup water
- 1 pound bulk Italian sausage
- 1 medium onion, chopped
- 1 medium green pepper, chopped
- 1 small zucchini, chopped
- 1 garlic clove, minced
- 1 can (15-1/2 ounces) great northern beans, rinsed and drained
- 1 can (14-1/2 ounces) Italian stewed tomatoes
- 1 teaspoon Italian seasoning
- 1/4 teaspoon seasoned salt

Shredded Parmesan cheese

1 Halve squash lengthwise and discard seeds. Pierce skin with a fork or knife; place, cut side down, in a microwave-safe dish. Add the water; cover and microwave on high for 6-9 minutes or until squash is tender. Let stand for 5 minutes.

2 Meanwhile, in a large skillet, brown sausage until meat is no longer pink; drain. Add the onion, green pepper, zucchini and garlic. Cook, uncovered, for 10 minutes or until the vegetables are crisp-tender, stirring occasionally; drain. Add the beans, tomatoes, Italian seasoning and salt. Cover and simmer for 10 minutes or until heated through.

3 Using a fork, scoop out the spaghetti squash strands; place in a serving dish. Top with sausage mixture. Sprinkle with Parmesan cheese. **Yield:** 6 servings.

EDITOR'S NOTE: This recipe was tested in a 1,100-watt microwave.

TIP . . . .
On a Roll

Some cabbage leaves have a thick rib, which keeps them from lying flat and being easily rolled up. In that case, trim the end of the leaf (and the thick end of the rib).

Pork and Cabbage Rolls

I received this recipe from my mother-in-law and made some adjustments. Because I'm allergic to tomatoes, I cover the rolls with chicken broth.

—Barbara Whitehouse, Huntley, Illinois

- 1   medium head cabbage (3 pounds)
- 1   pound ground pork
- 1/2   pound sage-flavored pork sausage
- 1   cup chopped onion
- 2   cups cooked brown rice
- 1/4   teaspoon pepper
- 2   cups chicken broth *or* 2 cans (15 ounces *each*) seasoned tomato sauce

1   Remove core from the cabbage. Place cabbage in a large saucepan and cover with water. Bring to a boil; boil until outer leaves loosen from head. Remove cabbage; set softened leaves aside. Return cabbage to boiling water to soften more leaves. Repeat until all leaves are softened. Remove tough center stalk from each leaf. Set aside 12 large leaves for rolls. Coarsely chop enough of the remaining leaves to measure 8 cups. Place chopped cabbage in an ungreased 13-in. x 9-in. x 2-in. baking dish.

2   In a skillet over medium heat, cook pork, sausage and onion until meat is no longer pink and onion is tender; drain. Stir in rice. Place 1/2 cup of the meat mixture on each cabbage leaf. Fold in the sides; starting at an unfolded edge, roll up the leaf completely to enclose meat. Repeat with remaining meat and leaves.

3   Place rolls, seam side down, in the baking dish. Sprinkle with pepper. Pour broth or tomato sauce over rolls. Cover and bake at 325° for 1 to 1-1/4 hours. **Yield: 6 servings.**

Pizza Patties

To cut preparation at mealtime, mix and shape these patties the night before and refrigerate. If you like lots of sauce, you may want to serve extra spaghetti sauce on the side for dipping.

—Taste of Home Test Kitchen

- 1/3   cup finely chopped green pepper
- 1   small onion, finely chopped
- 1/4   cup grated Parmesan cheese
- 1   pound bulk Italian sausage
- 1   cup spaghetti sauce
- 4   sandwich buns, split
- 1/2   cup shredded part-skim mozzarella cheese

1   In a large bowl, combine the green pepper, onion and Parmesan cheese. Crumble sausage over mixture and mix just until combined. Shape into four patties.

2   In a large skillet, cook patties over medium heat for 7-8 minutes on each side or until meat is no longer pink; drain.

3   Add the spaghetti sauce; bring to a boil. Reduce heat; cover and simmer for 7-8 minutes or until heated through. Place a patty on the bottom of each bun; drizzle with spaghetti sauce. Sprinkle with mozzarella cheese; replace tops. **Yield: 4 servings.**

Mexican Pork Roast

A friend who lives in Mexico shared this recipe with me some years ago. The leftovers make great burritos and tacos.

—Chuck Allen, Dana Point, California

2	medium onions, sliced
2	medium carrots, sliced
2	jalapeno peppers, seeded and chopped
3	garlic cloves, minced
2	tablespoons olive oil
1/2	cup water
1/2	cup chicken broth
1	teaspoon ground coriander
1/2	teaspoon salt
1/2	teaspoon ground cumin
1/2	teaspoon dried oregano
1/4	teaspoon pepper
1	boneless pork shoulder roast (3 pounds)

1 In a large skillet, saute the onions, carrots, jalapenos and garlic in oil for 3 minutes. Transfer to a 5-qt. slow cooker; add water and broth.

2 In a small bowl, combine the coriander, salt, cumin, oregano and pepper; rub over roast. Cut roast in half; place in the slow cooker. Cover and cook on low for 8-9 hours or until meat is tender.

3 Transfer roast and vegetables to a serving platter; keep warm. Strain cooking juices and skim fat. Pour into a small saucepan. Bring to a boil; cook until liquid is reduced to about 1 cup. Serve with roast and vegetables. **Yield:** 8 servings.

EDITOR'S NOTE: When cutting hot peppers, disposable gloves are recommended. Avoid touching your face.

Pork-Potato Meatballs

Ground pork, shredded potato, green onion and mustard combine to create this savory sensation.

—Julaine Roach, Mauston, Wisconsin

    1   cup finely shredded peeled potato
   1/4 cup chopped green onions
    1   egg, lightly beaten
    2   tablespoons milk
    1   teaspoon prepared mustard
   1/2 teaspoon salt
   1/8 teaspoon pepper
    1   pound ground pork
   1/4 cup dry bread crumbs
  1-1/3 cups water, *divided*
    1   teaspoon chicken bouillon granules
    2   tablespoons all-purpose flour

1 In a large bowl, combine the first seven ingredients. Crumble pork over mixture, sprinkle with bread crumbs and mix well. Shape into 1-in. balls. In a large skillet, brown meatballs in batches over medium heat; drain. Remove and keep warm.

2 Add 1 cup water and bouillon to skillet; stir until bouillon is dissolved. Return meatballs to the pan; cover and cook for 20 minutes or until no longer pink. Combine flour and remaining water until smooth; gradually add to skillet. Bring to a boil; cook and stir for 2 minutes or until thickened. **Yield:** 4 servings.

Slow-Cooked Ribs

Nothing says comfort like a plate full of mouthwatering ribs coated in barbecue sauce. These are delicious and tangy.

—Sharon Crider, St. Robert, Missouri

    4   pounds boneless country-style pork ribs
    1   cup barbecue sauce
    1   cup Catalina salad dressing
   1/2 teaspoon minced garlic
    2   tablespoons all-purpose flour
   1/4 cup cold water

1 Cut ribs into serving-size pieces. Place in a 5-qt. slow cooker. Combine barbecue sauce and salad dressing; pour over ribs. Sprinkle with garlic. Cover and cook on low for 6-7 hours or until meat is tender.

2 Remove ribs and keep warm. Strain cooking liquid into a small saucepan; skim fat. Combine flour and water until smooth; stir into cooking liquid. Bring to a boil; cook and stir for 2 minutes or until thickened. Serve sauce with ribs. **Yield:** 8 servings.

Sausage Scalloped Potatoes

My mom's creamy entree was excellent except for the time it took to cook. So I adapted it for the microwave with wonderful results.

—Erlene Crusoe, Litchfield, Minnesota

- 1   pound smoked kielbasa *or* Polish sausage, cut into 1/4-inch slices
- 2   tablespoons butter
- 2   tablespoons all-purpose flour
- 1   teaspoon salt
- 1/4   teaspoon pepper
- 2   cups milk
- 4   medium red potatoes, halved and thinly sliced (3-1/2 to 4 cups)
- 1/4   cup chopped onion
- 2   tablespoons minced fresh parsley, optional

1 Place the sausage in a microwave-safe bowl. Microwave, uncovered, on high for 3 minutes. Drain and set aside.

2 Place butter in a 2-1/2-qt. microwave-safe dish. Heat on high for 45-60 seconds or until melted. Whisk in flour, salt and pepper until smooth. Gradually whisk in milk. Microwave, uncovered, on high for 8-10 minutes or until thickened and bubbly, stirring every 2 minutes.

3 Stir in potatoes and onion. Cover and microwave on high for 4 minutes; stir. Heat 4 minutes longer. Stir in the sausage. Cover and cook for 8-10 minutes, stirring every 4 minutes or until potatoes are tender and sausage is heated through. Stir. Let stand, covered, for 5 minutes. Sprinkle with parsley if desired. **Yield:** 4-6 servings.

Creamed Ham on Corn Bread

I top pieces of corn bread with a cheesy sauce chock-full of ham to make a satisfying supper. This is one budget meal our family loves.

—Denise Hershman, Cromwell, Indiana

- 1   package (8-1/2 ounces) corn bread/muffin mix
- 1   egg
- 1/3   cup milk

CREAMED HAM:

- 2   tablespoons butter
- 2   tablespoons all-purpose flour
- 1/2   teaspoon ground mustard
- 1/4   teaspoon salt
- 1-1/2   cups milk
- 3/4   cup shredded cheddar cheese
- 1-1/2   cups cubed fully cooked ham

1 In a large bowl, combine the corn bread/muffin mix, egg and milk until blended. Spread into a greased 8-in. square baking pan. Bake at 400° for 18-20 minutes.

2 Meanwhile, in a saucepan, melt butter; stir in the flour, mustard and salt until smooth. Add milk. Bring to a boil; cook and stir for 2 minutes or until thickened. Stir in cheese until melted. Add ham and heat through. Cut corn bread into squares; top with creamed ham. **Yield:** 6 servings.

Saucy Pork Chops with Vegetables

Served with mashed potatoes, these savory chops satisfy any hearty appetite. It is a very colorful dish and is nice to share with guests, too.

—Mildred Sherrer, Fort Worth, Texas

- 6   pork chops (1/2 inch thick)
- 1   cup sliced carrots
- 1   medium green pepper, cut into strips
- 1   medium onion, chopped
- 1   can (10-3/4 ounces) condensed golden mushroom soup, undiluted
- 1/4   cup water
- 1/2   to 3/4 teaspoon rubbed sage

Hot cooked noodles *or* rice

1 In a large skillet coated with cooking spray, brown pork chops on both sides. Remove and set aside. Saute the carrots, green pepper and onion until crisp-tender, stirring to loosen any browned bits from pan. Stir in the soup, water and sage. Return chops to the pan. Cover and simmer for 15-20 minutes or until meat is tender. Serve with noodles or rice. **Yield:** 6 servings.

Sausage Vermicelli

This is a longtime family favorite. Sausage adds great flavor to a speedy skillet supper.

—Shauna Hamman, Mesa, Arizona

- 1   pound bulk pork sausage
- 1   medium onion, chopped
- 1   cup sliced celery
- 4-1/2   cups water
- 1   cup uncooked long grain rice
- 2   packages (2.1 ounces *each*) chicken noodle soup mix

1 In a large skillet, cook the sausage, onion and celery over medium heat until meat is no longer pink; drain. Remove meat and vegetables with a slotted spoon and set aside.

2 In the same skillet, combine the water, rice and soup mixes. Bring to a boil. Reduce heat; cover and simmer for 12-15 minutes or until rice is tender. Stir in sausage mixture; heat through. **Yield:** 5 servings.

Poultry

Country Roasted Chicken

This is my family's favorite way to eat poultry. It gets wonderful flavor from the celery, onion and parsley tucked inside.

—Judy Page, Edenville, Michigan

- 1 broiler/fryer chicken (3 pounds)
- 1/2 teaspoon dried thyme
- 2 teaspoons salt, *divided*
- 1 large onion, cut into eighths
- 2 celery ribs with leaves, cut into 4-inch pieces
- 4 fresh parsley sprigs
- 8 small red potatoes
- 1/4 cup chicken broth
- 1/4 cup minced fresh parsley

1 Sprinkle the inside of chicken with thyme and 1 teaspoon salt. Stuff chicken with the onion, celery and parsley sprigs. Place in a greased Dutch oven.

2 Cover and bake at 375° for 30 minutes. Sprinkle remaining salt over chicken. Add potatoes and broth to pan. Cover and bake 25 minutes longer.

3 Increase oven temperature to 400°. Bake, uncovered, for 10-15 minutes or until potatoes are tender and a meat thermometer inserted in the chicken thighs reads 180°. Sprinkle with minced parsley. **Yield:** 4 servings.

Turkey Enchiladas

These enchiladas are generously stuffed with cubed turkey, cheese and chilies in a mild, creamy sauce. My daughter first made these for us, and I asked for the recipe.

—Leona Therou, Overland Park, Kansas

- 1 medium onion, chopped
- 1/3 cup chopped green pepper
- 2 tablespoons vegetable oil
- 2 cups cubed cooked turkey
- 1 cup (4 ounces) shredded Colby-Monterey Jack cheese, *divided*
- 1 can (4 ounces) chopped green chilies
- 1 cup (8 ounces) sour cream
- 1 can (10-3/4 ounces) condensed cream of chicken soup, undiluted
- 1/4 teaspoon ground coriander
- 1/8 teaspoon ground cumin
- 6 flour tortillas (8 inches), warmed

1 In a large skillet, saute onion and green pepper in oil until tender; remove from the heat. Stir in the turkey, 1/2 cup of cheese and chilies; set aside. In a large saucepan, combine the sour cream, soup, coriander and cumin. Cook and stir over low heat until warm; stir 1/2 cup into the turkey mixture.

2 Spoon about 1/3 cup turkey filling down the center of each tortilla; roll up tightly. Place seam side down in a greased 13-in. x 9-in. x 2-in. baking dish. Spoon remaining soup mixture down center of tortillas. Sprinkle with remaining cheese.

3 Bake, uncovered, at 350° for 20-25 minutes or until heated through. **Yield:** 6 servings.

Oregano-Lemon Chicken

I've been known to make this recipe twice a week. I like to call it sticky chicken since the slightly sweet sauce of honey, lemon juice and herbs nicely coats the chicken thighs.

—Dorothy Reinhold, Malibu, California

- 6 bone-in chicken thighs (3 pounds)
- 3 tablespoons lemon juice
- 2 tablespoons honey
- 1 tablespoon olive oil
- 3 garlic cloves, minced
- 2 teaspoons dried oregano

1 Place the chicken in a greased 13-in. x 9-in. x 2-in. baking dish. Combine the lemon juice, honey, oil, garlic and oregano; pour over chicken.

2 Bake, uncovered, at 375° for 45 minutes or until a meat thermometer reads 180° and chicken juices run clear, basting occasionally with pan juices. **Yield:** 6 servings.

TIP . . . .
Crystallized Honey

If your honey crystallizes, place the jar in warm water and stir until the crystals dissolve. Or place honey in a microwave-safe container and microwave on high, stirring every 30 seconds, until the crystals dissolve.

Chicken Spareribs

Inexpensive chicken thighs get all gussied up in a zippy sparerib-style sauce that's irresistible.

—Janice Porterfield, Atlanta, Texas

8	bone-in chicken thighs
2	tablespoons vegetable oil
1	cup water
2/3	cup packed brown sugar
2/3	cup soy sauce
1/2	cup apple juice
1/4	cup ketchup
2	tablespoons cider vinegar
2	garlic cloves, minced
1	teaspoon crushed red pepper flakes
1/2	teaspoon ground ginger
2	tablespoons cornstarch
2	tablespoons cold water

1 In a Dutch oven, brown chicken over medium heat in oil in batches on both sides; drain. Return all of the chicken to the pan.

2 In a large bowl, combine the water, brown sugar, soy sauce, apple juice, ketchup, vinegar, garlic, pepper flakes and ginger; pour over chicken. Bring to a boil. Reduce heat; cover and simmer for 20 minutes or until chicken juices run clear.

3 Remove chicken to a platter and keep warm. Combine cornstarch and water until smooth; stir into cooking juices. Bring to a boil; cook and stir for 2 minutes or until thickened. Serve with chicken. **Yield:** 4 servings.

TIP
Cut Carrot Costs

When a recipe uses baby carrots (like Turkey Leg Pot Roast at right), you can purchase a more economical package of carrots and slice them into strips or chunks.

Turkey Leg Pot Roast

Well-seasoned turkey legs and tender veggies make this meal ideal for a crisp fall day. Moist and satisfying, the recipe couldn't be more comforting!

—Rick and Vegas Pearson, Cadillac, Michigan

3	medium potatoes, peeled and quartered
2	cups fresh baby carrots
2	celery ribs, cut into 2-1/2-inch pieces
1	medium onion, peeled and quartered
3	garlic cloves, peeled and quartered
1/2	cup chicken broth
3	turkey drumsticks (about 1/2 pound *each*)
2	teaspoons seasoned salt
1	teaspoon dried thyme
1	teaspoon dried parsley flakes
1/4	teaspoon pepper

1 In a greased 5-qt. slow cooker, combine the first six ingredients. Place drumsticks over vegetables. Sprinkle with the seasoned salt, thyme, parsley and pepper. Cover; cook on low for 5 to 5-1/2 hours or until a meat thermometer reads 180°. **Yield:** 3 servings.

Breaded Chicken with Orange Sauce

After cooking the chicken in its coating, you're left with browned bits in the pan that make a delightful sauce with orange juice and Italian seasoning.

—Soraida Angie Cannestra
Milwaukee, Wisconsin

1/4	cup milk
3/4	cup seasoned bread crumbs
4-1/2	teaspoons grated Parmesan cheese
3/4	teaspoon Italian seasoning, *divided*
1/2	teaspoon garlic powder
4	boneless skinless chicken breast halves (5 ounces *each*)
3	tablespoons vegetable oil
3/4	cup orange juice

Hot cooked rice

1 Place milk in a shallow bowl. In another shallow bowl, combine the bread crumbs, Parmesan cheese, 1/2 teaspoon Italian seasoning and garlic powder. Dip chicken in milk, then evenly coat with crumb mixture.

2 In a large skillet, cook chicken in oil over medium heat for 6-8 minutes on each side or until juices run clear. Remove and keep warm.

3 Add orange juice and remaining Italian seasoning to skillet, stirring to loosen browned bits. Bring to a boil; cook until sauce is reduced to about 1/4 cup. Serve with chicken and rice. **Yield:** 4 servings.

Braised Turkey Thighs

Folks who enjoy dark meat will appreciate this treatment for turkey thighs. An oven bag keeps them nice and moist during baking. Little bits of vegetables add taste and texture to the flavorful gravy.

—Loretta Paulus, Venice, Florida

1	cup *each* finely chopped onion, celery and carrot
1/3	cup ketchup
1-1/4	teaspoons salt
1/2	teaspoon paprika
1/8	teaspoon pepper
4	pounds turkey thighs
2	tablespoons all-purpose flour, *divided*
1	large oven roasting bag
1/2	cup reduced-sodium chicken broth
1/3	cup dry white wine *or* additional reduced-sodium chicken broth
1	teaspoon dried oregano
2	bay leaves
1/4	cup cold water

1 In a large bowl, combine the onion, celery, carrots, ketchup, salt, paprika and pepper. Pat onto turkey thighs. Place 1 tablespoon flour in oven bag; shake to coat. Transfer turkey thighs to oven bag.

2 Place in a 13-in. x 9-in. x 2-in. baking dish. Combine the broth, wine or additional broth, oregano and bay leaves. Put into bag; seal. Cut 2 slits into the top of the bag. Bake at 350° for 1-1/2 hours or until a meat thermometer reads 180° and the turkey juices run clear.

3 Remove turkey to a serving platter; keep warm. Pour pan juices into a small saucepan; skim fat and discard bay leaves. Bring to a boil. Reduce heat; simmer, uncovered, for 5 minutes or until mixture is reduced to 1-3/4 cups.

4 In a small bowl, combine remaining flour and water until smooth. Stir into saucepan. Bring to a boil; cook and stir for 2 minutes or until thickened. Remove skin and bones from turkey; cut turkey into slices. Serve gravy with the turkey. **Yield:** 8 servings.

Chicken Veggie Casserole

With chicken, corn, beans and potatoes, this casserole is a hot, complete meal in a dish.

—Martha Balser, Cincinnati, Ohio

1	can (10-3/4 ounces) condensed cream of chicken soup, undiluted
1/2	cup milk
1/4	teaspoon dried thyme
1/4	teaspoon salt
1/4	teaspoon pepper
2	cups cubed cooked chicken
1	can (15-1/4 ounces) whole kernel corn, drained
2	cups frozen cut green beans, thawed
2	cups sliced cooked potatoes

1 In a large bowl, combine the soup, milk, thyme, salt and pepper. Stir in the chicken, corn, beans and potatoes. Pour into a greased 1-1/2-qt. baking dish. Bake, uncovered, at 400° for 15 minutes or until heated through. **Yield:** 6 servings.

Orange Chicken

These golden chicken pieces are nicely seasoned with a tangy citrus marinade. The ingredients are easy to have on hand so you can whip up this special entree anytime.

—Rita Goshaw, South Milwaukee, Wisconsin

- 4 chicken leg quarters (3-1/2 pounds), skin removed
- 1 teaspoon salt
- 1/8 to 1/4 teaspoon pepper
- 3 tablespoons orange juice concentrate
- 1 tablespoon honey
- 1 teaspoon prepared mustard

1 Place chicken in a single layer in a greased 13-in. x 9-in. x 2-in. baking pan; sprinkle with salt and pepper. Bake, uncovered, at 375° for 25 minutes.

2 In a small bowl, combine the orange juice concentrate, honey and mustard. Baste chicken with half the marinade. Bake 15 minutes longer; baste with the remaining marinade. Bake 10 minutes more or until the meat juices run clear. **Yield:** 4 servings.

Chili Chicken 'n' Rice

Tender chicken breasts on top of hearty chili and rice make for a filling and frugal meal-in-one. Choose mild or hot chili to suit your family's taste.

—Kathy Duke, Anchorage, Alaska

- 4 boneless skinless chicken breast halves (4 ounces *each*)
- 2 cups cooked rice
- 1 can (15 ounces) chili with beans
- 2 tablespoons taco seasoning
- 4 slices process American cheese

1 In a large nonstick skillet, brown the chicken over medium heat on both sides. Spread rice in a greased 11-in. x 7-in. x 2-in. baking dish. Combine the chili and taco seasoning; spoon over the rice. Top with chicken.

2 Cover and bake at 350° for 25 minutes. Top with cheese slices. Bake, uncovered, for 5 minutes or until a meat thermometer reads 170°. **Yield:** 4 servings.

Garlic Rosemary Turkey

The house smells so good while this turkey is cooking that my family can hardly wait to eat! This is a beautiful, succulent main dish.

—Cathy Dobbins, Rio Rancho, New Mexico

- 1 whole turkey (10 to 12 pounds)
- 6 to 8 garlic cloves
- 2 large lemons, halved
- 2 teaspoons dried rosemary, crushed
- 1 teaspoon rubbed sage

1 Cut six to eight small slits in turkey skin; insert garlic between the skin and meat. Squeeze two lemon halves inside the turkey and stuff them in the turkey. Squeeze remaining lemon over outside of turkey. Spray the turkey with cooking spray; sprinkle with rosemary and sage.

2 Place on a rack in a roasting pan. Tie drumsticks together. Bake, uncovered, at 325° for 1 hour. Cover and bake 2-1/2 to 3-1/2 hours longer or until a meat thermometer reads 180°, basting occasionally with the pan drippings. (Cover loosely with foil if turkey browns too quickly.) **Yield:** 8-10 servings.

BBQ Chicken Sandwiches

These are great sandwiches and are a cinch to make. For a spicier taste, eliminate the ketchup and increase the amount of salsa to 1 cup.

—Leticia Lewis, Kennewick, Washington

- 1/2 cup chopped onion
- 1/2 cup diced celery
- 1 garlic clove, minced
- 1 tablespoon butter
- 1/2 cup salsa
- 1/2 cup ketchup
- 2 tablespoons brown sugar
- 2 tablespoons cider vinegar
- 1 tablespoon Worcestershire sauce
- 1/2 teaspoon chili powder
- 1/4 teaspoon salt
- 1/8 teaspoon pepper
- 2 cups shredded cooked chicken
- 6 hamburger buns, split and toasted

1 In a large saucepan, saute the onion, celery and garlic in butter until tender. Stir in the salsa, ketchup, brown sugar, vinegar, Worcestershire sauce, chili powder, salt and pepper. Stir in chicken. Bring to a boil. Reduce heat; cover and simmer for 15 minutes. Serve about 1/3 cup chicken mixture on each bun. **Yield:** 6 servings.

TIP
Prevent Sprouting Garlic

Store-bought garlic is sometimes last year's crop. If the cloves start to sprout, they pick up a very strong bitter taste. To prevent this, cut cloves in half before using and remove the green sprout in the middle.

Creamed Chicken Over Beans

This simple but tasty blend will surprise you. It uses leftover chicken and frozen green beans, so it's fast to fix for a brunch or light lunch.

—Louise Martin, Denver, Pennsylvania

- 1/4 cup butter
- 1/4 cup all-purpose flour
- 1/2 teaspoon salt
- 1/8 teaspoon pepper
- 1-1/2 cups water
- 1/4 cup milk
- 1 teaspoon chicken bouillon granules
- 2 cups cubed cooked chicken
- 1 package (16 ounces) frozen cut green beans, cooked and drained

Paprika, optional

1 In a large saucepan, melt butter. Stir in the flour, salt and pepper until smooth. Gradually add the water, milk and bouillon. Bring to a boil; cook and stir for 2 minutes or until thickened. Add the chicken and heat through. Serve over beans. Sprinkle with paprika if desired. **Yield:** 4 servings.

Asian Turkey Burgers

I use garlic, ginger and soy sauce to turn ground turkey into moist, tender patties. These better-for-you burgers are winners at my house.

—Jeanette Saskowski, Antioch, Tennessee

- 1 egg white
- 1 tablespoon soy sauce
- 1/2 cup dry bread crumbs
- 1 tablespoon finely chopped onion
- 1 garlic clove, minced
- 1/4 teaspoon ground ginger
- 1/8 teaspoon pepper
- 12 ounces ground turkey

1 In a large bowl, combine the first seven ingredients. Crumble turkey over mixture and mix just until combined. Shape into four patties. In a nonstick skillet coated with cooking spray, cook turkey over medium heat for 6-8 minutes on each side or until a meat thermometer reaches 165°. **Yield:** 4 servings.

Skillet Chicken Supper

This hearty main dish is gently spiced with a tasty vegetable medley. Frozen mixed vegetables can be used in place of the peas.

—Marlene Muckenhirn, Delano, Minnesota

- 1 cup all-purpose flour
- 1 teaspoon garlic powder
- 1 teaspoon pepper
- 1 broiler/fryer chicken (3 to 4 pounds), cut up
- 2 tablespoons vegetable oil
- 1-3/4 cups water, *divided*
- 1/2 cup soy sauce
- 1/2 teaspoon dried oregano
- 3 medium red potatoes, cut into 1-inch chunks
- 3 large carrots, cut into 1-inch pieces
- 3 celery ribs, cut into 1-inch pieces
- 1 package (10 ounces) frozen peas

1 In a small bowl, combine the flour, garlic powder and pepper. Pour half the flour mixture into a large resealable plastic bag. Add chicken, one piece at a time, and shake to coat; set the remaining flour mixture aside.

2 In a large skillet, cook chicken in oil until browned on all sides; drain. Combine 1-1/4 cups water, soy sauce and oregano; pour over chicken. Add the vegetables. Bring to a boil; reduce heat. Cover and simmer for 30-40 minutes or until the chicken juices run clear. Remove chicken and vegetables; keep warm.

3 Combine reserved flour mixture and remaining water until smooth; add to the cooking juices. Bring to a boil; cook and stir for 2 minutes or until thickened. Serve with the chicken and vegetables. **Yield:** 6 servings.

TIP . . . .
Cutting Up a Whole Chicken

Instead of buying a cut-up chicken, save money and do it yourself. Here's how:

Pull the leg and thigh away from the body of the bird. With a small, sharp knife, cut through the skin to expose the joint.

Cut through the joint, then cut the skin around thigh to free the leg. Repeat with the other leg.

Separate the drumstick from the thigh by cutting the skin at the joint. Bend drumstick to expose joint; cut through joint and skin.

Pull wing away from the body. Cut through skin to expose joint. Cut through joint and skin to separate wing from body. Repeat.

With kitchen or poultry shears, snip along each side of the backbone between rib joints.

Hold chicken breast in both hands (skin side down) and bend the breast back to snap the breastbone. Turn over and cut in half along the breastbone. The breastbone will remain attached to one of the halves.

Tex-Mex Turkey Casserole

Every time I make this for guests, I end up sharing my recipe. One bite and you'll see why!

—Debra Martin, Belleville, Michigan

- 1 pound lean ground turkey
- 1 medium green pepper, chopped
- 1 medium onion, chopped
- 3 garlic cloves, minced
- 2 cans (15 ounces *each*) black beans, rinsed and drained
- 1 jar (16 ounces) salsa
- 1 can (15 ounces) tomato sauce
- 1 can (14-1/2 ounces) Mexican stewed tomatoes
- 1 teaspoon *each* onion powder, garlic powder and ground cumin
- 12 corn tortillas (6 inches)
- 2 cups (8 ounces) shredded reduced-fat cheddar cheese, *divided*

1 In a large nonstick saucepan coated with cooking spray, cook the turkey, green pepper, onion and garlic over medium heat until meat is no longer pink. Stir in the beans, salsa, tomato sauce, tomatoes, onion powder, garlic powder and cumin. Bring to a boil. Reduce heat; simmer, uncovered, for 10 minutes.

2 Spread 1 cup meat sauce into a 13-in. x 9-in. x 2-in. baking dish coated with cooking spray. Top with six tortillas. Spread with half of the remaining meat sauce; sprinkle with 1 cup cheese. Layer with remaining tortillas and meat sauce.

3 Cover and bake at 350° for 20 minutes. Uncover; sprinkle with remaining cheese. Bake 5-10 minutes longer or until bubbly and cheese is melted. **Yield:** 10 servings.

Oven-Fried Chicken

Tarragon, ginger and cayenne pepper season the cornmeal coating that I use on my golden "fried" chicken. The moist meat and crunchy coating are sure to make this homey entree a mealtime mainstay at your house, too.

—Daucia Brooks, Westmoreland, Tennessee

- 1/2 cup cornmeal
- 1/2 cup dry bread crumbs
- 1 teaspoon dried tarragon
- 1 teaspoon ground ginger
- 1/2 teaspoon salt
- 1/4 teaspoon cayenne pepper
- 1/4 teaspoon pepper
- 3 egg whites
- 2 tablespoons fat-free milk
- 1/2 cup all-purpose flour
- 1 broiler/fryer chicken (3 to 4 pounds), cut up

Refrigerated butter-flavored spray

1 In a shallow bowl, combine the first seven ingredients. In another shallow bowl, combine egg whites and milk. Place flour in a third shallow bowl. Coat chicken with flour; dip in the egg white mixture, then roll in cornmeal mixture.

2 Place in a 15-in. x 10-in. x 2-in. baking pan coated with cooking spray. Bake, uncovered, at 350° for 40 minutes. Spritz with butter-flavored spray. Bake 10-15 minutes longer or until juices run clear. **Yield:** 6 servings.

Orange-Mustard Grilled Chicken

We love grilling out...and this is one of our favorite recipes. The ginger, orange and mustard flavors make a tantalizing sauce for the moist chicken.

—Paula Marchesi, Lenhartsville, Pennsylvania

- 1/4 cup lemon-lime soda
- 1/4 cup orange juice
- 1/4 cup Dijon mustard
- 1/4 cup reduced-sodium soy sauce
- 3 tablespoons honey
- 2 tablespoons minced fresh gingerroot
- 6 boneless skinless chicken breast halves (4 ounces each)

1 In a small bowl, combine the first six ingredients. Pour 3/4 cup marinade into a large resealable plastic bag; add the chicken. Seal bag and turn to coat; refrigerate for 45 minutes. Cover and refrigerate remaining marinade for basting.

2 Coat grill rack with cooking spray before starting the grill. Drain and discard marinade from chicken. Grill, covered, over medium heat 5-6 minutes on each side or until the juices run clear, basting occasionally with the reserved marinade. **Yield:** 6 servings.

TIP
Boning Chicken Breasts
To remove the bone from chicken breasts, insert a small boning or paring knife between the ribs and breast meat. Press knife along bones; cut to remove meat.

Szechuan Chicken Noodle Toss

My family loves Chinese food, so I came up with this quick and easy recipe to use up leftover chicken, pork or beef.

—Carol Roane, Sarasota, Florida

- 4 quarts water
- 6 ounces uncooked thin spaghetti
- 1 package (16 ounces) frozen stir-fry vegetable blend
- 1 tablespoon butter
- 1 pound boneless skinless chicken breasts, cut into 2-inch strips
- 2 garlic cloves, minced
- 1/8 teaspoon crushed red pepper flakes
- 1 tablespoon vegetable oil
- 1/3 cup stir-fry sauce
- 3 green onions, chopped

1 In a Dutch oven, bring water to a boil. Add spaghetti; cook for 4 minutes. Add vegetables; cook 3-4 minutes longer or until spaghetti and vegetables are tender. Drain. Toss with butter; set aside and keep warm.

2 In a nonstick skillet, stir-fry the chicken, garlic and red pepper flakes in oil until the chicken is no longer pink. Add the stir-fry sauce; heat through. Add the onions and spaghetti mixture; toss to coat. **Yield:** 4 servings.

Cranberry Turkey Loaf

This is a delightful alternative to meat loaf. It's very moist, and the cranberry sauce gives it a tasty twist.

—Paula Zsiray, Logan, Utah

- 1/2 cup herb-seasoned stuffing mix, crushed
- 1 egg, lightly beaten
- 3/4 cup whole-berry cranberry sauce, *divided*
- 1/4 teaspoon salt
- 1/8 teaspoon pepper
- 1 pound ground turkey

1 In a large bowl, combine the stuffing mix, egg, 1/4 cup cranberry sauce, salt and pepper. Crumble turkey over mixture and mix well.

2 Pat into an ungreased 8-in. x 4-in. x 2-in. loaf pan. Bake, uncovered, at 350° for 55-65 minutes or until a meat thermometer reads 165°.

3 Heat remaining cranberry sauce in a microwave on high for 1 minute or until heated through. Slice turkey loaf; serve with sauce. **Yield:** 4 servings.

Easy Chicken and Noodles

I prepare this stovetop supper in mere minutes. Canned soup makes the sauce a snap to throw together while the noodles boil.

—Shirley Heston, Lancaster, Ohio

- 1 can (10-3/4 ounces) condensed cream of chicken soup, undiluted
- 3/4 cup milk
- 1/3 cup grated Parmesan cheese
- 1/8 teaspoon pepper
- 3 cups cooked wide egg noodles
- 2 cups cubed cooked chicken

1 In a large saucepan, combine the soup, milk, Parmesan cheese and pepper. Stir in the noodles and chicken; heat through. **Yield:** 4 servings.

Turkey Biscuit Potpie

Refrigerated buttermilk biscuits cut the preparation time in this comforting classic.

—Vicki Kerr, Portland, Maine

- 1   pound ground turkey
- 3   tablespoons all-purpose flour
- 2   cups milk
- 2-1/2   cups frozen peas and carrots, thawed
- 1/4   to 1/2 teaspoon salt
- 1/4   teaspoon pepper
- 1   tube (12 ounces) refrigerated buttermilk biscuits, separated into 10 biscuits

1 In a large skillet coated with cooking spray, cook turkey until no longer pink; drain. Meanwhile, in a large saucepan, combine flour and milk until smooth. Bring to a boil; cook and stir for 2 minutes or until thickened. Stir in vegetables, salt, pepper and turkey; remove from heat and keep warm.

2 Place biscuits 2 in. apart on an ungreased baking sheet. Bake at 400° for 5 minutes. Transfer turkey mixture to a greased 8-in. square baking dish. Place nine biscuits over turkey mixture. Bake potpie and remaining biscuit for 5-7 minutes or until biscuits are golden brown. **Yield:** 5 servings.

Ranch Turkey Pasta Dinner

This entree is a great way to showcase leftover holiday turkey.

—Peggy Key, Grant, Alabama

- 2-1/2   cups uncooked penne pasta
- 6   to 8 tablespoons butter, cubed
- 1   envelope ranch salad dressing mix
- 1   cup frozen peas and carrots, thawed
- 3   cups cubed cooked turkey

1 Cook pasta according to package directions. Meanwhile, in a large skillet, melt butter. Stir in salad dressing; mix until smooth. Add peas and carrots; cook and stir for 2-3 minutes. Drain pasta and add to skillet. Stir in turkey; cook 3-4 minutes or until heated through. **Yield:** 4 servings.

Spicy Chicken Stew

When your family has a taste for Mexican food, reach for this slightly spicy recipe. Round out the meal with a tossed salad.

—Taste of Home Test Kitchen

- 3   pounds boneless skinless chicken thighs, cut into 1/2-inch pieces
- 2   teaspoons minced garlic
- 2   tablespoons olive oil
- 1   can (15 ounces) garbanzo beans or chickpeas, rinsed and drained
- 1   can (14-1/2 ounces) diced tomatoes with onions, undrained
- 1   cup lime-garlic salsa
- 1   teaspoon ground cumin
- 1/3   cup minced fresh cilantro

Sour cream, optional

1 In a Dutch oven, cook chicken and garlic in oil for 5 minutes. Stir in the beans, tomatoes, salsa and cumin. Cover and simmer for 15 minutes or until chicken is no longer pink. Stir in cilantro. Top with sour cream if desired. **Yield:** 6 servings.

Garlic Clove Chicken

My Greek neighbors made this roasted chicken frequently, and I couldn't get enough of it. If you like garlic, you'll love this chicken!

—Denise Hollebeke, Penhold, Alberta

1	roasting chicken (5 to 6 pounds)
1	small onion, quartered
40	garlic cloves, peeled
1/4	cup vegetable oil
1-1/2	teaspoons salt
1	teaspoon dried parsley flakes
1/2	teaspoon dried celery flakes
1/2	teaspoon *each* dried tarragon, thyme and rosemary, crushed
1/4	teaspoon pepper

1 Place chicken breast side up on a rack in a shallow roasting pan. Stuff onion in chicken; tie drumsticks together. Arrange garlic cloves around chicken. In a small bowl, combine the remaining ingredients. Drizzle over chicken and garlic.

2 Cover and bake at 350° for 1-3/4 hours. Uncover; bake 30-45 minutes longer or until a meat thermometer reads 180°, basting occasionally with pan drippings. (Cover loosely with foil if chicken browns too quickly.) Cover and let stand for 10 minutes before slicing. **Yield:** 6 servings.

Turkey Tetrazzini

This tasty main dish is popular with everyone. A delicious layer of melted cheese tops this hearty, creamy casserole.

—Sue Ross, Casa Grande, Arizona

2	cups uncooked spaghetti (broken into 2-inch pieces)
1	teaspoon chicken bouillon granules
3/4	cup boiling water
1	can (10-3/4 ounces) condensed cream of mushroom soup, undiluted
1/8	teaspoon celery salt
1/8	teaspoon pepper
1-1/2	cups cubed cooked turkey
1	small onion, finely chopped
2	tablespoons diced pimientos, drained
1-1/2	cups (6 ounces) shredded cheddar cheese, *divided*

1 Cook spaghetti according to package directions. Meanwhile, in a large bowl, dissolve bouillon in water. Add the soup, celery salt and pepper. Drain spaghetti; add to soup mixture. Stir in the turkey, onion, pimientos and 1/2 cup of cheese.

2 Transfer to a greased 8-in. square baking dish. Top with the remaining cheese. Bake, uncovered, at 350° for 35-40 minutes or until heated through. **Yield:** 6 servings.

Creamy Baked Chicken

Even when my grocery budget is tight, my family and I can enjoy full-flavored foods. This dish is comforting and easy to prepare.

—Barbara Clarke, Punta Gorda, Florida

- 1   broiler/fryer chicken (3 pounds), cut up
- 1   can (10-3/4 ounces) condensed cream of chicken soup, undiluted
- 1   can (10-3/4 ounces) condensed cream of mushroom soup, undiluted
- 1   cup (8 ounces) sour cream
- 1/2 cup water
- 1   teaspoon snipped chives

Salt and pepper to taste
- 1/2 teaspoon paprika

1 Place chicken in a greased 13-in. x 9-in. x 2-in. baking dish. In a large bowl, combine the soups, sour cream, water, chives, salt and pepper; spoon over chicken. Sprinkle with paprika.

2 Bake, uncovered, at 350° for 1 hour or until chicken juices run clear. **Yield:** 6 servings.

Apricot Honey Chicken

With its sweet, fruity sauce, this entree is a sheer delight. There's no need to heat up the oven, so you can even enjoy it during the summer...or any time of year.

—Kathy Hawkins, Ingleside, Illinois

- 4   boneless skinless chicken breast halves (5 ounces each)
- 1   tablespoon vegetable oil
- 3   tablespoons apricot preserves
- 2   tablespoons orange juice
- 4   teaspoons honey

1 In a large skillet, cook chicken in oil over medium heat for 7-9 minutes on each side or until juices run clear. Combine the preserves, orange juice and honey; pour over chicken. Cook for 2 minutes or until heated through. **Yield:** 4 servings.

Honey Barbecued Chicken

This chicken has plenty of taste and eye appeal. It's baked to perfection in an onion sauce that's both sweet and spunky.

—Debbi Smith, Crossett, Arkansas

- 2 broiler/fryer chickens (3 pounds *each*), cut up
- 1/2 teaspoon salt
- 1/2 teaspoon pepper
- 2 large onions, chopped
- 2 cans (8 ounces *each*) tomato sauce
- 1/2 cup cider vinegar
- 1/2 cup honey
- 1/4 cup Worcestershire sauce
- 2 teaspoons paprika
- 1/2 teaspoon hot pepper sauce

1 Place chicken, skin side down, in an ungreased 13-in. x 9-in. x 2-in. baking dish. Sprinkle with the salt and pepper. Combine the remaining ingredients; pour over chicken.

2 Bake, uncovered, at 375° for 30 minutes. Turn chicken and bake 20 minutes longer or until chicken juices run clear, basting occasionally. **Yield:** 8 servings.

TIP
Keep Onions Handy

Stock up on onions when on sale. Chop and place in a 15-in. x 10-in. x 1-in. pan in the freezer. When frozen, place in freezer bags or containers; freeze for up to 1 year. Frozen chopped onions are best used in recipes such as soups, sauces and casseroles.

Fish & Meatless

Tasty Lentil Tacos

Finding dishes that are healthy for my husband and yummy for our children is a challenge. This recipe is a huge hit with everyone.

—**Michelle Thomas, Bangor, Maine**

1	cup finely chopped onion
1	garlic clove, minced
1	teaspoon canola oil
1	cup dried lentils, rinsed
1	tablespoon chili powder
2	teaspoons ground cumin
1	teaspoon dried oregano
2-1/2	cups chicken *or* vegetable broth
1	cup salsa
12	taco shells

1-1/2	cups shredded lettuce
1	cup chopped fresh tomato
1-1/2	cups (6 ounces) shredded reduced-fat cheddar cheese
6	tablespoons fat-free sour cream

1 In a large nonstick skillet, saute the onion and garlic in oil until tender. Add the lentils, chili powder, cumin and oregano; cook and stir for 1 minute. Add broth; bring to a boil. Reduce heat; cover and simmer for 25-30 minutes or until the lentils are tender.

2 Uncover; cook for 6-8 minutes or until mixture is thickened. Mash lentils slightly. Stir in salsa.

3 Spoon about 1/4 cup lentil mixture into each taco shell. Top with lettuce, tomato, cheese and sour cream. **Yield:** 6 servings.

Creole Tuna

I know you'll enjoy this speedy recipe. It has been in my family for as long as I can remember. Because it relies on pantry staples, it's easy to make when you can't decide what to fix for dinner.

—Betty Bernat, Littleton, New Hampshire

- 1/4 cup chopped green pepper
- 2 tablespoons butter
- 2 tablespoons all-purpose flour
- 1/2 teaspoon sugar
- 1/2 teaspoon salt
- 1/8 teaspoon pepper
- 1/3 cup milk
- 1 can (14-1/2 ounces) stewed tomatoes
- 1 can (6 ounces) tuna, drained and flaked
- 1 teaspoon Creole seasoning

Hot cooked rice, optional

1 In a large saucepan, saute green pepper in butter until tender. Stir in the flour, sugar, salt and pepper until blended. Gradually add milk, stirring constantly. Stir in tomatoes. Bring to a boil; cook and stir for 2 minutes. Add tuna and Creole seasoning; heat through. Serve with rice if desired. **Yield:** 4 servings.

Cajun-Style Catfish

This dish features the green pepper, onion and celery combination common to Cajun dishes, but you'll find it's not too spicy.

—Irene Cliett, Cedar Bluff, Mississippi

- 1/2 cup chopped onion
- 1/2 cup chopped celery
- 1/2 cup chopped green pepper
- 1 tablespoon olive oil
- 1 can (14-1/2 ounces) diced tomatoes and green chilies, undrained
- 1/2 cup sliced fresh mushrooms
- 1 can (2-1/4 ounces) sliced ripe olives, drained
- 1/2 teaspoon garlic powder
- 4 catfish fillets (6 ounces each)
- 1/4 cup grated Parmesan cheese

1 In a large skillet, saute the onion, celery and green pepper in oil until tender. Add the tomatoes, mushrooms, olives and garlic powder. Bring to a boil. Reduce heat; simmer, uncovered, for 10 minutes or until heated through.

2 Place the catfish in an ungreased 13-in. x 9-in. x 2-in. baking dish. Top with vegetable mixture; sprinkle with Parmesan cheese. Bake, uncovered, at 400° for 15-20 minutes or until fish flakes easily with a fork. **Yield:** 4 servings.

TIP
Creole Seasoning Substitute
The following spices may be substituted for 1 teaspoon Creole seasoning: 1/4 teaspoon salt, garlic powder and paprika; and a pinch each of dried thyme, ground cumin and cayenne pepper.

Bean 'n' Rice Burritos

One night I wanted to make something different for dinner. I started with black beans and added things I thought would taste good. The end result was as delicious as it was economical.

—**Susie Kohler, Union, Missouri**

- 1 can (15 ounces) black beans, rinsed and drained
- 1 can (14-1/2 ounces) diced tomatoes, drained
- 2 teaspoons garlic powder
- 1 teaspoon ground cumin
- 2 cups cooked rice
- 12 flour tortillas (6 inches), warmed
- 4 ounces process cheese (Velveeta), cut into 12 slices
- 1 cup (8 ounces) sour cream

1 In a large skillet, combine the beans, tomatoes, garlic powder and cumin; heat through. Stir in the rice. Spoon about 1/3 cupful off-center on each tortilla. Top with cheese. Fold sides and ends over filling and roll up. Serve with sour cream. **Yield:** 6 servings.

Easy Fish Fillets

For folks who want to cook fish in a flash, this recipe is quite a catch. These fillets always turn out moist and flaky.

—**Theresa Stewart, New Oxford, Pennsylvania**

- 3/4 cup seasoned bread crumbs
- 1/3 cup reduced-fat Italian salad dressing
- 4 catfish fillets (5 ounces each), patted dry

1 Place bread crumbs in a shallow bowl. Place dressing in another shallow bowl. Dip fish in dressing, then coat with crumbs. Place fish on a rack in a 15-in. x 10-in. x 1-in. baking pan. Bake, uncovered, at 450° for 15-20 minutes or until the fish flakes easily with a fork. **Yield:** 4 servings.

Tuna Cheese Melts

This toasted, cheesy tuna sandwich gets an extra flavor boost from a garlicky sour cream spread.

—**Bernadine Dirmeyer, Harpster, Ohio**

- 1/2 cup sour cream
- 1/2 teaspoon garlic salt
- 8 slices rye *or* white bread
- 1 can (6 ounces) tuna, drained and flaked
- 2 tablespoons mayonnaise
- 4 slices process American cheese
- 4 tablespoons butter, *divided*

1 In a small bowl, combine sour cream and garlic salt; spread on one side of each slice of bread. In another small bowl, combine tuna and mayonnaise; spread on four slices of bread. Top with cheese and remaining bread; gently press together.

2 Melt 2 tablespoons butter in a large skillet over medium heat. Add two sandwiches; toast sandwiches until bread is lightly browned on both sides and cheese is melted. Repeat with remaining butter and sandwiches. **Yield:** 4 servings.

Garlic Salmon Linguine

This main dish calls for handy pantry ingredients, including pasta and canned salmon. I serve it with asparagus, rolls and fruit.

—**Theresa Hagan, Glendale, Arizona**

- 1 package (16 ounces) linguine
- 3 garlic cloves, minced
- 1/3 cup olive oil
- 1 can (14-3/4 ounces) salmon, drained, bones and skin removed
- 3/4 cup chicken broth
- 1/4 cup minced fresh parsley
- 1/2 teaspoon salt
- 1/8 teaspoon cayenne pepper

1 Cook the linguine according to package directions. Meanwhile, in a large skillet, saute garlic in oil until crisp-tender. Stir in the salmon, broth, parsley, salt and cayenne. Cook until heated through. Drain linguine; add to the salmon mixture and toss to coat. **Yield:** 6 servings.

Black Bean Nacho Bake

Pasta, black beans and nacho cheese soup combine in this speedy six-ingredient supper.

—**Melodie Gay, Salt Lake City, Utah**

- 1 package (7 ounces) small pasta shells, cooked and drained
- 1 can (15 ounces) black beans, rinsed and drained
- 1 can (11 ounces) condensed nacho cheese soup, undiluted
- 1/3 cup milk
- 1/2 cup crushed tortilla chips
- 1/2 cup shredded cheddar cheese

1 In a large bowl, combine pasta shells and beans. In a small bowl, combine soup and milk; stir into macaroni mixture.

2 Transfer to a greased 8-in. square baking dish. Cover and bake at 350° for 25 minutes. Uncover; sprinkle with tortilla chips and cheese. Bake 5-10 minutes longer or until pasta is tender and cheese is melted. **Yield:** 4 servings.

Dijon-Crusted Fish

Dijon, Parmesan and a hint of horseradish give this toasty fish lots of flavor. The preparation is so easy.

—Scott Schmidtke, Chicago, Illinois

3	tablespoons reduced-fat mayonnaise
2	tablespoons grated Parmesan cheese, *divided*
1	tablespoon lemon juice
2	teaspoons Dijon mustard
1	teaspoon horseradish
4	tilapia fillets (5 ounces *each*)
1/4	cup dry bread crumbs
2	teaspoons butter, melted

1 In a small bowl, combine the mayonnaise, 1 tablespoon Parmesan cheese, lemon juice, mustard and horseradish. Place fillets on a baking sheet coated with cooking spray. Spread mayonnaise mixture evenly over fillets.

2 In a small bowl, combine the bread crumbs, butter and remaining Parmesan cheese; sprinkle over the fish fillets.

3 Bake at 425° for 13-18 minutes or until fish flakes easily with a fork. **Yield:** 4 servings.

TIP
Buying and Storing Fish

Purchase fish that smells and looks good, whether it is refrigerated or frozen.

Prepackaged fish should be tightly wrapped with no liquid in the package. The fish should not have discoloration or browning around the edges.

Frozen fish should be frozen solid. The package should not contain ice crystals. The fish should not have any yellow or white discoloration.

Store fish in the coolest part of your refrigerator for up to 2 days. Frozen fish should be thawed in its original package in the refrigerator. Do not refreeze.

Ravioli Primavera

I rely on frozen vegetables and ravioli to hurry along this colorful main dish. It's pleasantly seasoned with minced garlic and fresh parsley.

—Lois McAtee, Oceanside, California

4	cups frozen cheese ravioli
1	package (16 ounces) frozen Italian vegetables, thawed
1/4	cup olive oil
2	garlic cloves, minced
1/4	cup vegetable broth
2	tablespoons minced fresh parsley
1/4	teaspoon salt
1/4	teaspoon pepper

1 Prepare ravioli according to package directions. Meanwhile, in a large skillet, saute vegetables in oil for 3 minutes or until tender. Add garlic; saute for 1 minute longer or until garlic is tender.

2 Stir in broth. Simmer, uncovered, for 2 minutes. Stir in the parsley, salt and pepper; cook 2 minutes longer or until vegetables are tender. Drain pasta. Add to vegetable mixture; toss to coat. **Yield:** 4 servings.

Fettuccine with Black Bean Sauce

When my husband needed to go on a heart-smart diet, I had to come up with new ways to get more vegetables into our daily menus. This meatless spaghetti sauce is a winner and especially delicious with spinach fettuccine.

—Marianne Neuman, East Troy, Wisconsin

- 6 ounces uncooked fettuccine
- 1 small green pepper, chopped
- 1 small onion, chopped
- 1 tablespoon olive oil
- 2 cups garden-style pasta sauce
- 1 can (15 ounces) black beans, rinsed and drained
- 2 tablespoons minced fresh basil *or* 2 teaspoons dried basil
- 1 teaspoon dried oregano
- 1/2 teaspoon fennel seed
- 1/4 teaspoon garlic salt
- 1 cup (4 ounces) shredded part-skim mozzarella cheese

1 Cook fettuccine according to package directions. Meanwhile, in a large saucepan, saute green pepper and onion in oil until tender. Stir in the pasta sauce, black beans and seasonings. Bring to a boil. Reduce heat; simmer, uncovered, for 5 minutes. Drain fettuccine. Top with sauce and sprinkle with mozzarella cheese. **Yield:** 5 servings.

EDITOR'S NOTE: This recipe was tested with Ragu Super Vegetable Primavera pasta sauce.

Soft Fish Tacos

My husband, Bill, and I created these tasty fish tacos. The combination of tilapia and cabbage may seem unusual, but after one bite, everyone's hooked!

—**Carrie Billups, Florence, Oregon**

4	cups coleslaw mix
1/2	cup fat-free tartar sauce
1/2	teaspoon salt
1/2	teaspoon ground cumin
1/4	teaspoon pepper
1-1/2	pounds tilapia fillets
2	tablespoons olive oil
1	tablespoon lemon juice
10	corn tortillas (6 inches), warmed

Shredded cheddar cheese, chopped tomato and sliced avocado, optional

1 In a large bowl, toss the coleslaw mix, tartar sauce, salt, cumin and pepper; set aside. In a large nonstick skillet coated with cooking spray, cook tilapia in oil and lemon juice over medium heat for 4-5 minutes on each side or until fish flakes easily with a fork.

2 Place tilapia on tortillas; top with coleslaw mixture. Serve with cheese, tomato and avocado if desired. **Yield:** 5 servings.

Fish Fillets Italiano

My husband is an avid fisherman, so we enjoy a lot of fresh ocean fish. I found this recipe in a cookbook but adjusted it to serve two and changed the seasonings to suit our tastes.

—**Margaret Risinger, Pacifica, California**

1/4	cup chopped onion
1	garlic clove, minced
2	teaspoons olive oil
1	cup diced zucchini
1/2	cup sliced fresh mushrooms
1/2	teaspoon dried oregano
1/4	teaspoon dried basil
1	can (8 ounces) tomato sauce
1	tablespoon tomato paste
3/4	pound cod, perch *or* haddock fillets
2	tablespoons shredded Parmesan cheese

1 In a large skillet, saute onion and garlic in oil until tender. Add the zucchini, mushrooms, oregano and basil. Cook for 3 minutes or until tender. Stir in the tomato sauce and paste. Cook for 8-10 minutes or until heated through.

2 Place fillets in an ungreased 11-in. x 7-in. x 2-in. baking dish; top with vegetable mixture. Bake, uncovered, at 350° for 20 minutes or until fish flakes easily with a fork. Sprinkle with Parmesan cheese. **Yield:** 2 servings.

Tuna Mushroom Casserole

I usually serve this casserole when I'm short on time and we need something hearty and comforting.

—**Connie Moore, Medway, Ohio**

1	package (12 ounces) wide noodles, cooked and drained
2	cans (6 ounces *each*) tuna, drained
1	can (4 ounces) mushroom stems and pieces, drained
1	can (10-3/4 ounces) condensed cream of mushroom soup, undiluted
1-1/3	cups milk
1/2	teaspoon salt
1/4	teaspoon pepper
1/2	cup crushed saltines
3	tablespoons butter, melted

Paprika, tomato slices and fresh thyme, optional

1 In a large bowl, combine the noodles, tuna and mushrooms. Combine soup, milk, salt and pepper; pour over noodle mixture and mix well. Pour into a greased 2-1/2-qt. baking dish. Combine saltines and butter; sprinkle over noodles.

2 Bake, uncovered, at 350° for 35-45 minutes or until heated through. Sprinkle with paprika and garnish with tomato slices and thyme if desired. **Yield:** 6 servings.

Lemony Salmon Patties

Topped with a zippy white sauce, these little patties bake up golden brown in a muffin pan. They're impressive enough for company.

—Lorice Britt, Severn, North Carolina

1	can (14-3/4 ounces) pink salmon, drained, skin and bones removed
3/4	cup milk
1	cup soft bread crumbs
1	egg, lightly beaten
1	tablespoon chopped fresh parsley
1	teaspoon minced onion
1/2	teaspoon Worcestershire sauce
1/4	teaspoon salt
1/8	teaspoon pepper

LEMON SAUCE:

2	tablespoons butter
4	teaspoons all-purpose flour
3/4	cup milk
2	tablespoons lemon juice
1/4	teaspoon salt
1/8	to 1/4 teaspoon cayenne pepper

1 In a large bowl, combine the first nine ingredients. Fill eight greased muffin cups with 1/4 cup salmon mixture. Bake at 350° for 45 minutes or until browned.

2 Meanwhile, melt butter in a saucepan; stir in the flour to form a smooth paste. Gradually stir in milk; bring to a boil over medium heat, stirring constantly. Cook and stir for 2 minutes or until thickened. Remove from the heat; stir in the lemon juice, salt and cayenne pepper. Serve with patties. **Yield:** 4 servings.

TIP
Salmon Bones
The bones from canned salmon are edible and can add calcium to your diet. If you don't like the texture, mash the drained salmon in a bowl with the back of a spoon. The bones will become undetectable.

Oven-Fried Fish Nuggets

My husband and I love fresh fried fish, but we're both trying to cut back on fats. I made up this recipe, and it was a huge hit. He tells me he likes it as much as deep-fried fish, and that's saying a lot!

—LaDonna Reed, Ponca City, Oklahoma

1/3	cup seasoned bread crumbs
1/3	cup crushed cornflakes
3	tablespoons grated Parmesan cheese
1/2	teaspoon salt
1/4	teaspoon pepper
1-1/2	pounds cod fillets, cut into 1-inch cubes

Butter-flavored cooking spray

1 In a shallow bowl, combine the bread crumbs, cornflakes, Parmesan cheese, salt and pepper. Coat fish with butter-flavored spray, then roll in crumb mixture.

2 Place on a baking sheet coated with cooking spray. Bake at 375° for 15-20 minutes or until fish flakes easily with a fork. **Yield:** 4 servings.

Crispy Catfish

Grilling is my family's favorite way to fix meals. Because my husband savors well-prepared meals, this recipe quickly became one of his most requested.

—**Rhonda Dietz, Garden City, Kansas**

3/4	cup finely crushed saltines (about 22 crackers)
1	teaspoon seasoned salt
1/2	teaspoon celery salt
1/2	teaspoon garlic salt
1/3	cup butter, melted
4	catfish fillets (about 8 ounces *each*)

1 In a shallow dish, combine the first four ingredients. Pat the fillets dry; dip in butter, then coat with crumb mixture.

2 Coat grill rack with cooking spray before starting grill. Grill fillets, covered, over medium-hot heat for 5 minutes on each side or until fish flakes easily with a fork. **Yield:** 4 servings.

Pasta Primavera

This colorful pasta and vegetable toss is a great quick meal. It has such a special taste it's hard to believe it costs less than a dollar a serving.

—**Charlotte McDaniel, Jacksonville, Alabama**

2	cups broccoli florets
1	can (10-3/4 ounces) condensed cream of mushroom soup, undiluted
1	large carrot, julienned
1/2	cup milk
1/4	cup grated Parmesan cheese
1	garlic clove, minced
1/8	teaspoon pepper
3	cups cooked spaghetti

1 In a large saucepan, combine the first seven ingredients. Cook, uncovered, over medium heat until vegetables are tender, about 12 minutes. Stir in spaghetti; heat through. **Yield:** 4 servings.

Linguine in Clam Sauce

My father-in-law makes this special dish for my birthday. Zucchini adds a tasty twist.

—Louise Fabin Vouk, Kirkand, Ohio

- 1 package (1 pound) linguine
- 1 large onion, finely chopped
- 2 tablespoons olive oil
- 1 medium zucchini, diced
- 3 cans (6-1/2 ounces each) chopped clams
- 1/2 pound sliced fresh mushrooms
- 2 teaspoons chicken bouillon granules
- 1 teaspoon minced fresh basil
- 1/8 teaspoon pepper

Shredded Parmesan cheese

1 Cook linguine according to package directions. Meanwhile, in a large skillet, saute onion and garlic in oil until tender. Add zucchini; cook for 2 minutes or until crisp-tender.

2 Drain clams, reserving 1/2 cup juice. Add the clams, mushrooms, bouillon, basil, pepper and reserved juice to the skillet. Bring to a boil. Reduce heat; simmer, uncovered, for 5 minutes or until vegetables are tender. Drain linguine; top with clam mixture. Sprinkle with Parmesan cheese. **Yield:** 4-6 servings.

Planned Overs

Garden Fish Packets

I frequently serve this flavorful combination of fish, vegetables and cheese over a bed of rice. It's quick to prepare, and the foil packets make cleanup a breeze.

—Sally Davis, Warren, Pennsylvania

- 3 tablespoons butter, melted
- 3 pounds frozen cod *or* haddock fillets, thawed
- 2 teaspoons seasoned salt
- 3/4 teaspoon lemon-pepper seasoning
- 2 medium tomatoes, thinly sliced
- 2 medium green peppers, thinly sliced
- 1/2 cup thinly sliced green onions
- 1/2 pound sliced fresh mushrooms
- 2 cups (8 ounces) shredded part-skim mozzarella cheese

1 Drizzle the butter over eight pieces of heavy-duty foil (about 18 in. x 12 in.). Cut fish into eight portions; place one portion on each piece of foil. Sprinkle all with seasoned salt and lemon-pepper. Top with vegetables and cheese.

2 Loosely wrap foil around fish; seal top and sides. Place in two ungreased 15-in. x 10-in. x 1-in. baking pans. Bake at 350° for 23-25 minutes or until fish flakes easily with a fork. Carefully open foil; transfer fish and vegetables to serving plates. **Yield:** 8 servings.

Gone Fishin' Chowder

My grandpa and his brother, who are twins, love to fish. For years, they've used cooked fish to make this colorful chowder. It's so good that when I entered it in our 4-H Food Show, I received a top award.

—Jasmina Kocurek, Palacios, Texas

- 4 bacon strips
- 1 cup chopped onion
- 1 teaspoon dried thyme
- 5 cups water
- 3 cups diced peeled potatoes
- 1-1/2 cups coarsely chopped carrots
- 1/2 cup chopped celery
- 2 teaspoons salt
- 1/8 to 1/4 teaspoon pepper
- 1 can (28 ounces) diced tomatoes, undrained
- 1 tablespoon dried parsley flakes
- 1-1/2 cups cubed cooked fish

1 In a Dutch oven or soup kettle over medium heat, cook bacon until crisp. Drain, reserving 1 teaspoon drippings. Crumble bacon and set aside. Saute onion and thyme in reserved drippings.

2 Add the water, potatoes, carrots, celery, salt and pepper. Cover and simmer for 20-25 minutes or until vegetables are tender. Add tomatoes, parsley and bacon; cook for 10 minutes. Add fish; heat through. **Yield:** 12 servings (about 3 quarts).

EDITOR'S NOTE: To prepare with fresh fish, dice 3/4 pound fresh fish and add to chowder at the same time as the tomatoes. Cook for 10-15 minutes or until fish is opaque.

Fried Fish Nuggets

My family always requests these cheesy fish bites during our annual fishing trip to Canada.

—Lynn Negaard, Litchfield, Minnesota

- 2 eggs, lightly beaten
- 1/2 cup dry bread crumbs
- 1/2 cup shredded cheddar cheese
- 1/4 cup finely chopped onion
- 1 garlic clove, minced
- 1-1/2 teaspoons minced fresh parsley
- 1/4 teaspoon dill weed
- 1/4 teaspoon pepper
- 1-1/2 cups flaked cooked fish

Oil for deep-fat frying
Tartar sauce, optional

1 In a large bowl, combine the first eight ingredients. Stir in the fish. Roll into 1-in. balls.

2 In an electric skillet or deep-fat fryer, heat oil to 375°. Fry fish nuggets, a few at a time, until golden brown on both sides; drain on paper towels. Serve with tartar sauce if desired. **Yield:** about 2-1/2 dozen.

Four-Bean Taco Chili

Heat up the dinner table on a cold night with this zesty chili. It's chock-full of ground beef, beans, green chilies and taco seasoning. Be sure to save leftovers for my two other recipes that follow.

—Amy Martell, Canton, Pennsylvania

- 2 pounds ground beef
- 3 cups tomato juice
- 1 jar (16 ounces) salsa
- 1 can (16 ounces) kidney beans, rinsed and drained
- 1 can (15-1/2 ounces) great northern beans, rinsed and drained
- 1 can (15 ounces) butter beans, rinsed and drained
- 1 can (15 ounces) black beans, rinsed and drained
- 1 can (8 ounces) tomato sauce
- 1 can (6 ounces) tomato paste
- 1 can (4 ounces) chopped green chilies
- 1 envelope taco seasoning

1 In a Dutch oven or soup kettle, cook beef over medium heat until no longer pink; drain. Stir in the remaining ingredients. Bring to a boil. Reduce heat; simmer, uncovered, for 15 minutes, stirring occasionally. **Yield:** 12 cups.

Cheesy Chili Dip

Three ingredients are all I add to a few cups of chili to create this fast-to-fix snack. Simply zap the lip-smacking appetizer in the microwave, serve it with tortilla chips and stand back as the zesty party-pleaser disappears.

—Amy Martell

- 2 cups Four-Bean Taco Chili (recipe on this page)
- 1 jar (8 ounces) salsa
- 1 can (4 ounces) chopped green chilies
- 1 package (16 ounces) process cheese (Velveeta), cubed

Tortilla chips

1 In a microwave-safe bowl, combine the chili, salsa, chilies and cheese. Cover and microwave on high for 3-4 minutes or until cheese is melted, stirring occasionally. Serve with tortilla chips. **Yield:** 5 cups.

EDITOR'S NOTE: This recipe was tested in a 1,100-watt microwave.

Chili Manicotti

No one will guess that the secret to this tasty entree is yesterday's chili. A jar of spaghetti sauce combined with my specialty creates the ideal sauce for this cheese-filled manicotti.

—Amy Martell

- 10 uncooked manicotti shells
- 2 cups (8 ounces) shredded part-skim mozzarella cheese, *divided*
- 1 carton (15 ounces) ricotta cheese
- 1/4 cup shredded Parmesan cheese
- 1 egg, lightly beaten
- 3 cups Four-Bean Taco Chili (recipe on this page)
- 1 jar (14 ounces) meatless spaghetti sauce

Minced fresh parsley, optional

1 Cook manicotti according to package directions. Meanwhile, in a large bowl, combine 1 cup mozzarella cheese, ricotta cheese, Parmesan cheese and egg; set aside. Combine the chili and spaghetti sauce; pour half into a greased 13-in. x 9-in. x 2-in. baking dish.

2 Rinse and drain manicotti shells; stuff with cheese mixture. Place over sauce. Top with remaining sauce; sprinkle with remaining cheese.

3 Bake, uncovered, at 350° for 40-45 minutes or until heated through. Sprinkle with parsley if desired. **Yield:** 5 servings.

Mom's Meatballs

I bake a large batch of moist meatballs that are tender and flavorful. Serve some for dinner and freeze the extras for future meals.

—Dorothy Smith, El Dorado, Arkansas

- 1-1/2 cups chopped onion
- 1/3 cup ketchup
- 3 tablespoons lemon juice
- 1 tablespoon Worcestershire sauce
- 3/4 cup crushed saltines (about 24 crackers)
- 3 pounds ground beef

1 In a large bowl, combine onion, ketchup, lemon juice, Worcestershire sauce and crackers. Crumble beef over mixture, mix well. Shape into 1-in. balls.

2 Place meatballs on a greased rack in a shallow baking pan. Bake, uncovered, at 400° for 10 minutes or until meat is no longer pink; drain. Serve meatballs immediately, or refrigerate or freeze for use in other recipes. **Yield:** 7 dozen.

Meatball Minestrone

As the busy parents of two boys, my husband and I are always on the lookout for quick meals. You don't have to thaw the frozen meatballs for this satisfying soup, so it's table-ready in moments.

—Linda de Beaudrap, Calgary, Alberta

- 6 cups water
- 1 can (16 ounces) kidney beans, rinsed and drained
- 1 package (16 ounces) frozen mixed vegetables
- 2 tablespoons beef bouillon granules
- 1 tablespoon dried minced onion
- 1 bay leaf
- 1 teaspoon dried basil
- 1 teaspoon salt
- 1/2 teaspoon pepper
- 4 ounces spaghetti, broken into 2-inch pieces
- 24 cooked meatballs
- 1 can (14-1/2 ounces) stewed tomatoes

1 In a Dutch oven or soup kettle, combine the first nine ingredients. Bring to a boil; add spaghetti. Reduce heat; cover and simmer for 10 minutes or until spaghetti is tender. Add the meatballs and tomatoes; heat through. Discard bay leaf. **Yield:** 10-12 servings.

Meatball Lasagna

My family wants me to make this dish all the time. It goes over well at reunions, too.

—Addella Thomas, Mt. Sterling, Illinois

- 2 cans (14-1/2 ounces *each*) diced tomatoes, undrained
- 1 can (8 ounces) tomato sauce
- 1 cup water
- 1 can (6 ounces) tomato paste
- 1 medium onion, chopped
- 1 garlic clove, minced
- 1 tablespoon dried basil
- 4 teaspoons dried parsley flakes
- 2 teaspoons sugar

Garlic salt to taste

- 8 uncooked lasagna noodles
- 24 cooked meatballs
- 1 egg
- 1 cup ricotta cheese
- 2 cups (8 ounces) shredded part-skim mozzarella cheese
- 3/4 cup grated Parmesan cheese

1 In a large saucepan, combine the first 10 ingredients. Bring to a boil. Reduce heat; cover and simmer for 20 minutes. Meanwhile, cook lasagna noodles according to package directions; drain.

2 Crumble meatballs into the sauce. In a small bowl, combine egg and ricotta cheese. Spoon 1 cup of the meat sauce into a greased 13-in. x 9-in. x 2-in. baking dish. Layer with half of the noodles, ricotta mixture, meat sauce, mozzarella and Parmesan cheeses. Repeat layers.

3 Cover and bake at 350° for 45 minutes. Uncover; bake 5-10 minutes longer or until golden brown. Let stand for 15 minutes before cutting. **Yield:** 8-10 servings.

Favorite Pot Roast

I love cooking a pot roast on the weekend because it can simmer for hours while I'm doing other things. My recipe makes enough for a family of four with plenty left over.

—Leona Therou, Overland Park, Kansas

- 1 boneless beef rump roast (4 pounds)
- 2 tablespoons vegetable oil
- 2 teaspoons salt
- 1/2 teaspoon pepper
- 1/2 teaspoon dried thyme
- 1 bay leaf
- 3 cups water, *divided*
- 8 medium potatoes, peeled and quartered
- 8 large carrots, cut into 2-inch chunks
- 1 pound small onions, peeled
- 1/2 cup all-purpose flour
- 1/2 teaspoon browning sauce, optional

Additional salt and pepper to taste

1 In a Dutch oven, brown the roast on all sides in oil. Combine the salt, pepper and thyme; sprinkle evenly over meat. Add bay leaf and 2 cups water; bring to a boil. Reduce heat; cover and simmer for 2-1/2 hours.

2 Add the potatoes, carrots and onions. Cover and simmer 45 minutes longer or until meat and vegetables are tender. Remove roast and vegetables to a serving platter; keep warm. Discard bay leaf.

3 Skim fat from pan juices; add enough water to pan juices to measure 2 cups. In a bowl, combine flour and remaining water until smooth; stir into juices. Bring to a boil; cook and stir for 2 minutes or until thickened and bubbly. Stir in browning sauce if desired. Season with salt and pepper. Slice roast; serve with vegetables and gravy. **Yield:** 8 servings.

Beef Pasties

Our home economists came up with this recipe for pasties as a way to put leftover pot roast to deliciously good use.

—Taste of Home Test Kitchen

- 2 cups cubed cooked roast beef (1/4-inch pieces)
- 1-1/2 cup diced cooked potatoes
- 1 cup beef gravy
- 1/2 cup diced cooked carrots
- 1/2 cup diced cooked onion
- 1 tablespoon chopped fresh parsley
- 1/4 teaspoon dried thyme
- 1/2 teaspoon salt
- 1/8 to 1/4 teaspoon pepper

Pastry for double-crust pie (9 inches)
Half-and-half cream

1 In a large bowl, combine the first nine ingredients; set aside. On a lightly floured surface, roll out a fourth of the pastry into an 8-in. circle. Mound 1 cup filling on half of circle. Moisten edges with water; fold dough over filling and press the edges with a fork to seal.

2 Place on an ungreased baking sheet. Repeat with remaining pastry and filling. Cut slits in top of each; brush with cream. Bake at 450° for 20-25 minutes or until golden brown. **Yield:** 4 servings.

Easy Beef Sandwiches

With only three ingredients, our food staff assembled these sandwiches in short order. Use store-bought barbecue sauce to flavor your leftover beef if you like.

—Taste of Home Test Kitchen

- 2 cups shredded cooked roast beef
- 1 bottle (18 ounces) barbecue sauce
- 5 kaiser rolls, split

1 In a large saucepan, combine beef and barbecue sauce; heat through. Serve on rolls. **Yield:** 5 servings.

Three-Meat Sauce

This authentic Italian spaghetti sauce recipe is a longtime family favorite. Very hearty with lots of meat and a zippy flavor, it's wonderful over a plateful of your favorite pasta.

—Lillian Di Senso, Lake Havasu City, Arizona

- 1 boneless chuck roast (2-1/2 to 3 pounds), trimmed and cut into 1-inch cubes
- 1 pork shoulder roast (2 to 2-1/2 pounds), trimmed and cut into 1-inch cubes
- 1 pound Italian sausage links, cut into 1-inch slices
- 3 tablespoons olive oil
- 3 large onions, chopped
- 5 cans (15 ounces *each*) tomato sauce
- 3 cans (6 ounces *each*) tomato paste
- 1 cup water
- 1/2 cup minced fresh parsley *or* 3 tablespoons dried parsley flakes
- 1/2 cup minced fresh oregano *or* 3 tablespoons dried oregano
- 5 teaspoons salt
- 2 teaspoons pepper

1. In a large Dutch oven or soup kettle, brown beef, pork and sausage in oil; drain. Add onions; cook until tender. Add the tomato sauce and paste, water, parsley, oregano, salt and pepper. Bring to a boil. Reduce heat; cover and simmer for 2-1/2 to 3 hours or until beef and pork are tender.

2. For 4-6 people, serve 4 cups of the meat sauce over 1 pound of cooked and drained spaghetti. Refrigerate or freeze remaining sauce (may be frozen up to 3 months). **Yield: 18 cups.**

Easy Lasagna

For a supper to please a crowd, I layer lasagna noodles with meat sauce and a cottage cheese mixture to make this fast version of a traditional favorite.

—**Pam Beerens, Evart, Michigan**

- 1-1/2 cups (12 ounces) 4% cottage cheese
- 1 egg
- 1/4 cup grated Parmesan cheese
- 1 tablespoon minced fresh parsley
  or 1 teaspoon dried parsley flakes
- 1/2 teaspoon dried oregano
- 1/4 teaspoon dried basil
- 9 lasagna noodles, cooked, rinsed and drained
- 4 cups Three-Meat Sauce (recipe on opposite page)
- 2 cups (8 ounces) shredded part-skim mozzarella cheese

1. In a large bowl, combine the cottage cheese, egg, Parmesan cheese, parsley, oregano and basil. In a greased 13-in. x 9-in. x 2-in. baking dish, layer a third of the noodles, meat sauce, cottage cheese mixture and mozzarella. Repeat layers.

2. Cover and bake at 350° for 30 minutes; uncover and bake 15-20 minutes longer or until bubbly. Let stand for 15 minutes before cutting. **Yield: 12 servings.**

EDITOR'S NOTE: 1 pound of browned ground beef and one 26-1/2 ounce can of spaghetti sauce may be substituted for the Three-Meat Sauce.

Quick Calzones

Here's a winning way to use up leftover meat sauce—hearty calzones that taste like they're made from scratch. Frozen bread dough makes them a snap to assemble and creates a tasty crust, thanks to the Parmesan topping.

—**Taste of Home Test Kitchen**

- 1 loaf (1 pound) frozen bread dough, thawed
- 1 cup Three-Meat Sauce (recipe on opposite page)
- 1/4 cup shredded part-skim mozzarella cheese
- 1 to 2 tablespoons milk
- 1 tablespoon grated Parmesan cheese
- 1/2 teaspoon Italian seasoning

1. Divide bread dough into four portions; roll each into a 6-in. circle. Spoon 1/4 cup of meat sauce on half of each circle to within 1/2 in. of edges. Sprinkle each with 1 tablespoon of mozzarella cheese.

2. Fold dough over the filling and press the edges firmly to seal. Brush with milk. Combine Parmesan cheese and Italian seasoning; sprinkle evenly over the calzones.

3. Place on a greased baking sheet. Bake at 350° for 20 minutes or until golden brown. **Yield: 4 servings.**

TIP . . . .
A Lesson in Lasagna

To give your favorite lasagna recipe a twist, try replacing a quarter of the mozzarella cheese with shredded sharp cheddar. It greatly heightens the flavor.

Whenever you cook more lasagna noodles than needed, cut the leftovers into 1/4- or 1/2-inch strips and put them in a heavy-duty resealable plastic bag. They freeze well and make quick, hearty additions to soups.

Ham with Cherry Sauce

This tangy fruit sauce with almonds is so wonderful over baked ham...and the ruby-red color is gorgeous, too! I usually round out this dinner with sweet potatoes, coleslaw or applesauce and rolls.

—Joan Laurenzo, Johnstown, Ohio

- 1/2 fully cooked bone-in ham (6 to 7 pounds)
- 1 jar (12 ounces) cherry preserves
- 1/4 cup red wine vinegar
- 2 tablespoons light corn syrup
- 1/4 teaspoon *each* ground cloves, cinnamon and nutmeg
- 3 tablespoons slivered almonds

1 Place ham on a rack in a shallow roasting pan. Score the surface of the ham, making diamond shapes 1/2 in. deep. Bake, uncovered, at 325° for 1-1/2 to 2 hours or until a meat thermometer reads 140°.

2 In a large saucepan, combine the preserves, vinegar, corn syrup, cloves, cinnamon and nutmeg. Bring to a boil, stirring often. Reduce heat; simmer, uncovered, for 2 minutes. Remove from the heat; stir in almonds. Serve with ham. **Yield:** 10-12 servings (1-1/2 cups sauce).

Pretty Ham Primavera

I give leftover ham a face-lift in this tasty pasta dish. The mild cream sauce gets fresh flavor from sauteed mushrooms and a boost of color from frozen peas.

—Joan Laurenzo, Johnstown, Ohio

- 1/2 pound sliced fresh mushrooms
- 1/3 cup chopped onion
- 2 tablespoons olive oil
- 2 tablespoons all-purpose flour
- 2 teaspoons Italian seasoning
- 2 teaspoons chicken bouillon granules
- 1/2 teaspoon salt
- 1/8 teaspoon pepper
- 2 cups milk
- 1 package (7 ounces) thin spaghetti, cooked and drained
- 2 cups cubed fully cooked ham
- 1 package (10 ounces) frozen peas, thawed

Grated Parmesan cheese, optional

1 In a large skillet, saute the mushrooms and onion in oil until tender. Stir in the flour, Italian seasoning, bouillon, salt and pepper until smooth.

2 Gradually add the milk, stirring constantly. Bring to a boil; cook and stir for 2 minutes or until thickened. Stir in the spaghetti, ham and peas; heat through. Sprinkle with the Parmesan cheese if desired. **Yield:** 4 servings.

Plantation Ham Pie

A pretty parsley pinwheel tops this hearty casserole filled with a saucy mixture of broccoli, ham and onion. It can also be made with asparagus.

—Sharon White, Morden, Manitoba

- 4 cups cubed fully cooked ham (2 pounds)
- 1 medium onion, chopped
- 2 tablespoons butter
- 2 cans (10-3/4 ounces *each*) condensed cream of chicken soup, undiluted
- 1 cup milk
- 2 cups fresh *or* frozen broccoli florets
- 2 cups biscuit/baking mix
- 1/2 cup water
- 1/2 cup minced fresh parsley

1 In a large skillet, saute ham and onion in butter until onion is tender. Combine soup and milk; stir into ham mixture. Add broccoli; heat through. Pour into an ungreased shallow 2-1/2-qt. baking dish.

2 Combine biscuit mix and water until a soft dough forms. On a lightly floured surface, knead dough 10 times. Roll out into a 12-in. square; sprinkle with parsley.

3 Roll up jelly-roll style. Cut into 12 pieces; place over the ham mixture. Bake, uncovered, at 425° for 20-25 minutes or until biscuits are golden and ham mixture is bubbly. **Yield:** 6 servings.

Italian Sausage Sandwiches

There's no need for other condiments when you jazz up sausages with zippy peppers. This is a favorite of mine in the summer, when bell peppers are at their peak and more affordable.

—Bonnie Jost, Manitowoc, Wisconsin

- 16 Italian sausage links (4 ounces *each*)
- 1 *each* medium green, sweet red, yellow and orange peppers, julienned
- 1 banana pepper, julienned, optional
- 1 onion, halved and sliced
- 2 tablespoons vegetable oil
- 8 brat *or* hot dog buns, split

1 In a large skillet, cook sausages over medium heat until no longer pink. Meanwhile, in another large skillet, saute peppers and onion in oil. Drain sausages; place a sausage in each bun.

2 Top each with about 1/3 cup pepper mixture. Refrigerate remaining sausages. **Yield:** 8 sandwiches plus 8 extra sausages.

Italian Sausage Spaghetti

Spicy slices of leftover sausage and Italian seasoning lend plenty of flavor to this effortless spaghetti sauce. The chunky mixture turns last night's extras into a great second-day supper.

—Joyce Hostetler, Midway, Arkansas

- 1 small onion, chopped
- 1 small green pepper, chopped
- 3 garlic cloves, minced
- 2 teaspoons olive oil
- 5 cooked Italian sausage links, cut into 1/4-inch slices
- 1 can (28 ounces) diced tomatoes, undrained
- 1 can (6 ounces) tomato paste
- 1/4 cup water
- 1 tablespoon Italian seasoning
- 1 teaspoon sugar
- 1/2 teaspoon salt
- 1/2 teaspoon pepper

Hot cooked spaghetti

1 In a large saucepan, saute the onion, green pepper and garlic in oil until tender. Stir in the sausage, tomatoes, tomato paste, water and seasonings. Bring to a boil. Reduce heat; cover and simmer for 15 minutes. Serve with the spaghetti. **Yield:** 5 servings.

Sausage French Bread Pizza

I never seem to have pizza dough on hand, but that doesn't stop our family from enjoying pizza. I simply top crusty French bread with creamy Alfredo sauce, sausage and veggies.

—Cherie Sweet, Evansville, Indiana

- 1 loaf (1 pound) unsliced French bread
- 1-1/3 cups prepared Alfredo sauce
- 3 cooked Italian sausage links, chopped
- 1 can (2-1/4 ounces) sliced ripe olives, drained
- 1 small sweet red pepper, chopped
- 1 small onion, chopped
- 1/2 cup chopped fresh broccoli
- 1/2 cup fresh cauliflowerets
- 2-1/4 cups sliced fresh mushrooms
- 1-1/2 cups (6 ounces) shredded pizza cheese blend

1 Cut the bread in half horizontally; place on a baking sheet. Spread cut sides with Alfredo sauce. Sprinkle with the sausage, olives, red pepper, onion, broccoli, cauliflower, mushrooms and cheese.

2 Bake at 350° for 15-20 minutes or until heated through. Cut into serving-size pieces. **Yield:** 8 servings.

Corny Corn Bread

I bake a big pan of this golden corn bread for my growing family. Each moist square is chock-full of sweet kernels. Since the recipe makes a lot, it's handy for large gatherings...or use the leftovers in other recipes.

—Diana Leskauskas, Chatham, New Jersey

- 2 cups cornmeal
- 2/3 cup all-purpose flour
- 1/4 cup sugar
- 4 teaspoons baking powder
- 1-1/2 teaspoons salt
- 1 teaspoon baking soda
- 4 eggs, lightly beaten
- 2 cups milk
- 1 cup vegetable oil
- 2 cans (15-1/4 ounces *each*) whole kernel corn, drained
- 1 small onion, finely chopped

1 In a large bowl, combine the cornmeal, flour, sugar, baking powder, salt and baking soda. In a small bowl, whisk the eggs, milk and oil. Stir into the dry ingredients just until moistened. Fold in corn and onion.

2 Pour into a greased 13-in. x 9-in. x 2-in. baking dish. Bake at 400° for 25-30 minutes or until a toothpick inserted near the center comes out clean. Serve warm. **Yield:** 12-15 servings.

Corn Bread Salad

My family loves this cool, crisp medley. It's a unique treatment for extra corn bread. You can fix this refreshing salad ahead of time and vary the vegetables to suit your tastes.

—Martha Spears, Lenoir, North Carolina

- 1 cup coarsely crumbled corn bread
- 1 can (8-3/4 ounces) whole kernel corn, drained
- 1/2 cup *each* chopped onion, cucumber, broccoli, green pepper, sweet red pepper and seeded tomato
- 1/2 cup peppercorn ranch salad dressing
- Salt and pepper to taste
- Lettuce leaves, optional

1 In a bowl, combine the corn bread, vegetables, salad dressing, salt and pepper. Cover and refrigerate for 4 hours. Serve on a lettuce-lined plate if desired. **Yield:** 6 servings.

Corn Bread Chicken Bake

To make the most of leftover corn bread, try this hearty main-dish casserole. It's moist, delicious and good on any occasion.

—Madge Britton, Afton, Tennessee

- 1-1/4 pounds boneless skinless chicken breasts
- 6 cups cubed corn bread
- 8 bread slices, cubed
- 1 medium onion, chopped
- 2 cans (10-3/4 ounces *each*) condensed cream of chicken soup, undiluted
- 1 cup chicken broth
- 2 tablespoons butter, melted
- 1-1/2 to 2 teaspoons rubbed sage
- 1 teaspoon salt
- 1/2 to 1 teaspoon pepper

1 Place chicken in a large skillet and cover with water; bring to a boil. Reduce heat; cover and simmer for 12-14 minutes or until juices run clear. Drain and cut into cubes.

2 In a large bowl, combine remaining ingredients. Add chicken. Transfer to a greased 13-in. x 9-in. x 2-in. baking dish. Bake, uncovered, at 350° for 45 minutes or until heated through. **Yield:** 8-10 servings.

Teriyaki Turkey Breast

Marinating turkey breast overnight gives it great flavor and a juicy tenderness.

—Marvin Hayes, Delano, Minnesota

- 1 cup packed brown sugar
- 3/4 cup soy sauce
- 1/2 cup sherry *or* apple juice
- 1/4 cup olive oil
- 1 tablespoon ground ginger
- 1 tablespoon ground mustard
- 1 teaspoon garlic powder
- 1 bone-in turkey breast (8 pounds)

1 In a small bowl, combine the first seven ingredients. Pour 1 cup marinade into a large resealable plastic bag; add the turkey. Seal bag and turn to coat; refrigerate overnight. Cover and refrigerate remaining marinade.

2 Drain and discard marinade. Place turkey on a rack in a shallow roasting pan. Bake, uncovered, at 350° for 2 to 2-1/2 hours or until a meat thermometer reads 170°, basting every 30 minutes with reserved marinade. Let stand for 10 minutes before slicing. **Yield:** 8-10 servings plus carcass and 3 cups cubed leftover meat.

Turkey Soup

I make the most of my turkey by simmering the carcass to create this comforting soup.

—Myrna Sisel, Green Bay, Wisconsin

- 1 leftover turkey breast carcass (from an 8-pound turkey breast)
- 3 quarts water
- 4 teaspoons chicken bouillon granules
- 2 bay leaves
- 1/2 cup uncooked instant rice
- 1/2 cup uncooked quick-cooking barley
- 1-1/2 cups sliced carrots
- 1 cup chopped onion
- 1 cup sliced celery
- 1 garlic clove, minced
- 1 teaspoon salt
- 1/4 teaspoon pepper
- 1 cup cubed cooked turkey
- 2 tablespoons minced fresh parsley *or* 2 teaspoons dried parsley flakes

1 Place carcass, water, bouillon and bay leaves in a Dutch oven or soup kettle; bring to a boil. Reduce heat; cover and simmer for 1-1/2 hours. Remove carcass; cool.

2 Remove meat from bones and cut into bite-size pieces; set meat aside. Discard bones. Strain broth and skim fat; discard bay leaves. Add rice and barley to broth; bring to a boil. Reduce heat; cover and simmer for 30 minutes.

3 Stir in the carrots, onion, celery, garlic, salt and pepper; cover and simmer 20-25 minutes longer or until the vegetables are tender. Add cubed turkey, parsley and reserved turkey; heat through. **Yield:** 12 servings.

Turkey Macaroni Bake

A coworker gave me this recipe when we were discussing ways to use leftover turkey.

—Cherry Williams, St. Albert, Alberta

- 2 cups cubed cooked turkey
- 1-1/2 cups uncooked elbow macaroni
- 2 cups (8 ounces) shredded cheddar cheese, *divided*
- 1 can (10-3/4 ounces) condensed cream of chicken soup, undiluted
- 1 cup milk
- 1 can (8 ounces) mushroom stems and pieces, drained
- 1/4 teaspoon pepper

1 In a large bowl, combine the turkey, macaroni, 1-1/2 cups cheese, soup, milk, mushrooms and pepper. Pour into a greased 2-qt. baking dish.

2 Cover and bake at 350° for 60-65 minutes or until macaroni is tender. Uncover; sprinkle with remaining cheese. Bake 5-10 minutes longer or until cheese is melted. **Yield:** 6 servings.

Broiled Sirloin

Serve this succulent beef with fluffy mashed potatoes, fresh greens and crusty bread—it's a meal fit for company!

—Sue Ross, Casa Grande, Arizona

- 3 pounds boneless beef sirloin *or* round steak (about 1 inch thick)
- 1 medium onion, chopped
- 1/2 cup lemon juice
- 1/4 cup vegetable oil
- 1 teaspoon garlic salt
- 1 teaspoon dried thyme
- 1 teaspoon dried oregano
- 1/2 teaspoon celery salt
- 1/2 teaspoon pepper
- 2 tablespoons butter, melted

1 With a meat fork, pierce holes in both sides of steak. Place in a large resealable bag. Combine the onion, lemon juice, oil, garlic salt, thyme, oregano, celery salt and pepper; pour over meat. Cover and refrigerate for 6 hours or overnight.

2 Drain and discard marinade. Broil steak 6 in. from the heat for 8 minutes. Brush with butter and turn. Broil 6 minutes longer or until meat reaches desired doneness (for medium-rare, a meat thermometer should read 145°; medium, 160°; well-done, 170°). **Yield:** 10 servings.

Pepper Steak Sandwiches

Stack up a big platter of these sandwiches for your next buffet. The steak is so tender and delicious, and the peppers add pretty color.

—Ruby Williams, Bogalusa, Louisiana

- 2 medium green peppers, julienned
- 1 small onion, sliced
- 4 garlic cloves, minced, *divided*
- 1 tablespoon olive oil
- 2 cups cooked sirloin *or* round steak (3/4 pound), thinly sliced
- 1/2 teaspoon salt, optional
- 1/8 teaspoon pepper
- 1/4 cup butter, softened
- 4 French *or* Italian sandwich rolls, split and toasted

1 In a large skillet, saute the green peppers, onion and half of the garlic in oil until vegetables are tender. Add the steak, salt if desired and pepper; heat through.

2 Blend butter and remaining garlic; spread over cut side of rolls. Place steak mixture on bottom halves; replace roll tops. **Yield:** 4 servings.

Sirloin Stir-Fry

This delicious stir-fry is quick to stir up and is perfect for a casual meal during the week when time is always at a premium.

—Kim Shea, Wethersfield, Connecticut

- 1 medium onion, chopped
- 1 medium green pepper, chopped
- 1 medium sweet red pepper, chopped
- 3 garlic cloves, minced
- 2 tablespoons butter
- 1 can (14-1/2 ounces) Italian stewed tomatoes
- 2 to 3 teaspoons dried basil
- 2 teaspoons sugar
- 1 teaspoon garlic salt *or* 1/8 teaspoon garlic powder
- 1/4 teaspoon pepper
- 2 cups cooked sirloin *or* round steak (3/4 pound), cut into thin strips

Hot cooked rice

1 In a skillet or wok, stir-fry the onion, peppers and garlic in butter until vegetables are tender. Add the tomatoes, basil, sugar, garlic salt and pepper. Bring to a boil. Reduce heat; cover and simmer for 5 minutes. Add steak; cover and simmer until heated through. Serve with rice. **Yield:** 4 servings.

Seasoned Taco Meat

This party-size recipe blends plenty of ground beef and zippy seasonings. Turn the big batch of meat into a taco supper for hungry guests.

—Margaret Peterson, Forest City, Iowa

- 4 pounds ground beef
- 3 tablespoons chopped onion
- 1 can (14-1/2 ounces) beef broth
- 1 can (8 ounces) tomato sauce
- 1/4 cup chili powder
- 2 tablespoons paprika
- 1 tablespoon beef bouillon granules
- 1 tablespoon ground cumin
- 1 teaspoon chicken bouillon granules
- 1 teaspoon garlic powder
- 1 teaspoon cayenne pepper
- 1/2 teaspoon pepper
- 1/2 teaspoon lime juice
- 1/4 teaspoon onion powder
- 1/4 teaspoon sugar
- 1/4 teaspoon salt
- 1/4 teaspoon garlic salt

Taco shells or flour tortillas
Shredded cheese and salsa

1 In a Dutch oven, cook the beef and onion over medium heat until meat is no longer pink; drain. Stir in the next 15 ingredients. Bring to a boil. Reduce heat; cover and simmer for 10 minutes.

2 Serve in taco shells with shredded cheese and salsa. **Yield:** 8 cups.

Taco Pizza Squares

Your gang will come running the minute you take this zesty pizza out of the oven. I top convenient refrigerated pizza dough with leftover taco meat, tomatoes and cheese, bringing a flavor-filled fiesta to the table.

—Sarah Vovos, Middleton, Wisconsin

- 2 tubes (13.8 ounces each) refrigerated pizza crust
- 1 can (8 ounces) pizza sauce
- 2 cups Seasoned Taco Meat (recipe on this page)
- 2 medium tomatoes, seeded and chopped
- 2 cups (8 ounces) shredded part-skim mozzarella cheese

Shredded lettuce or sour cream, optional

1 Unroll pizza dough and place in a 15-in. x 10-in. x 1-in. baking pan. Spread with pizza sauce; sprinkle with the taco meat, tomatoes and cheese. Bake at 400° for 15-20 minutes or until crust is golden brown. Top with shredded lettuce and sour cream if desired. **Yield:** 8-10 servings.

Taco Pinwheels

Extra taco meat makes these appealing appetizers easy to assemble. I add the seasoned meat to a cream cheese mixture that I roll up in tortillas.

—Cindy Reams, Philipsburg, Pennsylvania

- 4 ounces cream cheese, softened
- 3/4 cup Seasoned Taco Meat (recipe on this page)
- 1/4 cup finely shredded cheddar cheese
- 1/4 cup salsa
- 2 tablespoons mayonnaise
- 2 tablespoons chopped ripe olives
- 2 tablespoons finely chopped onion
- 5 flour tortillas (8 inches), room temperature
- 1/2 cup shredded lettuce

Additional salsa

1 In a small bowl, beat the cream cheese until smooth. Stir in the taco meat, cheese, salsa, mayonnaise, olives and onion. Spread over tortillas. Sprinkle with lettuce; roll up tightly. Wrap in plastic wrap and refrigerate for at least 1 hour.

2 Unwrap and cut into 1-in. pieces. Serve with additional salsa. **Yield:** about 3 dozen appetizers.

Roasted Chicken

This moist and tender chicken is a real time-saver on a busy weekend. A simple blend of seasonings makes it a snap to prepare, and it smells heavenly as it roasts.

—Marian Platt, Sequim, Washington

- 2 roasting chickens (about 5 pounds *each*)
- 1 teaspoon *each* salt, seasoned salt, celery salt and onion salt
- 1/2 teaspoon pepper

1 Pat chickens dry. Place with breast side up in an ungreased 13-in. x 9-in. x 2-in. baking pan. Combine seasonings; rub over and inside chickens.

2 Cover tightly and bake at 400° for 1 hour. Uncover and bake 30 minutes longer or until a meat thermometer reads 180°. Serve one chicken immediately.

3 Cool the second chicken; debone and cube the meat and refrigerate or freeze (may be frozen for up to 3 months). **Yield:** 4-6 servings per chicken.

Chicken Enchiladas

Leftover chicken is used to create a rich and creamy meal-in-one. This colorful dish has zippy flavor. It's a nice change of pace from beef enchiladas.

—Julie Moutray, Wichita, Kansas

- 1 can (16 ounces) refried beans
- 10 flour tortillas (8 inches), warmed
- 1 can (10-3/4 ounces) condensed cream of chicken soup, undiluted
- 1 cup (8 ounces) sour cream
- 3 to 4 cups cubed cooked chicken
- 3 cups (12 ounces) shredded cheddar cheese, *divided*
- 1 can (15 ounces) enchilada sauce
- 1/4 cup sliced green onions
- 1/4 cup sliced ripe olives
- Shredded lettuce, optional

1 Spread about 2 tablespoons of beans on each tortilla. Combine soup and sour cream; stir in chicken. Spoon 1/3 to 1/2 cup down the center of each tortilla; top with 1 tablespoon cheese.

2 Roll up and place enchiladas seam side down in a greased 13-in. x 9-in. x 2-in. baking dish. Pour enchilada sauce over the top; sprinkle with the onions, olives and remaining cheese.

3 Bake, uncovered, at 350° for 35 minutes or until heated through. Just before serving, sprinkle lettuce around the enchiladas if desired. **Yield:** 10 servings.

Fast Chicken Divan

Frozen broccoli and leftover chicken get an easy but elegant treatment in this delicious dish. I dress them up with a saucy blend of cream soup and mayonnaise, then cover it all with a golden, cheesy crumb topping.

—Bertille Cooper, California, Maryland

- 2 packages (10 ounces *each*) frozen broccoli florets *or* chopped broccoli
- 3 cups cubed cooked chicken
- 2 cans (10-3/4 ounces *each*) condensed cream of chicken soup, undiluted
- 1 cup mayonnaise
- 1 teaspoon lemon juice
- 1 cup (4 ounces) shredded sharp cheddar cheese
- 3/4 cup dry bread crumbs
- 3 tablespoons butter, melted
- 1 tablespoon sliced pimientos, optional

1 In a large saucepan, cook the broccoli in boiling water for 1 minute; drain. Transfer to a greased 11-in. x 7-in. x 2-in. baking dish; top with chicken. Combine the soup, mayonnaise and lemon juice; spread over chicken. Sprinkle with cheese. Combine bread crumbs and butter; sprinkle over top.

2 Bake, uncovered, at 325° for 30 minutes or until bubbly and golden brown. Let stand for 10 minutes before serving. Garnish with pimientos if desired. **Yield:** 4-6 servings.

EDITOR'S NOTE: Reduced-fat or fat-free mayonnaise is not recommended for this recipe.

Cinnamon Swirl Bread

Your family will be impressed with the appealing swirls of cinnamon in these lovely loaves.

—Diane Armstrong, Elm Grove, Wisconsin

- 2 packages (1/4 ounce *each*) active dry yeast
- 1/3 cup warm water (110° to 115°)
- 1 cup warm milk (110° to 115°)
- 1 cup sugar, *divided*
- 2 eggs, lightly beaten
- 6 tablespoons butter, softened
- 1-1/2 teaspoons salt
- 5-1/2 to 6 cups all-purpose flour
- 2 tablespoons ground cinnamon

1 In a large bowl, dissolve yeast in water. Add the milk, 1/2 cup sugar, eggs, butter, salt and 2-1/2 cups flour; beat until smooth. Stir in enough remaining flour to form a soft dough.

2 Turn onto a floured surface; knead until smooth and elastic, about 6-8 minutes. Place in a greased bowl, turning once to grease top. Cover and let rise in a warm place until doubled, about 1 hour.

3 Punch dough down; divide in half. Roll each half into an 18-in. x 8-in. rectangle. Combine cinnamon and remaining sugar; sprinkle over the dough. Roll up each rectangle from a short side; pinch seam to seal.

4 Place seam side down in two greased 9-in. x 5-in. x 3-in. loaf pans. Cover and let rise until doubled, about 1-1/2 hours.

5 Bake at 350° for 30-35 minutes or until golden brown. Remove from pans and cool on wire racks. **Yield:** 2 loaves (16 slices each).

Orange French Toast

With a hint of orange flavor, this awesome overnight brunch dish is a special way to wake up the taste buds of weekend guests.

—Kristy Martin, Circle Pine, Minnesota

- 6 eggs, lightly beaten
- 3/4 cup orange juice
- 1/2 cup half-and-half cream
- 2 tablespoons sugar

- 1 teaspoon vanilla extract
- 1/2 teaspoon grated orange peel
- 8 thick slices cinnamon bread
- 1/4 cup butter, melted

1 In a shallow bowl, combine the first six ingredients. Dip both sides of bread into egg mixture; let soak for 5 minutes. Place in a greased 15-in. x 10-in. x 1-in. baking pan. Cover and refrigerate overnight.

2 Uncover; drizzle with butter. Bake at 325° for 35-40 minutes or until browned. **Yield:** 8 servings.

Rhubarb Betty

Try this speedy fruit dessert once and you'll rave about its taste and convenience. The cinnamon flavor of the bread complements the tart, tender rhubarb quite nicely.

—Sharon Keys, Spencerport, New York

- 5 cups diced fresh *or* frozen rhubarb, thawed
- 3/4 to 1 cup sugar
- 1/2 teaspoon ground cinnamon
- 4 cups cubed cinnamon bread
- 1/4 cup butter, melted

Vanilla ice cream *or* whipped cream, optional

1 In a large bowl, combine the rhubarb, sugar and cinnamon. Add half of the bread cubes; toss gently. Transfer to an ungreased 2-qt. microwave-safe dish. Top with remaining bread cubes; drizzle with butter.

2 Microwave, uncovered, on high for 7-9 minutes or until rhubarb is tender. Serve warm with ice cream or whipped cream if desired. **Yield:** 8 servings.

EDITOR'S NOTE: This recipe was tested in a 1,100-watt microwave. If using frozen rhubarb, measure rhubarb while still frozen, then thaw completely. Drain in a colander, but do not press liquid out. It can also be prepared in a conventional oven. Use an ungreased 2-qt. baking dish. Cover and bake at 350° for 40 minutes; uncover and bake 10 minutes longer or until the rhubarb is tender.

Pork Chop Potato Casserole

This rich-tasting casserole features tender pork chops, hearty hash browns and a golden topping of cheese and french-fried onions.

—Norma Shepler, Lake Wales, Florida

- 8 bone-in pork loin chops (1/2 inch thick and 6 ounces each)
- 1 teaspoon seasoned salt
- 1 tablespoon vegetable oil
- 1 can (10-3/4 ounces) condensed cream of celery soup, undiluted
- 2/3 cup milk
- 1/2 cup sour cream
- 1/2 teaspoon salt
- 1/4 teaspoon pepper
- 1 package (26 ounces) frozen shredded hash brown potatoes
- 1 cup (4 ounces) shredded cheddar cheese, *divided*
- 1 can (2.8 ounces) french-fried onions, *divided*

1 Sprinkle pork chops with seasoned salt. In a large skillet, brown chops on both sides in oil.

2 In a large bowl, combine the soup, milk, sour cream, salt and pepper; stir in hash browns, 3/4 cup cheese and half of the onions. Spread into a greased 13-in. x 9-in. x 2-in. baking dish. Arrange pork chops on top.

3 Cover and bake at 350° for 40 minutes. Uncover; sprinkle with the remaining cheese and onions. Bake, uncovered, 5-10 minutes longer or until meat juices run clear. **Yield: 8 servings.**

Italian Pork and Rice

When I have a few extra pork chops, I use them to prepare this colorful stovetop meal. I serve it with garlic bread and a tossed salad for a fresh-tasting dinner with Italian flair.

—Loreen McAllister, Elsie, Michigan

- 1 cup sliced fresh mushrooms
- 1/3 cup chopped onion
- 1 garlic clove, minced
- 1 tablespoon butter
- 1 can (14-1/2 ounces) Italian diced tomatoes, undrained
- 1 cup cubed cooked pork (about 2 pork chops)
- 1/2 cup chopped green pepper
- 1/2 cup chopped sweet red pepper
- 1 teaspoon Italian seasoning
- 1/2 teaspoon salt, optional

Pinch sugar

- 1/2 cup uncooked instant rice

1 In a large saucepan, saute the mushrooms, onion and garlic in butter until tender. Stir in tomatoes, pork, peppers, Italian seasoning, salt if desired and sugar; bring to a boil. Stir in rice. Cover and remove from the heat; let stand for 5 minutes. Stir before serving. **Yield: 3 servings.**

Country Skillet Supper

With hearty potatoes and bright green peas, this dish is creamy, comforting and so tasty.

—Arlene Snyder, Millerstown, Pennsylvania

- 1 small onion, chopped
- 1 tablespoon vegetable oil
- 1 can (10-3/4 ounces) condensed cream of celery soup, undiluted
- 1/2 cup milk
- 1 teaspoon Worcestershire sauce
- 1/4 teaspoon salt
- 1/8 teaspoon pepper
- 1 cup cubed cooked pork
- 1 cup cubed cooked potatoes
- 1 cup frozen peas, thawed

Biscuits, optional

1 In a large skillet, saute onion in oil until tender. Stir in the soup, milk, Worcestershire, salt and pepper; mix well. Add the pork, potatoes and peas; heat through. Serve with biscuits if desired. **Yield: 2-3 servings.**

Pork with Apricot Sauce

I dress up pork tenderloin with a sweet apricot sauce mildly seasoned with ginger. It makes an impressive entree, yet leaves plenty of extra pork for meals later in the week.

—Kris Wells, Hereford, Arizona

- 4 pork tenderloins (1 pound each)
- 1 jar (12 ounces) apricot preserves
- 1/3 cup lemon juice
- 1/3 cup ketchup
- 1/4 cup sherry or chicken broth
- 3 tablespoons honey
- 1 tablespoon soy sauce
- 1/8 to 1/4 teaspoon ground ginger

1 Place tenderloins on a rack in a shallow roasting pan. Bake, uncovered, at 450° for 30-35 minutes or until a meat thermometer reads 160°.

2 Meanwhile, in a saucepan, combine the remaining ingredients. Cook and stir until heated through.

3 Slice the pork; serve 1-1/2 pounds with the apricot sauce. Refrigerate or freeze remaining pork for another use. **Yield:** 4-6 servings (2 cups sauce) plus 2-1/2 pounds leftover pork.

Barbecued Pork Sandwiches

I found this recipe in one of my great-aunt's cookbooks. The original recipe called for beef, but I used leftover pork roast I had on hand. My family loves these tangy sandwiches.

—Melissa Norris, Churubusco, Indiana

- 1/4 cup sugar
- 4 teaspoons cornstarch
- 1-1/2 teaspoons dried minced onion
- 1 teaspoon salt
- 1/4 teaspoon pepper
- 1-1/2 cups ketchup
- 3/4 cup water
- 1/4 cup cider vinegar
- 1/4 cup butter, cubed
- 3 tablespoons Worcestershire sauce
- 2 tablespoons lemon juice
- 1 tablespoon prepared mustard
- 3 cups sliced cooked pork (about 1-1/2 pounds)
- 8 sandwich buns, split

1 In a large saucepan, combine the first 12 ingredients. Bring to a boil; cook and stir for 2 minutes or until thickened. Add pork; heat through. Serve on buns. **Yield:** 8 servings.

Chili Verde

Leftover pork adds heartiness to this zippy chili. It's great on a cool night with a stack of tortillas. I've taken it to many gatherings, and it's always gone when the party's over.

—Jo Oliverius, Alpine, California

- 2 cups cubed cooked pork (about 1 pound)
- 1 can (16 ounces) kidney beans, rinsed and drained
- 1 can (15 ounces) pinto beans, rinsed and drained
- 1 can (15 ounces) chili with beans, undrained
- 1 can (14-1/2 ounces) stewed tomatoes
- 1-1/2 to 2 cups green salsa
- 1 large onion, chopped
- 2 cans (4 ounces each) chopped green chilies
- 2 garlic cloves, minced
- 1 tablespoon minced fresh cilantro
- 2 teaspoons ground cumin

1 In a large saucepan, combine all ingredients. Bring to a boil. Reduce the heat; simmer, uncovered, for 10 minutes or until heated through. **Yield:** 8 servings.

Green Pepper Meat Loaf

My husband and I can't get enough of this classic main dish. Leftover slices are terrific made into sandwiches for lunch the next day.

—Edna Lauderdale, Milwaukee, Wisconsin

- 2 eggs, lightly beaten
- 2 medium green peppers, chopped
- 1 large onion, finely chopped
- 1/4 cup chopped celery leaves
- 1/4 cup minced fresh parsley
- 1 envelope onion soup mix
- 2 pounds ground beef
- 1 pound bulk pork sausage
- 4 bacon strips, optional

1 In a large bowl, combine the eggs, green peppers, onion, celery leaves, parsley and soup mix. Crumble beef and sausage over the mixture and mix well. Shape into a 12-in. x 4-in. loaf.

2 Place on a rack in a shallow baking pan. Bake, uncovered, at 350° for 1 hour. Place bacon strips over top if desired. Bake 45-60 minutes longer or until no pink remains and a meat thermometer reads 160°. **Yield:** 14 slices.

Meat Loaf Burritos

I deliciously disguise leftover meat loaf in these hearty burritos. They get plenty of flavor from cheese, salsa and other colorful toppings.

—Lori Thompson, New London, Texas

- 1 tablespoon butter
- 1 can (15 ounces) pinto beans, rinsed and drained
- 2 cups crumbled cooked meat loaf (3 slices)
- 6 flour tortillas (6 inches), warmed

Shredded cheddar cheese, shredded lettuce, chopped tomatoes and salsa, optional

1 Melt butter in a skillet; add half of the beans and mash with a fork. Stir in meat loaf and remaining beans; heat through.

2 Spoon about 1/2 cup meat loaf mixture onto each tortilla. Top with cheese if desired. Fold up bottom and sides over filling. Serve with lettuce, tomatoes and salsa if desired. **Yield:** 6 burritos.

Meat Loaf Shepherd's Pie

I don't have a lot of time to spend cooking. This meal-in-one is quick and easy to make.

—Jennifer Haines, Redford, Michigan

- 5 slices cooked meat loaf
- 1 jar (12 ounces) beef gravy
- 1 can (15-1/4 ounces) whole kernel corn, drained
- 4 cups warm mashed potatoes (prepared with milk and butter)
- 3/4 cup shredded cheddar cheese, *divided*
- 1/2 cup sour cream
- 1/4 cup sliced green onions

1 Place meat loaf slices in a greased 2-1/2-qt. baking dish. Cover with gravy; top with corn. Combine potatoes, 1/2 cup cheese, sour cream and onions; spread over corn.

2 Bake, uncovered, at 375° for 25-30 minutes or until heated through. Sprinkle with remaining cheese. Bake 2 minutes longer or until the cheese is melted. **Yield:** 4-6 servings.

TIP
Mixing Meat Loaf

For moist meat loaf, handle the mixture as little as possible. In a large bowl, combine all ingredients except the beef. Crumble the meat over the mixture. With a sturdy spoon or by hand, gently mix the ingredients just until combined.

Savory Pork Roast

I love this herbed roast so much that I make it as often as I can. It's wonderful for special occasions, particularly when served with sweet potatoes and corn muffins. It makes a lot so you will have plenty of pork left over for several other recipes.

—Edie DeSpain, Logan, Utah

- 1 garlic clove, minced
- 2 teaspoons dried marjoram
- 1 teaspoon salt
- 1 teaspoon rubbed sage
- 1 boneless whole pork loin roast (about 4 pounds)

1 Combine the seasonings; rub over roast. Place on a rack in a shallow roasting pan.

2 Bake, uncovered, at 350° for 80 minutes or until a meat thermometer reads 160°. Let stand for 10-15 minutes before slicing. **Yield:** 9-12 servings (or 3-4 servings plus leftover).

Pork Fried Rice

My husband anxiously awaits the nights we have pork because he knows I'll use the leftovers in this recipe. That's because the dish can be prepared in less than 30 minutes. Add a few fortune cookies to make the meal special.

—Norma Reynolds, Overland Park, Kansas

- 1/2 cup diced carrots
- 1/2 cup diced celery
- 1/2 cup diced sweet red pepper
- 1/2 cup sliced green onions
- 2 tablespoons vegetable oil, *divided*
- 3 eggs, lightly beaten
- 2 cups cubed cooked pork (about 1 pound)
- 2 cups cold cooked rice
- 4 to 5 teaspoons soy sauce

Salt and pepper to taste

1 In a large skillet, saute the vegetables in 1 tablespoon of oil until crisp-tender; remove and keep warm. Heat remaining oil over medium heat.

2 Add eggs; cook and stir until completely set. Add the pork, rice, soy sauce, salt, pepper and vegetables; cook and stir until heated through. **Yield:** 5 servings.

Italian Pork Hoagies

I like to prepare these quick toasted sandwiches whenever I have extra pork. I spread pizza sauce over hoagie buns before adding sliced pork, Italian salad dressing and mozzarella cheese.

—Jackie Hannahs, Fountain, Michigan

- 6 hoagie buns, split
- 1/2 cup pizza sauce
- 12 slices cooked pork (1/4 inch thick and 2 ounces *each*)
- 1/2 cup Italian salad dressing
- 1/2 cup shredded part-skim mozzarella cheese

1 Place bottom and top halves of buns, cut side up, on an ungreased baking sheet. Spread pizza sauce on the bottom half of each bun. Top with pork; drizzle with salad dressing. Sprinkle with cheese.

2 Bake at 350° for 5-10 minutes or until cheese is melted and tops of buns are lightly toasted. Replace bun tops. **Yield:** 6 servings.

TIP
Rice at the Ready

Whenever preparing rice for a recipe, you may want to make some extra.

Cooked rice can be refrigerated for several days to be used in other dishes (like Pork Fried Rice at left).

You can also package rice in 1/2- and 1-cup portions and freeze in heavy-duty resealable plastic bags for up to 6 months.

To reheat cooked rice, add 2 tablespoons of liquid for each cup of rice. Cook in a saucepan or microwave in a microwave-safe bowl until heated through.

Garden-Fresh Spaghetti

This thick pasta sauce with fresh-from-the-garden flavor is chock-full of peppers, mushrooms, carrots and onion. It makes a big batch, so you'll have plenty to serve over spaghetti with leftovers for some other meals.

—Sue Yaeger, Boone, Iowa

- 4 cups sliced fresh mushrooms
- 3 medium carrots, coarsely chopped
- 1 cup chopped celery
- 1 cup chopped onion
- 1/2 cup chopped green pepper
- 1/2 cup chopped sweet red pepper
- 4 garlic cloves, minced
- 1/4 cup vegetable oil
- 2 cans (28 ounces *each*) crushed tomatoes
- 2 cans (15 ounces *each*) tomato sauce
- 1 can (12 ounces) tomato paste
- 1 cup beef broth
- 2 teaspoons dried basil
- 2 teaspoons dried oregano
- 1-1/2 teaspoons brown sugar
- 1 teaspoon salt
- 1/2 teaspoon pepper
- 1 cup grated Parmesan cheese

Hot cooked spaghetti

1 In a Dutch oven, saute the mushrooms, carrots, celery, onion, peppers and garlic in oil until tender. Add the next 10 ingredients. Bring to a boil. Reduce heat; cover and simmer for 1 hour. Serve with spaghetti. **Yield: 15 cups sauce.**

Sausage Broccoli Manicotti

Even kids will gobble up their broccoli when it's served this way. I doctor up spaghetti sauce with Italian sausage and garlic, then drizzle it over shells stuffed with broccoli and cheese.

—Jason Jost, Manitowoc, Wisconsin

- 1 package (8 ounces) manicotti shells
- 2 cups (16 ounces) 4% cottage cheese
- 3 cups frozen chopped broccoli, thawed and well drained
- 1-1/2 cups (6 ounces) shredded part-skim mozzarella cheese, *divided*
- 3/4 cup shredded Parmesan cheese, *divided*

- 1 egg
- 2 teaspoons minced fresh parsley
- 1/2 teaspoon onion powder
- 1/2 teaspoon pepper
- 1/8 teaspoon garlic powder
- 1 pound bulk Italian sausage
- 4 cups meatless spaghetti sauce
- 2 garlic cloves, minced

1 Cook manicotti according to package directions. Meanwhile, in a large bowl, combine the cottage cheese, broccoli, 1 cup mozzarella cheese, 1/4 cup Parmesan cheese, egg, parsley, onion powder, pepper and garlic powder; set aside.

2 In a large skillet, cook the sausage over medium heat until no longer pink; drain. Add spaghetti sauce and garlic. Spread 1 cup meat sauce in a greased 13-in. x 9-in. x 2-in. baking dish.

3 Rinse and drain shells; stuff with broccoli mixture. Arrange over sauce. Top with remaining sauce. Sprinkle with remaining mozzarella and Parmesan. Bake, uncovered, at 350° for 40-50 minutes or until heated through. **Yield: 6-8 servings.**

Parmesan Chicken

I like to make this yummy recipe when I have extra spaghetti sauce on hand. The herbed coating on the tender chicken gets nice and golden.

—Margie Eddy, Ann Arbor, Michigan

- 1/2 cup seasoned bread crumbs
- 1/2 cup grated Parmesan cheese, *divided*
- 1-1/2 teaspoons dried oregano, *divided*
- 1/2 teaspoon dried basil
- 1/2 teaspoon salt
- 1/4 teaspoon pepper
- 1 egg
- 1 tablespoon water
- 4 boneless skinless chicken breast halves (4 ounces *each*)
- 2 tablespoons butter
- 2 cups meatless spaghetti sauce
- 1/2 teaspoon garlic salt
- 1 cup (4 ounces) shredded part-skim mozzarella cheese

Hot cooked fettuccine *or* pasta of your choice

1 In a shallow bowl, combine the bread crumbs, 1/4 cup Parmesan cheese, 1 teaspoon oregano, basil,

salt and pepper. In another shallow bowl, combine the egg and water. Dip chicken in egg mixture, then coat with crumb mixture.

2 In a large skillet, cook chicken in butter on both sides until juices run clear.

3 Meanwhile, in a large saucepan, combine the spaghetti sauce, garlic salt and remaining oregano, Cook over medium heat until heated through. Spoon over chicken; sprinkle with mozzarella cheese and remaining Parmesan cheese. Serve with pasta. **Yield:** 4 servings.

Heavenly Angel Food Cake

This light, moist cake is my favorite. It tastes heavenly and is special enough for most any occasion.

—Fayrene De Koker, Vancouver, Washington

- 12 eggs
- 1-1/4 cups confectioners' sugar
- 1 cup all-purpose flour
- 1-1/2 teaspoons cream of tartar
- 1-1/2 teaspoons vanilla extract
- 1/2 teaspoon almond extract
- 1/4 teaspoon salt
- 1 cup sugar

1 Separate eggs; discard yolks or refrigerate for another use. Measure egg whites, adding or removing whites as needed to equal 1-1/2 cups. Place in a large bowl; let stand at room temperature for 30 minutes. Sift confectioners' sugar and flour together twice; set aside.

2 Add cream of tartar, extracts and salt to egg whites; beat on medium speed until soft peaks form. Gradually add sugar, about 2 tablespoons at a time, beating on high until stiff glossy peaks form and sugar is dissolved. Gradually fold in flour mixture, about 1/2 cup at a time.

3 Gently spoon into an ungreased 10-in. tube pan. Cut through the batter with a knife to remove air pockets. Bake on the lowest oven rack at 350° for 40-45 minutes or until lightly browned and entire top appears dry. Immediately invert pan; cool completely, about 1 hour.

4 Run a knife around side and center tube of pan. Remove cake to a serving plate. **Yield:** 20 servings.

Caramelized Angel Dessert

This quick-and-easy treat is wonderful. Featuring a broiled, caramel-like sauce, the cake slices get an elegant treatment when topped with a little sour cream and mandarin oranges.

—Sharon Bickett, Chester, South Carolina

- 1/2 cup butter, softened
- 1/2 cup packed brown sugar
- 1 tablespoon lemon juice
- 1/4 teaspoon ground cinnamon
- Dash ground nutmeg
- 6 slices angel food cake
- 1 cup mandarin oranges
- Sour cream, optional

1 In a large bowl, cream butter and brown sugar until light and fluffy. Beat in the lemon juice, cinnamon and nutmeg until blended.

2 Spread about 1 tablespoon on the top and sides of each cake slice. Place on a baking sheet. Broil 4-6 in. from the heat for 1-2 minutes or until bubbly. Top with oranges and sour cream if desired. **Yield:** 6 servings.

Cranberry Ribbon Loaf

I use leftover angel food cake to create a refreshing cranberry dessert perfect for holiday gatherings. It's convenient, too, because it can be assembled ahead.

—Patricia Kile, Greentown, Pennsylvania

- 1 package (3 ounces) cream cheese, softened
- 1/4 cup sugar
- Dash salt
- 1 can (16 ounces) whole-berry cranberry sauce
- 1 cup heavy whipping cream, whipped
- 6 slices angel food cake (1/2 inch thick)

1 Line the bottom and sides of a 9-in. x 5-in. x 3-in. loaf pan with heavy-duty foil; set aside. In a large bowl, beat the cream cheese, sugar and salt until smooth. Stir in cranberry sauce. Fold in the whipped cream.

2 Spread a third of the mixture in prepared pan; top with three cake slices (cut cake if needed to fit). Repeat layers. Top with remaining cranberry mixture. Cover and freeze.

3 Remove from the freezer 15 minutes before serving. Use foil to remove loaf from pan; discard foil. Cut into slices. **Yield:** 8 servings.

Gingerbread Cake

I drizzle a basic orange sauce over homemade gingerbread for this old-fashioned dessert. Cut just the number of squares needed, and freeze the rest.

—Shannon Sides, Selma, Alabama

- 1/2 cup butter-flavored shortening
- 1/3 cup sugar
- 1 cup molasses
- 3/4 cup water
- 1 egg
- 2-1/3 cups all-purpose flour
- 1 teaspoon baking soda
- 1 teaspoon ground ginger
- 1 teaspoon ground cinnamon
- 3/4 teaspoon salt

ORANGE SAUCE:
- 1 cup confectioners' sugar
- 2 tablespoons orange juice
- 1/2 teaspoon grated orange peel

1 In a large bowl, cream shortening and sugar until light and fluffy. Add the molasses, water and egg. Combine the flour, baking soda, ginger, cinnamon and salt; add to the creamed mixture and beat until combined.

2 Pour into a greased 15-in. x 10-in. x 1-in. baking pan. Bake at 350° for 18-22 minutes or until a toothpick inserted near the center comes out clean. Cool on a wire rack.

3 In a small bowl, combine the sauce ingredients until blended. Serve with cake. **Yield: 4 servings with sauce plus leftovers.**

Gingerbread Men

Cookie cutters work well to form these fun and festive fellows. Kids of all ages will enjoy spreading the cutouts with soft, sweet white chocolate frosting, then giving them character by decorating with colorful store-bought candies.

—Taste of Home Test Kitchen

- 1 piece (10 inches x 7 inches) Gingerbread Cake (recipe on this page)
- 1/4 cup butter, softened

- 1-1/2 squares (1-1/2 ounces) white baking chocolate, melted
- 1/2 cup confectioners' sugar

Assorted candies

1 Using a 3-1/2-in. gingerbread man cookie cutter, cut out six men from the gingerbread cake. In a small bowl, combine the butter, chocolate and confectioners' sugar; beat for 2 minutes or until light and fluffy. Frost the gingerbread men and decorate with candies as desired. **Yield: 6 gingerbread men.**

Gingerbread Trifle

This tasty dessert was a hit when I served it to our Bible study group. It's a wonderful blend of flavors and a great ending to holiday meals. If you don't have leftover gingerbread, bake some from a boxed mix to assemble this trifle.

—Betty Kleberger, Florissant, Missouri

- 2 cups cold milk
- 1 package (3.4 ounces) instant French vanilla pudding mix
- 7 cups cubed Gingerbread Cake (recipe on this page)
- 3/4 cup English toffee bits or almond brickle chips
- 1 carton (8 ounces) frozen whipped topping, thawed
- 1 maraschino cherry

1 In a large bowl, whisk the milk and pudding mix for 2 minutes. Let stand for 2 minutes or until soft-set.

2 In a 2-qt. serving bowl, layer half of the cake cubes and pudding. Sprinkle with 1/2 cup toffee bits. Top with remaining cake and pudding. Spread whipped topping over the top; sprinkle with the remaining toffee bits. Garnish with a cherry. **Yield: 8-10 servings.**

Herbed Pork Roast

A combination of dry herbs gives pork an out-of-this-world flavor. This wonderful, moist roast is a family favorite—and it makes great company fare, too.

—Carolyn Pope, Mason City, Iowa

    2   tablespoons sugar
    2   teaspoons dried marjoram
    2   teaspoons rubbed sage
    1   teaspoon salt
    1/2 teaspoon celery seed
    1/2 teaspoon ground mustard
    1/8 teaspoon pepper
    1   boneless whole pork loin roast (5 pounds)

1 Combine the first seven ingredients; rub over roast. Cover and refrigerate for 4 hours or overnight.

2 Place roast on a rack in a shallow roasting pan. Bake, uncovered, at 325° for 2-1/2 hours or until a meat thermometer reads 160°.

3 Let stand for 15 minutes before slicing. Refrigerate or freeze remaining pork (may be frozen for up to 3 months). **Yield:** 12-14 servings.

Spicy Pork Sandwiches

I blend a flavorful sandwich spread that's a fun alternative to standard mustard or mayo. It adds interest to leftover pork or most any sandwich meat, including turkey and roast beef.

—Myra Innes, Auburn, Kansas

    1/2   cup mayonnaise
    1-1/2 teaspoons finely chopped onion
    1-1/2 teaspoons minced fresh parsley
    1-1/2 teaspoons finely chopped celery
    1-1/2 teaspoons picante sauce
    1-1/2 teaspoons Dijon mustard
    1/4   teaspoon salt
    1/4   teaspoon pepper
    10   slices whole wheat bread
    5   slices cooked pork
Lettuce leaves

1 In a small bowl, combine the first eight ingredients. Spread about 1 tablespoon on each slice of bread. Top five slices with pork and lettuce; top with remaining bread. Refrigerate any leftover spread for another use. **Yield:** 5 sandwiches.

Pork Noodle Casserole

I learned to make this hearty dish from my grandmother. We never have a family get-together without it. It's a great addition to a buffet and makes a filling meal with warm rolls.

—Barbara Beyer, Two Rivers, Wisconsin

    3   cups cubed cooked pork
    1   can (14-3/4 ounces) cream-style corn
    1   cup chicken broth
    4   ounces process cheese (Velveeta), diced
    2/3 cup chopped green pepper
    2/3 cup chopped onion
    1   jar (4-1/2 ounces) whole mushrooms, drained
    2   tablespoons diced pimientos
    1/2 teaspoon salt
    1/4 teaspoon pepper
    8   ounces uncooked egg noodles

1 In a large bowl, combine the first 10 ingredients. Add noodles; gently toss to coat. Transfer to a greased 2-1/2-qt. baking dish.

2 Cover and bake at 325° for 1 hour or until noodles are tender, stirring every 20 minutes. **Yield:** 6 servings.

Freezer
Pleasers

Southern Vegetable Soup

This recipe for a chunky, vegetable-filled soup is a
surefire way to warm up on those cold winter nights.

—Christy Hinrichs, Parkville, Missouri

1/2	cup chopped onion
2	teaspoons minced garlic
2	teaspoons olive oil
2	cans (14-1/2 ounces *each*) vegetable broth
1	can (28 ounces) crushed tomatoes
1	package (16 ounces) frozen mixed vegetables
1	cup sliced fresh *or* frozen okra
1	can (4 ounces) chopped green chilies
2	teaspoons dried savory
1	teaspoon sugar
1/2	teaspoon salt
1/2	teaspoon dried tarragon
1/8	teaspoon white pepper

1 In a Dutch oven, saute onion and garlic in oil for
3 minutes or until tender. Stir in the remaining
ingredients. Bring to a boil. Reduce heat; cover and
simmer for 15-20 minutes or until vegetables are
crisp-tender.

2 Serve immediately or transfer to freezer containers.
May be frozen for up to 3 months.

3 **To use frozen soup:** Thaw in the refrigerator
overnight. Transfer to a saucepan. Cover and
cook over medium heat until heated through.
Yield: 6 servings (2-1/2 quarts).

Corn Bread Turkey Casserole

Folks who love turkey and stuffing will appreciate the flavor and convenience of this golden casserole. The recipe makes three pans, so there's plenty to share.

—Michelle Flynn, Philadelphia, Pennsylvania

- 3 packages (6 ounces *each*) crushed corn bread stuffing mix
- 10 to 11 cups cubed cooked turkey
- 2 cups (8 ounces) shredded cheddar cheese
- 2 cans (10-3/4 ounces *each*) condensed cream of celery soup, undiluted
- 2 cans (10-3/4 ounces *each*) condensed cream of chicken soup, undiluted
- 1 can (10-3/4 ounces) condensed cream of mushroom soup, undiluted
- 1 can (12 ounces) evaporated milk
- 1-1/2 cups (6 ounces) shredded Swiss cheese

1 Prepare stuffing mix according to package directions. Add turkey and cheddar cheese. In a large bowl, combine soups and milk. Layer three greased 13-in. x 9-in. x 2-in. baking dishes with 1 cup turkey mixture and 1 cup soup mixture. Repeat layers. Sprinkle with Swiss cheese.

2 Cover and freeze two casseroles for up to 3 months. Cover and bake the remaining casserole at 350° for 30-35 minutes or until bubbly. Let stand for 5-10 minutes before serving.

3 **To use frozen casserole:** Thaw in the refrigerator overnight. Bake, uncovered, at 350° for 35-40 minutes or until bubbly. Let stand for 5-10 minutes before serving. **Yield:** 3 casseroles (8-10 servings each).

Spaghetti Casserole

This is an easy dish to prepare ahead of time, refrigerate and bake just before company arrives. Canned soup makes this casserole creamy, but it still cuts well for serving.

—Kim Rocker, LaGrange, Georgia

- 1 package (16 ounces) angel hair pasta
- 1-1/2 pounds ground beef
- 1 jar (26 ounces) spaghetti sauce
- 2 cans (8 ounces *each*) tomato sauce
- 1 can (10-3/4 ounces) condensed cream of mushroom soup, undiluted
- 1 cup (8 ounces) sour cream
- 2 cups (8 ounces) shredded Colby-Monterey Jack cheese

1 Cook pasta according to package directions. Meanwhile, in a large skillet, cook beef over medium heat until no longer pink; drain. Stir in spaghetti sauce and tomato sauce. Remove from the heat.

2 Drain pasta. Combine soup and sour cream. In two 8-in. square baking dishes, layer half of the meat sauce, pasta, soup mixture and cheese. Repeat the layers.

3 Cover and freeze one casserole for up to 3 months. Cover and bake the remaining casserole at 350° for 55-65 minutes or until cheese is melted.

4 **To use frozen casserole:** Thaw in the refrigerator overnight. Remove from the refrigerator 30 minutes before baking. Bake as directed. **Yield:** 2 casseroles (6 servings each).

Double Meat Loaf

This tender meat loaf with beef and pork is a delicious entree for everyday or when company comes to call.

—Shirley L. Snyder, Payson, Arizona

- 1 egg
- 1 cup beef broth
- 1/2 cup quick-cooking oats
- 1 tablespoon dried minced onion
- 2 teaspoons dried parsley flakes
- 1 teaspoon salt
- 1/2 teaspoon pepper
- 1-1/2 pounds lean ground beef
- 1 pound bulk pork sausage
- 1 can (8 ounces) tomato sauce

1 In a large bowl, combine the first seven ingredients. Crumble beef and sausage over mixture; mix well. Pat into two greased 8-in. x 4-in. x 2-in. loaf pans. Top with tomato sauce.

2 Cover and freeze one meat loaf for up to 3 months. Bake the remaining loaf, uncovered, at 350° for 55-60 minutes or until a meat thermometer reads 160°.

3 **To use frozen meat loaf:** Thaw in the refrigerator overnight. Bake as directed. **Yield:** 2 loaves (4-6 servings each).

Breaded Chicken Patties

As a mother of three, I like to make a few batches of these patties at one time and freeze the extras for another meal. I remember helping my mother make big batches, too—there were 11 of us, so it took a lot of food to fill us all up!

—Brenda Martin, Lititz, Pennsylvania

- 1/4 cup finely chopped onion
- 1/4 cup finely chopped celery
- 6 tablespoons butter, *divided*
- 3 tablespoons all-purpose flour
- 1-1/3 cups milk, *divided*
- 2 tablespoons minced fresh parsley
- 1 teaspoon salt
- 1 teaspoon onion salt
- 1/2 teaspoon celery salt
- 1/4 teaspoon pepper
- 2 cups finely chopped cooked chicken
- 1 cup dry bread crumbs

Sandwich rolls, split
Lettuce leaves and tomato slices, optional

1 In a large saucepan, saute onion and celery in 3 tablespoons butter until tender. Combine flour and 1 cup milk. Gradually add to pan. Bring to a boil; cook and stir for 2 minutes or until thickened. Add parsley, seasonings and chicken. Remove from the heat. Chill until completely cooled.

2 Shape chicken mixture into six patties, using about 1/3 cup mixture for each patty. Place crumbs and remaining milk in separate shallow bowls. Roll patties in crumbs, then dip into milk; roll again in the crumbs.

3 In a large skillet, cook patties in remaining butter for 3 minutes on each side or until golden brown. Serve on rolls with lettuce and tomato if desired.

4 Uncooked patties may be frozen for up to 3 months. **To prepare frozen patties:** Cook in butter for 5-6 minutes on each side or until golden brown. **Yield:** 6 servings.

Sweet Barbecued Pork Chops

These tangy chops are so easy and taste so fresh, family and friends never guess this quick entree was frozen.

—Susan Holderman, Fostoria, Ohio

- 8 boneless pork loin chops
  (3/4 inch thick and 8 ounces *each*)
- 2 tablespoons vegetable oil
- 1/2 cup packed brown sugar
- 1/2 cup chopped sweet onion
- 1/2 cup *each* ketchup, barbecue sauce,
  French salad dressing and honey

1 In a large skillet, brown pork chops in oil in batches on both sides. Return all to the skillet. Combine the remaining ingredients; pour over chops. Bring to a boil. Reduce heat; cover and simmer for 12-14 minutes or until meat is tender.

2 Serve immediately, or cool before placing in a freezer container. Cover and freeze for up to 3 months.

3 **To use frozen pork chops:** Thaw in the refrigerator overnight. Place in a skillet; bring to a boil. Reduce heat; cover and simmer for 6-8 minutes or until heated through. **Yield:** 8 servings.

Three-Cheese Kielbasa Bake

This hearty, tasty casserole takes advantage of garden-fresh vegetables and handy convenience ingredients. I fix it any night of the week.

—Kate Beckman, Hemet, California

- 12 ounces uncooked elbow macaroni
- 2 pounds kielbasa *or* Polish sausage, halved lengthwise and sliced
- 1 tablespoon olive oil
- 2 medium onions, chopped
- 2 medium zucchini, quartered and sliced
- 2 medium carrots, grated
- 1/2 teaspoon minced garlic
- 1 jar (26 ounces) spaghetti sauce
- 1 can (14-1/2 ounces) stewed tomatoes
- 1 egg, lightly beaten
- 1 carton (15 ounces) ricotta cheese
- 2 cups (8 ounces) shredded cheddar cheese
- 2 cups (8 ounces) part-skim shredded mozzarella cheese
- 2 green onions, chopped

1 Cook macaroni according to package directions. Meanwhile, in a large skillet, brown sausage in oil over medium heat; drain. Add the onions, zucchini, carrots and garlic; cook and stir for 5-6 minutes or until crisp-tender.

2 Stir in spaghetti sauce and tomatoes. Bring to a boil. Reduce heat; simmer, uncovered, for 15 minutes. Drain macaroni.

3 In each of two greased 13-in. x 9-in. x 2-in. baking dishes, layer a fourth of the macaroni and meat sauce. Combine egg and ricotta cheese; spoon a fourth over sauce. Sprinkle with a fourth of the cheddar and mozzarella. Repeat layers. Top with green onions.

4 Cool one casserole; cover and freeze for up to 2 months. Cover and bake the remaining casserole at 350° for 15 minutes. Uncover; bake 15 minutes longer or until cheese is melted.

5 **To use frozen casserole:** Thaw in the refrigerator for 24 hours. Remove from the refrigerator 30 minutes before baking. Cover and bake at 350° for 35-40 minutes or until heated through. **Yield:** 2 casseroles (8-10 servings each).

Hominy Taco Chili

Canned items make this robust chili easy to prepare, and it always receives rave reviews.

—Barbara Wheless, Sheldon, South Carolina

- 1 pound ground beef
- 1 large onion, chopped
- 2 cans (15-1/2 ounces each) hominy, drained
- 2 cans (14-1/2 ounces each) stewed tomatoes, undrained
- 1 can (15-1/4 ounces) whole kernel corn, drained
- 1 can (15 ounces) pinto beans, rinsed and drained
- 1 can (15 ounces) black beans, rinsed and drained
- 1 cup water
- 1 envelope taco seasoning
- 1 envelope ranch salad dressing mix
- 2 teaspoons ground cumin
- 1/2 teaspoon garlic salt
- 1/2 teaspoon pepper

Corn chips, optional

1 In a Dutch oven, cook beef and onion over medium heat until meat is no longer pink; drain. Stir in the next 11 ingredients.

2 Bring to a boil. Reduce heat; cover and simmer for 30 minutes. Serve half of the chili with corn chips if desired. Freeze remaining chili in a freezer container for up to 3 months.

3 **To use frozen chili:** Thaw in the refrigerator. Transfer to a saucepan; heat through, adding water if desired. **Yield:** 2 batches (5 servings each).

Italian Chicken Roll-Ups

Coated with golden crumbs, these chicken rolls seem fancy enough for company.

—Barbara Wobser, Sandusky, Ohio

- 8 boneless skinless chicken breast halves (2 pounds)
- 8 thin slices (4 ounces) deli ham
- 4 slices provolone cheese, halved
- 2/3 cup seasoned bread crumbs
- 1/2 cup grated Romano or Parmesan cheese
- 1/4 cup minced fresh parsley
- 1/2 cup milk

Cooking spray

1 Flatten chicken to 1/4-in. thickness. Place a slice of ham and half slice of cheese on each piece of chicken. Roll up from a short side and tuck in ends; secure with a toothpick.

2 In a shallow bowl, combine the crumbs, Romano cheese and parsley. Pour milk into another bowl. Dip the chicken rolls in milk, then roll in the crumb mixture.

3 Wrap each of four chicken roll-ups in plastic wrap; place in a large freezer bag. Seal and freeze for up to 2 months. Place the remaining roll-ups seam side down on a greased baking sheet. Spritz the chicken with cooking spray. Bake, uncovered, at 425° for 25 minutes or until juices run clear. Remove the toothpicks.

4 **To use frozen chicken:** Completely thaw in the refrigerator. Unwrap roll-ups and place on a greased baking sheet. Spritz with cooking spray. Bake, uncovered, at 425° for 30 minutes or until juices run clear. **Yield:** 8 servings.

Beans and Franks Bake

I have made this casserole several times, and it's always a hit. The kid-pleasing combo has a sweet flavor from the baked beans and the corn bread topping.

—Roxanne VanGelder, Rochester, New Hampshire

- 2 packages (8-1/2 ounces *each*) corn bread/muffin mix
- 1 can (28 ounces) baked beans
- 4 hot dogs, halved lengthwise and sliced
- 1/2 pound sliced bacon, cooked and crumbled
- 1 cup ketchup
- 1/2 cup packed brown sugar
- 1/2 cup chopped onion
- 2 cups (8 ounces) shredded part-skim mozzarella cheese

1 Prepare corn bread batter according to package directions; set aside. In a large bowl, combine the beans, hot dogs, bacon, ketchup, brown sugar and onion. Transfer to two greased 8-in. square baking dishes. Sprinkle with the cheese; top with corn bread batter.

2 Cover and freeze one casserole for up to 3 months. Bake the second casserole, uncovered, at 350° for 40-45 minutes or until a toothpick inserted near the center comes out clean.

3 **To use frozen casserole:** Remove from the freezer 30 minutes before baking (do not thaw). Cover and bake at 350° for 40 minutes. Uncover; bake 15-20 minutes longer or until heated through. **Yield:** 2 casseroles (4 servings each).

Shepherd's Pie

This classic recipe makes one pie to eat right away and one batch of meat mixture to freeze for another day. Just pull out the frozen beef any time you have some leftover mashed potatoes.

—Paula Zsiray, Logan, Utah

- 2 pounds ground beef
- 2 cans (10-1/4 ounces *each*) beef gravy
- 2 cups frozen corn
- 2 cups frozen peas and carrots
- 2 teaspoons dried minced onion

ADDITIONAL INGREDIENTS (for each casserole):
- 2 to 3 cups mashed potatoes
- 2 tablespoons butter, melted

Paprika

1 In a Dutch oven, cook beef over medium heat until no longer pink; drain. Add the gravy, vegetables and onion. Spoon half into a greased 2-qt. baking dish. Top with mashed potatoes. Drizzle with butter and sprinkle with paprika.

2 Bake, uncovered, at 350° for 30-35 minutes or until heated through. Place the remaining beef mixture in a freezer container and freeze for up to 3 months.

3 **To prepare frozen casserole:** Thaw in the refrigerator; transfer to a greased 2-qt. baking dish. Top with the potatoes, butter and paprika; bake as directed. **Yield:** 2 casseroles (4 servings each).

Crescent Chicken Bundles

When I was expecting our third child, this was one of the meals I put in the freezer ahead of time.

—Jo Groth, Plainfield, Iowa

- 2 packages (3 ounces *each*) cream cheese, softened
- 4 tablespoons butter, melted, *divided*
- 2 tablespoons minced chives
- 2 tablespoons milk
- 1/2 teaspoon salt
- 1/4 teaspoon pepper
- 4 cups cubed cooked chicken
- 2 tubes (8 ounces *each*) refrigerated crescent rolls
- 1 cup crushed seasoned stuffing

1 In a small bowl, beat cream cheese, 2 tablespoons butter, chives, milk, salt and pepper until blended. Stir in chicken.

2 Unroll crescent roll dough and separate into eight rectangles; press perforations together. Spoon about 1/2 cup chicken mixture in the center of each rectangle. Bring edges up to the center and pinch to seal. Brush with remaining butter. Sprinkle with crushed croutons, lightly pressing down.

3 Transfer to two ungreased baking sheets. Cover one baking sheet and freeze until firm; transfer squares to a covered freezer container. May be frozen for up to 2 months. Bake remaining squares at 350° for 20-25 minutes or until golden brown.

4 **To use frozen squares:** Thaw in the refrigerator and bake as directed. **Yield:** 8 servings.

TIP
Freeze Cheese
Purchase large quantities of cheddar, Monterey jack and mozzarella, then shred them in a food processor. Store the shredded cheese in the freezer in heavy-duty resealable plastic bags.

Pizza Meat Loaf Cups

These little pizza-flavored loaves are convenient to reheat as an after-school snack or quick dinner. We like to drizzle extra pizza sauce on top.

—Susan Wollin, Marshall, Wisconsin

- 1 egg, beaten
- 1/2 cup pizza sauce
- 1/4 cup seasoned bread crumbs
- 1/2 teaspoon Italian seasoning
- 1-1/2 pounds ground beef
- 1-1/2 cups (6 ounces *each*) shredded part-skim mozzarella cheese

Additional pizza sauce, optional

1 In a large bowl, combine the egg, pizza sauce, bread crumbs and Italian seasoning. Crumble beef over mixture and mix well. Divide among 12 greased muffin cups; press onto the bottom and up the sides. Fill centers with cheese.

2 Bake at 375° for 15-18 minutes or until meat is no longer pink. Serve immediately with additional pizza sauce if desired. Or cool, place in freezer bags and freeze for up to 3 months.

3 **To use frozen pizza cups:** Thaw in the refrigerator for 24 hours. Heat on a microwave-safe plate on high for 2-3 minutes or until heated through. **Yield:** 1 dozen.

Meat Sauce for Pasta

I freeze a batch of this chunky sauce when I know I'll be entertaining weekend guests. It easily defrosts and reheats for a hearty meal in no time.

—Alberta McKay, Bartlesville, Oklahoma

- 2 pounds bulk Italian sausage *or* ground beef
- 1 large onion, chopped
- 2 cans (15 ounces *each*) tomato sauce
- 2 cans (14-1/2 ounces *each*) diced tomatoes, undrained
- 2 cans (4 ounces *each*) mushroom stems and pieces, drained
- 1/2 cup minced fresh parsley
- 2 teaspoons garlic salt
- 1 teaspoon dried oregano
- 1/2 teaspoon *each* dried basil, chili powder and pepper
- 2 bay leaves

Hot cooked pasta

1 In a Dutch oven, cook meat and onion over medium heat until meat is no longer pink; drain. Add the tomato sauce, tomatoes, mushrooms, parsley and seasonings. Bring to a boil. Reduce heat; cover and simmer for 45 minutes, stirring occasionally.

2 Uncover; simmer 15 minutes longer or until sauce reaches desired consistency. Discard bay leaves. Freeze in meal-size portions.

3 **To use frozen meat sauce:** Thaw in the refrigerator overnight. Place in a saucepan; heat through. Serve over pasta. **Yield:** about 14 (3/4-cup) servings.

Chicken Potpie

Comfort food can come with a low cost. Chock-full of chicken, potatoes, peas and corn, this autumn favorite makes two golden pies.

—Karen Johnson, Bakersfield, California

2	cups diced peeled potatoes
1-3/4	cups sliced carrots
2/3	cup chopped onion
1	cup butter, cubed
1	cup all-purpose flour
1-3/4	teaspoons salt
1	teaspoon dried thyme
3/4	teaspoon pepper
3	cups chicken broth
1-1/2	cups milk
4	cups cubed cooked chicken
1	cup frozen peas
1	cup frozen corn

Pastry for two double-crust pies (9 inches)

1 Place potatoes and carrots in a large saucepan; cover with water. Bring to a boil. Reduce heat; cover and simmer for 8-10 minutes or until crisp-tender. Drain and set aside.

2 In a large skillet, saute onion in butter until tender. Stir in the flour, salt, thyme and pepper until blended. Gradually stir in broth and milk. Bring to a boil; cook and stir for 2 minutes or until thickened. Add the chicken, peas, corn, potatoes and carrots; remove from the heat.

3 Line two 9-in. pie plates with bottom pastry; trim pastry even with edge. Fill pastry shells with chicken mixture. Roll out remaining pastry to fit top of pies. Cut slits or decorative cutouts in pastry. Place over filling; trim, seal and flute edges.

4 Bake one potpie at 425° for 35-40 minutes or until crust is lightly browned. Let stand for 15 minutes before cutting. Cover and freeze remaining potpie for up to 3 months.

5 **To use frozen potpie:** Shield frozen pie crust edges with foil; place on a baking sheet. Bake at 425° for 30 minutes. Reduce heat to 350°; bake 70-80 minutes longer or until crust is golden brown. **Yield:** 2 potpies (6-8 servings each).

Mini Sausage Pizzas

I dress up English muffins with sausage and cheese to make these handheld breakfast pizzas. My husband and son enjoy them in the morning.

—Janice Garvert, Plainville, Kansas

1	pound bulk pork sausage
2	jars (5 ounces *each*) sharp American cheese spread
1/4	cup butter, softened
1/8	to 1/4 teaspoon cayenne pepper
12	English muffins, split

1 In a large skillet, cook sausage over medium heat until no longer pink; drain well. In a small bowl, beat the cheese, butter and pepper until blended. Stir in the sausage. Spread on cut sides of muffins.

2 Place on a baking sheet, bake at 425° for 8-10 minutes or until golden brown.

3 Unbaked pizzas can be wrapped individually and frozen for up to 2 months. **To use frozen pizzas:** Unwrap pizza and place on a baking sheet. Bake at 425° for 10-15 minutes or until golden brown. **Yield:** 2 dozen.

Chicken and Bows

I first made this recipe when I was a professional nanny. It comes together quickly at dinnertime when the kids are hungry.

—Danette Forbes, Overland Park, Kansas

- 1 package (16 ounces) bow tie pasta
- 2 pounds boneless skinless chicken breasts, cut into strips
- 1 cup chopped sweet red pepper
- 1/4 cup butter, cubed
- 2 cans (10-3/4 ounces *each*) condensed cream of chicken soup, undiluted
- 2 cups frozen peas
- 1-1/2 cups milk
- 1 teaspoon garlic powder
- 1/4 to 1/2 teaspoon salt
- 1/4 teaspoon pepper
- 2/3 cup grated Parmesan cheese

1 Cook pasta according to package directions. Meanwhile, in a Dutch oven, cook chicken and red pepper in butter over medium heat for 5-6 minutes or until chicken juices run clear.

2 Stir in the soup, peas, milk, garlic powder, salt and pepper. Bring to a boil. Reduce heat; simmer, uncovered, for 1-2 minutes or until heated through. Stir in Parmesan cheese. Drain pasta; add to chicken mixture and toss to coat.

3 Serve half of the mixture immediately. Cool remaining mixture; transfer to a freezer container. Cover and freeze for up to 3 months.

4 **To use frozen casserole:** Thaw in the refrigerator overnight. Transfer to an ungreased shallow 3-qt. microwave-safe dish. Cover and microwave on high for 8-10 minutes or until heated through, stirring once. **Yield:** 2 casseroles (6 servings each).

EDITOR'S NOTE: This recipe was tested in a 1,100-watt microwave.

Baked Ham Sandwiches

Minced onion and prepared mustard put a flavorful spin on these ham and cheese sandwiches. I simply take a few foil-wrapped favorites from the freezer and warm them in the oven for effortless lunches.

—Charlotte Rowe, Alto, New Mexico

- 1/3 cup butter, softened
- 1/2 cup dried minced onion
- 1/3 to 1/2 cup prepared mustard
- 2 tablespoons poppy seeds
- 8 hamburger buns, split
- 16 slices deli ham
- 8 slices Swiss cheese

1 In a bowl, combine the butter, onion, mustard and poppy seeds; spread about 2 tablespoons on each bun. Layer with ham and cheese; replace tops. Wrap each sandwich in foil. Bake at 350° for 6-10 minutes or until cheese is melted. Uncooked sandwiches can be frozen for up to 2 months.

2 **To use frozen sandwiches:** Bake at 350° for 30-35 minutes or until cheese is melted. **Yield:** 8 servings.

Chicken Stuffing Casserole

This tasty chicken casserole is easy to assemble using handy pantry items. It's a great way to use up leftover cooked chicken.

—Cathy Smith, Wyoming, Michigan

- 2 packages (6 ounces *each*) chicken stuffing mix
- 2 cans (10-3/4 ounces *each*) condensed cream of mushroom soup, undiluted
- 1 cup milk
- 4 cups cubed cooked chicken
- 2 cups frozen corn
- 2 cans (8 ounces *each*) mushroom stems and pieces, drained
- 4 cups (16 ounces) shredded cheddar cheese

1 Prepare stuffing mixes according to package directions. Meanwhile, in a large bowl, combine soup and milk; set aside. Spread the stuffing into two greased 8-in. square baking dishes. Layer with the chicken, corn, mushrooms, soup mixture and cheese.

2 Cover and freeze one casserole for up to 3 months. Cover and bake the second casserole at 350° for 30-35 minutes or until cheese is melted.

3 **To use frozen casserole:** Remove from the freezer 30 minutes before baking (do not thaw). Bake at 350° for 1-1/2 hours. Uncover; bake 10-15 minutes longer or until heated through. **Yield:** 2 casseroles (6 servings each).

Beef Enchiladas

This spicy entree is a good dish to feed a large group of people.

—Rosemary Gonser, Clay Center, Kansas

2-1/2   pounds ground beef
2/3   cup chopped onion
2   cans (15 ounces *each*) enchilada sauce
1   can (10-3/4 ounces) condensed cream of mushroom soup, undiluted
1   can (10-3/4 ounces) condensed tomato soup, undiluted
20   flour tortillas (8 inches), warmed
2-1/2   cups (10 ounces) shredded cheddar cheese
Additional shredded cheddar cheese

1   In a large skillet, cook beef and onion over medium heat until meat is no longer pink; drain. Combine enchilada sauce and soups; pour 1 cup into each of two ungreased 13-in. x 9-in. x 2-in. baking dishes. Stir 1-1/2 cups of sauce into beef mixture; set remaining sauce aside.

2   Spoon 1/4 cup beef mixture down the center of each tortilla; top with 2 tablespoons cheese. Roll up tightly; place 10 enchiladas seam side down in each prepared dish. Top with remaining sauce.

3   Cover and freeze one pan for up to 3 months. Cover and bake the remaining pan at 350° for 25-30 minutes. Uncover; sprinkle with additional cheese. Bake 5-10 minutes longer or until cheese is melted.

4   **To use frozen enchiladas:** Thaw in the refrigerator overnight. Bake as directed. **Yield:** 2 pans (10 enchiladas each).

TIP

Keep Cooked Beef on Hand

One day when you have time, crumble and brown several pounds of ground beef. Spread on a cookie sheet; freeze until solid. Transfer to freezer bags in 1/2- or 1-pound amounts. On busy days, pull out a bag and add to any recipe that calls for browned ground beef.

Ham 'n' Cheese Quiche

I make and freeze these cheesy quiches to have on hand when I'm too tired to cook.

—Christena Palmer, Green River, Wyoming

2   pastry shells (9 inches)
2   cups diced fully cooked ham
2   cups (8 ounces) shredded sharp cheddar cheese
2   teaspoons dried minced onion
4   eggs
2   cups half-and-half cream
1/2   teaspoon salt
1/4   teaspoon pepper

1   Line unpricked pastry shells with a double thickness of heavy-duty foil. Bake at 400° for 5 minutes. Remove foil; bake 5 minutes longer.

2   Divide ham, cheese and onion between the shells. In a bowl, whisk eggs, cream, salt and pepper. Pour into shells.

3   Cover and freeze one quiche for up to 3 months. Cover edges of the remaining quiche with foil. Bake at 400° for 35-40 minutes or until a knife inserted near the center comes out clean. Let stand for 5-10 minutes before cutting.

4   **To use frozen quiche:** Completely thaw in the refrigerator. Remove from the refrigerator 30 minutes before baking as directed. **Yield:** 2 quiches (6 servings each).

Cheddar Turkey Casserole

This recipe makes two creamy casseroles, so you can serve one for dinner and freeze the second for a night when you're racing the clock.

—Carol Dilcher, Emmaus, Pennsylvania

- 2 cups chicken broth
- 2 cups water
- 4 teaspoons dried minced onion
- 2 cups uncooked long grain rice
- 2 cups frozen peas, thawed
- 4 cups cubed cooked turkey
- 2 cans (10-3/4 ounces each) condensed cheddar cheese soup, undiluted
- 2 cups milk
- 1 teaspoon salt
- 2 cups finely crushed butter-flavored crackers (about 60 crackers)
- 6 tablespoons butter, melted

1 In a large saucepan, bring the broth, water and onion to a boil. Reduce heat. Add rice; cover and simmer for 15 minutes. Remove from the heat; fluff with a fork.

2 Divide rice between two greased 9-in. square baking pans. Sprinkle each with peas and turkey. In a bowl, combine the soup, milk and salt until smooth; pour over turkey. Toss the cracker crumbs and butter; sprinkle over the top.

3 Cover and freeze one casserole for up to 3 months. Bake the second casserole, uncovered, at 350° for 35 minutes or until golden brown.

4 **To use frozen casserole:** Thaw in the refrigerator for 24 hours. Bake, uncovered, at 350° for 45-50 minutes or until heated through. **Yield:** 2 casseroles (4-6 servings each).

Sausage Rice Casserole

I fiddled around with this recipe, trying to adjust it to my family's tastes. When my pickiest child cleaned her plate, I knew I'd found the exact right flavor combination.

—Jennifer Trost, West Linn, Oregon

- 2   packages (7.2 ounces each) rice pilaf
- 2   pounds bulk pork sausage
- 6   celery ribs, chopped
- 4   medium carrots, sliced
- 1   can (10-3/4 ounces) condensed cream of chicken soup, undiluted
- 1   can (10-3/4 ounces) condensed cream of mushroom soup, undiluted
- 2   teaspoons onion powder
- 1/2 teaspoon garlic powder
- 1/4 teaspoon pepper

1 Prepare rice mixes according to package directions. Meanwhile, in a large skillet, cook the sausage, celery and carrots over medium heat until meat is no longer pink; drain.

2 In a large bowl, combine the sausage mixture, rice, soups, onion powder, garlic powder and pepper. Transfer to two greased 11-in. x 7-in. x 2-in. baking dishes.

3 Cover and freeze one casserole for up to 3 months. Cover and bake the remaining casserole at 350° for 40-45 minutes or until vegetables are tender.

4 **To use frozen casserole:** Thaw in the refrigerator overnight. Remove from the refrigerator 30 minutes before baking. Bake as directed. Yield: 2 casseroles (6-8 servings each).

Wild Rice Mushroom Chicken

I use a wild rice mix to put a tasty spin on a traditional chicken and rice bake. It's simple and delicious with leftover chicken or turkey.

—Jacqueline Graves, Lawrenceville, Georgia

- 2 packages (6 ounces *each*) long grain and wild rice mix
- 8 boneless skinless chicken breast halves
- 5 tablespoons butter, *divided*
- 1 large sweet red pepper, chopped
- 2 jars (4-1/2 ounces each) sliced mushrooms, drained

1 Prepare rice according to package directions. Meanwhile, in a large skillet, cook chicken in 3 tablespoons butter for 10 minutes on each side or until browned and juices run clear. Remove chicken and keep warm.

2 Add remaining butter to pan drippings; saute red pepper until tender. Stir in mushrooms; heat through. Add to rice. Serve four chicken breasts with half of the rice mixture.

3 Place remaining chicken in a greased 11-in. x 7-in. x 2-in. baking dish; top with remaining rice mixture. Cool. Cover and freeze for up to 3 months.

4 **To use frozen casserole:** Thaw in the refrigerator. Cover and bake casserole at 350° for 35-40 minutes or until heated through. **Yield:** 2 casseroles (4 servings each).

Taco-Filled Pasta Shells

I've been stuffing pasta shells with different fillings for years, but my family enjoys this version with taco-seasoned meat the most.

—Marge Hodel, Roanoke, Illinois

- 2 pounds ground beef
- 2 envelopes taco seasoning
- 1 package (8 ounces) cream cheese, cubed
- 24 uncooked jumbo pasta shells
- 1/4 cup butter, melted

ADDITIONAL INGREDIENTS (for each casserole):
- 1 cup salsa
- 1 cup taco sauce

- 1 cup (4 ounces) shredded cheddar cheese
- 1 cup (4 ounces) shredded Monterey Jack cheese
- 1-1/2 cups crushed tortilla chips
- 1 cup (8 ounces) sour cream
- 3 green onions, chopped

1 In a Dutch oven, cook beef over medium heat until no longer pink; drain. Add taco seasoning; prepare according to package directions. Add cream cheese; cook and stir for 5-10 minutes or until melted. Transfer to a bowl; chill for 1 hour.

2 Cook pasta shells according to package directions; drain. Gently toss with butter. Fill each shell with about 3 tablespoons of meat mixture. Place 12 shells in a freezer container. Cover and freeze for up to 3 months.

3 To prepare remaining shells, spoon salsa into a greased 9-in. square baking dish. Top with stuffed shells and taco sauce. Cover and bake at 350° for 30 minutes. Uncover; sprinkle with cheeses and chips. Bake 15 minutes longer or until heated through. Serve with sour cream and onions.

4 **To use frozen shells:** Thaw in the refrigerator for 24 hours (shells will be partially frozen). Spoon salsa into a greased 9-in. square baking dish; top with shells and taco sauce. Cover and bake at 350° for 40 minutes. Uncover and continue as above. **Yield:** 2 casseroles (6 servings each).

Chicken Tetrazzini

This is my revised version of a recipe a friend shared with me more than 35 years ago. It's nice to give to friends who are unable to cook.

—Helen McPhee, Savoy, Illinois

- 1 package (12 ounces) spaghetti
- 1/3 cup butter, cubed
- 1/3 cup all-purpose flour
- 3/4 teaspoon salt
- 1/4 teaspoon white pepper
- 1 can (14-1/2 ounces) chicken broth
- 1-1/2 cups half-and-half cream
- 1 cup heavy whipping cream
- 4 cups cubed cooked chicken
- 3 cans (4 ounces each) mushroom stems and pieces, drained
- 1 jar (4 ounces) sliced pimientos, drained
- 1/2 cup grated Parmesan cheese

1 Cook spaghetti according to package directions. Meanwhile, in a Dutch oven, melt butter. Stir in flour, salt and pepper until smooth. Gradually add the chicken broth, half-and-half and whipping cream. Bring to a boil; cook and stir for 2 minutes or until thickened.

2 Remove from the heat. Stir in the chicken, mushrooms and pimientos. Drain spaghetti; add to the chicken mixture and toss to coat. Transfer to two greased 11-in. x 7-in. x 2-in. baking dishes. Sprinkle with Parmesan cheese.

3 Cover and freeze one casserole for up to 2 months. Bake the second casserole, uncovered, at 350° for 20-25 minutes or until heated through.

4 **To use frozen casserole:** Thaw in the refrigerator overnight. Cover and bake at 350° for 30 minutes. Uncover; bake 15-20 minutes longer or until heated through. Stir before serving. **Yield:** 2 casseroles (3-4 servings each).

TIP . . . .
Seeding Tomatoes

Seeding a tomato eliminates some of the juice that can make a dish too watery. To seed a tomato, cut it in half and, using the tip of a spoon, scoop out the seeds. You can also gently squeeze each tomato half to remove the seeds.

Veggie Calzones

Bread dough makes it a breeze to assemble these savory turnovers. If you have a favorite pizza dough, use it instead.

—Lee Ann Arey, Gray, Maine

- 1/2 pound fresh mushrooms, chopped
- 1 medium onion, chopped
- 1 medium green pepper, chopped
- 2 tablespoons vegetable oil
- 3 plum tomatoes, seeded and chopped
- 1 can (6 ounces) tomato paste
- 1 cup (4 ounces) shredded Monterey Jack cheese
- 1 cup (4 ounces) shredded part-skim mozzarella cheese
- 1/2 cup grated Parmesan cheese
- 2 loaves (1 pound each) frozen bread dough, thawed
- 1 egg
- 1 tablespoon water

1 In a large skillet, saute the mushrooms, onion and green pepper in oil until tender. Add tomatoes; cook and stir for 3 minutes. Stir in tomato paste; set aside. Combine cheeses and set aside.

2 On a lightly floured surface, divide dough into eight pieces. Roll each piece into a 7-in. circle. Spoon a scant 1/2 cup of vegetable mixture and 1/4 cup of cheese mixture over one side of each circle. Brush edges of dough with water; fold dough over filling

and press edges with a fork to seal. Place calzones 3 in. apart on greased baking sheets. Cover and let rise in a warm place for 20 minutes.

3 Beat egg and water; brush over calzones. Bake at 375° for 15 minutes. Cool desired number of calzones; place in freezer bags. Seal and freeze for up to 3 months. Bake the remaining calzones 18-22 minutes longer or until golden brown. Serve immediately.

4 **To use frozen calzones:** Place 2 in. apart on a greased baking sheet. Bake at 350° for 30-35 minutes or until golden brown. **Yield:** 8 servings.

Make-Ahead Sloppy Joes

When our children were growing up, I frequently made big batches of these stuffed beef-and-sausage buns. Having them in the freezer was such a time-saver on busy weekends.

—Alyne Fuller, Odessa, Texas

- 1 pound bulk pork sausage
- 1 pound ground beef
- 1 medium onion, chopped
- 14 to 16 sandwich buns, split
- 2 cans (8 ounces *each*) tomato sauce
- 2 tablespoons prepared mustard
- 1 teaspoon dried parsley flakes
- 1 teaspoon garlic powder
- 1 teaspoon salt
- 1/4 teaspoon pepper
- 1/4 teaspoon dried oregano

1 In a large skillet, cook the sausage, beef and onion over medium heat until meat is no longer pink; drain. Remove the centers from the tops and bottoms of each bun. Tear removed bread into small pieces; add to skillet. Set buns aside.

2 Stir remaining ingredients into the sausage mixture. Spoon about 1/3 cupful onto the bottom of each bun; replace tops. Wrap individually in heavy-duty foil.

3 Bake at 350° for 20 minutes or until heated through or freeze for up to 3 months.

4 **To use frozen sandwiches:** Bake at 350° for 35 minutes or until heated through. **Yield:** 14-16 servings.

Hearty Ham Loaves

This easy-to-prepare recipe yields two ham loaves. They're so nicely flavored with a variety of savory seasonings that everyone raves about them.

—Audrey Thibodeau, Gilbert, Arizona

1	cup crushed butter-flavored crackers (about 25)
2/3	cup finely chopped onion
1/2	cup finely chopped green pepper
2	eggs, lightly beaten
2	tablespoons lemon juice
1	teaspoon ground mustard
1	teaspoon ground ginger
1	teaspoon Worcestershire sauce
1/4	teaspoon pepper

Dash ground nutmeg
Dash paprika

1-1/3	pounds finely ground fully cooked ham
1	pound bulk pork sausage

GLAZE:

1/2	cup packed brown sugar
1/4	cup cider vinegar
1/4	cup water
1	teaspoon ground mustard

1 In a large bowl, combine the first 11 ingredients. Sprinkle ham and sausage over the cracker mixture and mix well. Shape into two loaves. Place in ungreased 9-in. x 5-in. x 3-in. loaf pans.

2 Cover and freeze one meat loaf for up to 2 months. Bake the remaining loaf at 350° for 60 minutes.

3 Meanwhile, in a small saucepan, combine glaze ingredients. Bring to a boil; boil for 2 minutes. Remove loaf from the oven; drain. Baste with half of the glaze. Cool remaining glaze and set aside. Bake meatloaf 30-40 minutes longer or until a meat thermometer reads 160°, basting occasionally. Cover and freeze reserve glaze for up to 2 months.

4 **To prepare frozen ham loaf with frozen glaze:** Thaw both in the refrigerator overnight and bake as directed. **Yield:** 2 loaves (6-8 servings each).

Hamburger Stroganoff

I've been making this simple yet satisfying dish for more than 25 years. Just last year, I tried freezing the ground beef mixture so I'd have a head start on a future dinner. It works great!

—Aline Christenot, Chester, Montana

> 1 pound ground beef
> 1/4 cup chopped onion
> 1 garlic clove, minced
> 1 can (10-1/2 ounces) condensed beef consomme, undiluted
> 1 can (4 ounces) mushroom stems and pieces, undrained
> 3 tablespoons lemon juice
> 1/4 teaspoon pepper

ADDITIONAL INGREDIENTS (for each dish):

> 2 cups cooked spiral pasta
> 1/2 cup sour cream
> 2 tablespoons water

1 In a large skillet over medium heat, cook beef, onion and garlic until meat is no longer pink; drain. Stir in the consomme, mushrooms, lemon juice and pepper.

2 Place half of the mixture in a freezer container; cover and freeze for up to 3 months. To the remaining meat mixture, add pasta, sour cream and water; heat through (do not boil).

3 **To use frozen meat mixture:** Thaw in the refrigerator. Transfer to a saucepan or skillet and prepare as directed. **Yield:** 2 main dishes (2 servings each).

Pizza Pasta Casserole

Kids will line up for this zippy, pizza-flavored dish. The recipe makes two casseroles, so you can serve one to your family right away and keep one in the freezer for another night.

—Nancy Scarlett, Graham, North Carolina

> 2 pounds ground beef
> 1 large onion, chopped
> 2 jars (28 ounces *each*) spaghetti sauce
> 1 package (16 ounces) spiral pasta, cooked and drained
> 4 cups (16 ounces) shredded part-skim mozzarella cheese
> 8 ounces sliced pepperoni

1 In a large skillet, cook beef and onion over medium heat until meat is no longer pink; drain. Stir in spaghetti sauce and pasta.

2 Transfer to two greased 13-in. x 9-in. x 2-in. baking dishes. Sprinkle with cheese. Arrange pepperoni over the top.

3 Cover and freeze one casserole for up to 3 months. Bake the second casserole, uncovered, at 350° for 25-30 minutes or until heated through.

4 **To use frozen casserole:** Thaw in the refrigerator overnight. Bake casserole at 350° for 35-40 minutes or until heated through. **Yield:** 2 casseroles (8-10 servings each).

Hearty Meat Pie

Savory mushroom gravy is served alongside this homey meat-and-vegetable pie. I spend a little extra time making two of them, but the reward comes later when I pull the second pie out of the freezer and pop it in the oven.

—Twila Burkholder, Middleburg, Pennsylvania

Pastry for two double-crust pies
2	cups grated peeled potatoes
1-1/4	cups diced celery
1	cup grated carrots
1/4	cup chopped onion
2	tablespoons Worcestershire sauce
1	teaspoon salt
1/4	teaspoon pepper
3/4	pound lean ground beef

MUSHROOM GRAVY (for each pie):
1	can (4 ounces) mushroom stems and pieces
2	tablespoons all-purpose flour
2	tablespoons vegetable oil
1	teaspoon beef bouillon granules
4	drops browning sauce, optional

1 Divide pastry into fourths. On a lightly floured surface, roll out one portion to fit a 9-in. pie plate. In a large bowl, combine the next seven ingredients; crumble beef over mixture and mix well. Spoon half into crust.

2 Roll out another portion of pastry to fit top of pie; place over filling and seal edges. Cut vents in top pastry. Repeat with remaining pastry and filling.

3 Cover and freeze one pie for up to 3 months. Bake second pie at 375° for 15 minutes. Reduce heat; bake at 350° for 1 hour. Meanwhile, drain mushrooms, reserving liquid. Add water to liquid to measure 1 cup; set aside.

4 In a small saucepan, cook mushrooms and flour in oil until bubbly. Remove from the heat; stir in bouillon and reserved mushroom liquid. Bring to a boil; cook and stir for 1 minute or until thickened. Stir in browning sauce if desired. Serve with pie.

5 **To use frozen pie:** Bake at 375° for 70 minutes. Prepare gravy as directed. Serve with pie.
Yield: 2 pies (6-8 servings each).

Side Dishes

Fried Apples and Onions

I was surprised to see how quickly my friends gobbled this dish up. Excusing myself, I flew into the kitchen, chopped up more onions and apples, quickly fried them and brought out another steaming dish. That one disappeared, too!

—Sue Davis, Wausau, Wisconsin

6	medium onions, sliced and separated into rings
2	tablespoons butter
6	medium tart red apples, cut into 1/4-inch wedges
3	tablespoons brown sugar

1 In a large skillet, cook the onions in butter over medium heat for 3-5 minutes or until crisp-tender. Top with apples; sprinkle with brown sugar. Cover and cook for 15-20 minutes or until apples are tender. **Yield:** 8 servings.

Homemade Refried Beans

These refried beans are full of Southwestern flair. The recipe makes a big batch, which is great for entertaining a large crowd.

—Myra Innes, Auburn, Kansas

1	large onion, chopped
4	garlic cloves, minced
6	tablespoons olive oil, *divided*
5	cans (15 ounces *each*) pinto beans, rinsed and drained
1-1/2	teaspoons ground cumin
1	teaspoon salt
1/2	teaspoon ground coriander
1/4	teaspoon pepper
1/4	teaspoon hot pepper sauce
1	cup (4 ounces) shredded Monterey Jack cheese

1 In a large skillet, saute onion and garlic in 2 tablespoons oil until crisp-tender. Place 2 tablespoons oil in a blender; add half of the onion mixture, and half of the beans, cumin, salt, coriander, pepper, hot pepper sauce and cheese. Cover and process until smooth. Repeat with remaining ingredients.

2 Transfer to a large skillet. Cook, uncovered, over medium heat until heated through. Leftover refried beans may be frozen for up to 3 months. **Yield:** 7 cups.

Honey-Spice Acorn Squash

I've made this simple side dish for more than 35 years. Cinnamon and ginger give a nice spiced taste to the moist and tender squash halves.

—Alpha Wilson, Roswell, New Mexico

3	tablespoons honey
2	tablespoons butter, melted
1/4	teaspoon salt
1/8	teaspoon ground cinnamon
1/8	teaspoon ground ginger
2	medium acorn squash

1 In a large bowl, combine the honey, butter, salt, cinnamon and ginger. Cut squash in half; discard the seeds. Fill squash halves with butter mixture.

2 Place in a greased 15-in. x 10-in. x 1-in. baking pan. Cover and bake at 375° for 1 hour or until squash is tender. Uncover; bake 10 minutes longer or until filling is bubbly. **Yield:** 4 servings.

Curried Butternut Squash Kabobs

Squash cubes pick up a mouthwatering grilled taste along with a mild curry butter flavor. The pretty orange-colored side dish adds interest alongside more traditional summer entrees.

—Mary Relyea, Canastota, New York

- 1 butternut squash (2 pounds), peeled, seeded and cut into 1-inch cubes
- 3 tablespoons butter, melted
- 1 teaspoon curry powder
- 1/4 teaspoon salt

1 Place squash in a greased 13-in. x 9-in. x 2-in. baking dish. Combine the butter, curry powder and salt; drizzle over squash and toss to coat.

2 Bake, uncovered, at 450° for 20-25 minutes or until tender and lightly browned, stirring twice. Cool on a wire rack.

3 Thread squash cubes onto 12 metal or soaked wooden skewers. Grill, covered, over medium heat for 3-5 minutes on each side or until heated through. **Yield:** 12 servings.

Onion Barley Casserole

I always felt I was giving my family the best when I prepared this side dish. They loved the nutty flavor and chewy texture of the barley, and it was a delicious departure from rice.

—Elaine Kremenak, Grants Pass, Oregon

- 1/2 cup medium pearl barley
- 1 tablespoon vegetable oil
- 1-1/2 cups water
- 1 teaspoon beef bouillon granules
- 1/4 teaspoon salt
- 1/2 cup sliced green onions
- 1 can (4 ounces) whole button mushrooms, drained

1 In an ovenproof skillet, saute barley in oil until golden brown. Stir in water, bouillon and salt; bring to boil. Remove from the heat; add onions and mushrooms. Cover and bake at 350° for 40-50 minutes or until the barley is tender. **Yield:** 2-4 servings.

Roasted Beet Wedges

This recipe makes ordinary beets taste delicious. They come out sweet and tender every time.

—Wendy Stenman, Germantown, Wisconsin

- 1 pound medium fresh beets, peeled
- 4 teaspoons olive oil
- 1/2 teaspoon kosher salt
- 3 to 5 fresh rosemary sprigs

1 Cut each beet into six wedges; place in a large resealable plastic bag. Add olive oil and salt; seal and shake to coat.

2 Place a piece of heavy-duty foil (about 12 in. long) in a 15-in. x 10-in. x 1-in. baking pan. Arrange beets on foil and top with rosemary. Fold foil around beet mixture and seal tightly. Bake at 400° for 1-1/4 to 1-1/2 hours or until beets are tender. Discard rosemary sprigs. **Yield:** 4 servings.

EDITOR'S NOTE: For a milder herb flavor, try using fresh thyme instead of rosemary. You may make the beets a day ahead, then slice and serve cold in a salad.

Sausage Corn Bread Dressing

I dress up stuffing mix with pork sausage and jarred mushrooms to create this in-a-dash dressing. The hearty side dish is terrific with chicken, turkey or pork.

—Ruby Harman, Carrollton, Missouri

- 1 pound bulk pork sausage
- 3-1/2 cups water
- 1 jar (7 ounces) sliced mushrooms, drained
- 2 packages (6 ounces each) corn bread stuffing mix

1 In a large skillet, brown the sausage; drain. Add water and mushrooms. Bring to a boil. Remove from the heat; add the stuffing mix. Cover and let stand for 5 minutes. **Yield:** 8 servings.

Pear Cranberry Sauce

We don't care for regular cranberry sauce, so I usually perk it up with other fruit. This pear version is the one my family requests most often. It's tangy and has a beautiful ruby-red color.

—Joyce Bowman, Lady Lake, Florida

- 2-1/2 cups cubed peeled ripe pears (about 3 medium)
- 1 cup water
- 1/2 teaspoon ground ginger
- 1 cinnamon stick (3 inches), broken in half
- 1 package (12 ounces) fresh or frozen cranberries
- 1 to 1-1/4 cups sugar

1 In a large saucepan, combine the pears, water, ginger and cinnamon. Bring to a boil. Reduce heat; simmer, uncovered, for 5 minutes. Stir in cranberries and sugar. Bring to a boil. Reduce heat; simmer, uncovered, for 10-12 minutes or until the cranberries have popped and sauce is slightly thickened, stirring several items.

2 Discard cinnamon sticks. Mash sauce if desired. Cool. Cover and refrigerate until serving. **Yield:** about 2 cups.

Broccoli Au Gratin

With only four ingredients, this crumb-topped gratin costs just pennies a serving. It's a comforting casserole that pairs well with meaty entrees.

—M. McNeil, Germantown, Tennessee

- 1 package (16 ounces) frozen chopped broccoli
- 1 can (10-3/4 ounces) condensed cream of chicken soup, undiluted
- 1/2 cup shredded cheddar cheese
- 1/3 cup crushed butter-flavored crackers

1 Cook broccoli according to package directions; drain. Stir in the soup and cheese.

2 Transfer to a greased 1-1/2 qt. baking dish; sprinkle with cracker crumbs. Bake, uncovered, at 350° for 15-20 minutes or until heated through. **Yield:** 4 servings.

Parsnip Saute

This recipe proves that dishes don't need to be complicated to be delicious. Simple seasonings flavor garden-fresh vegetables.

—Janice Van Wassehnova
South Rockwood, Michigan

- 3 large parsnips, peeled and diced
- 1/2 cup diced carrot
- 1/2 cup sliced celery
- 1/2 cup diced onion
- 2 tablespoons butter
- 3/4 teaspoon salt
- 1/8 teaspoon pepper

1 Place parsnips in a saucepan and cover with water. Bring to a boil. Reduce heat; cover and simmer for 12-18 minutes or until crisp-tender. Drain.

2 Meanwhile, in a large skillet, saute the carrot, celery and onion in butter for 6-7 minutes or until crisp-tender. Add the parsnips, salt and pepper; cook and stir for 4 minutes or until vegetables are tender. **Yield:** 6 servings.

Grilled Corn in Husks

Seasoned with butter, Parmesan cheese and parsley, this grilled corn is especially good. Be sure to give the ears a soak before putting them on the grill.

—Nancy Zimmerman
Cape May Court House, New Jersey

- 4 large ears sweet corn in husks
- 1/4 cup butter, softened
- 2 tablespoons minced fresh parsley
- 1/4 cup grated Parmesan cheese

1 Carefully peel back husks from corn to within 1-in. of bottom; remove silk. Combine the butter and parsley; spread over corn. Rewrap corn in husks and secure with string. Soak in cold water for 20 minutes; drain.

2 Grill corn, covered, over medium heat for 20-25 minutes or until tender, turning often. Serve with Parmesan cheese. **Yield:** 4 servings.

𝒯𝒾𝒫 . . . .
Parsnip Pointers
Purchase small to medium parsnips that are firm and have smooth skin. Don't buy ones that are shriveled, limp, cracked or spotted. Store in a plastic bag for up to 2 weeks.

Stewed Tomatoes with Dumplings

When I was young and did not feel well, my mother would always make this because it was one of my favorite dishes. Just smelling it cook made me feel better, along with her tender loving care.

—Viola Stutz, Greenwood, Delaware

1   can (14-1/2 ounces) diced tomatoes, undrained
1   tablespoon sugar
1/4   teaspoon salt
1/4   teaspoon pepper
2   tablespoons butter
1/2   cup biscuit/baking mix
3   tablespoons milk

1   In a large saucepan, combine the tomatoes, sugar, salt, pepper and butter. Bring to a boil over medium heat, stirring occasionally.

2   In a small bowl, combine biscuit mix and milk. Drop batter in four mounds onto the tomatoes. Reduce heat; cover and simmer for 10 minutes or until a toothpick inserted in a dumpling comes out clean (do not lift cover while simmering).
Yield: 2 servings.

Penne with Cannellini Beans

With spinach, beans and tomatoes, this is so filling that it could be served as a light main dish.

—Brenda Harrell, Joplin, Missouri

- 8 ounces uncooked penne pasta
- 2 cans (14-1/2 ounces *each*) Italian diced tomatoes
- 1 can (15 ounces) cannellini *or* white kidney beans, rinsed and drained
- 1 package (10 ounces) fresh baby spinach, chopped
- 1/2 cup shredded Romano cheese

1 Cook pasta according to package directions. Meanwhile, in a large saucepan, bring the tomatoes and beans to a boil. Reduce heat; simmer, uncovered, for 10 minutes. Add spinach; cook and stir for 2 minutes or until spinach is wilted. Drain pasta; top with tomato mixture. Sprinkle with cheese. **Yield:** 5 servings.

Vibrant Veggie Stir-Fry

Over the years, my husband and I have learned to cook with less fat and sugar so we can enjoy good health as we grow older.

—Betty Claycomb, Alverton, Pennsylvania

- 4 cups fresh broccoli florets
- 3/4 cup fresh baby carrots, quartered lengthwise
- 2 teaspoons vegetable oil

- 1 medium zucchini, halved lengthwise and sliced
- 1/2 teaspoon salt
- 1/4 teaspoon pepper

1 In a nonstick skillet or wok, stir-fry broccoli and carrots in oil for 5 minutes. Add the zucchini, salt and pepper; stir-fry 4-5 minutes longer or until vegetables are crisp-tender. **Yield:** 4 servings.

Bulgur with Pine Nuts

Bulgur wheat is not only good for you...it's great for your budget! Here our home economists use simple ingredients to flavor it wonderfully.

—Taste of Home Test Kitchen

- 1 cup uncooked bulgur
- 2 cups chicken broth
- 3 tablespoons chopped green onions
- 1/4 cup pine nuts, toasted

1 In a large saucepan, combine the bulgur, broth and onions; bring to a boil over high heat. Reduce heat; cover and simmer for 15-18 minutes or until broth is absorbed. Add pine nuts; stir to combine. **Yield:** 4 servings.

Apricot Casserole

This sweet fruit dish is a terrific complement to salty ham at any brunch. Apricot is a tasty change from the more common pineapple.

—Janice Montiverdi, Sugar Land, Texas

- 2 cans (15 ounces *each*) apricot halves
- 1/2 cup plus 2 tablespoons butter, *divided*
- 1 cup packed brown sugar
- 1/4 cup all-purpose flour
- 1-1/3 cups crushed butter-flavored crackers (about 36 crackers)

1 Drain apricots, reserving 3/4 cup juice. Place apricots in a greased 11-in. x 7-in. x 2-in. baking dish. Melt 1/2 cup butter; add the brown sugar, flour and reserved juice. Pour over apricots.

2 Bake, uncovered, at 350° for 20 minutes. Melt remaining butter; toss with cracker crumbs. Sprinkle over top. Bake 15-20 minutes longer or until golden brown. **Yield:** 6-8 servings.

Spinach Combo

My mother and I get recipe ideas from watching TV cooking shows and looking through magazines. We then substitute ingredients we prefer.

—Amy Brosnan, Kansas City, Kansas

- 3/4 cup chopped onion
- 2 tablespoons vegetable oil
- 1 package (10 ounces) frozen chopped spinach, thawed and squeezed dry
- 1 cup uncooked long grain rice
- 2-1/4 cups water
- 2 medium tomatoes, diced
- 1 teaspoon salt
- 1/8 teaspoon pepper

1 In a large skillet, saute onion in oil until tender. Add the spinach, rice and water. Bring to a boil. Reduce heat; cover and simmer for 20-25 minutes or until rice is tender and water is absorbed. Stir in the tomatoes, salt and pepper; heat through. **Yield:** 6 servings.

Roasted Parmesan Potato Wedges

These potatoes have an irresistible cheese and herb coating. The aroma released from the oven while baking is heavenly.

—Linda Rock, Stratford, Wisconsin

- 4 potatoes (2 pounds)
- 2 teaspoons vegetable oil
- 1/2 cup grated Parmesan cheese
- 1 teaspoon dried basil
- 1 teaspoon seasoned salt
- 1/4 teaspoon onion powder
- 1/4 teaspoon garlic powder
- 1/4 teaspoon pepper

1 Cut each potato lengthwise in half. Cut each half into three wedges. In a large bowl, sprinkle potatoes with oil; toss to coat. Combine the remaining ingredients. Add to potatoes; toss to coat.

2 Arrange potatoes in a single layer on a 15-in. x 10-in. x 1-in. baking pan coated with cooking spray. Sprinkle with any remaining coating. Bake at 350° for 45-55 minutes or until golden brown and tender. **Yield:** 6 servings.

Card shows handwritten recipe:
3 medi...
cut len...
1 tablespoon butter or
margarine, melted
1/4 teaspoon dill weed
salt & pepper, optional
...cepan

Dilled Zucchini

These super squash couldn't be easier to prepare, and their mild flavor goes so well with chicken. I often rely on this recipe when I have a bumper crop of zucchini to use up.

—Sundra Hauck, Bogalusa, Louisiana

    3   medium zucchini, halved lengthwise
    1   tablespoon butter, melted
  1/4   teaspoon dill weed
Salt and pepper, optional

1 Place zucchini in a large skillet and cover with water; bring to a boil over medium heat. Cook 12-14 minutes or until tender. Drain; brush with butter. Sprinkle with dill, salt and pepper if desired. **Yield:** 6 servings.

Orzo with Zucchini and Feta

This pasta dish is simple to prepare and never fails to please. You can serve it hot as a side dish or cold as a salad.

—**Andrea Jones, McKinney, Texas**

- 1 cup uncooked orzo pasta
- 1 medium zucchini, cut into 1/4-inch pieces
- 2 tablespoons water
- 3/4 cup crumbled feta cheese
- 4 teaspoons olive oil
- 2 teaspoons dried oregano

Salt and pepper to taste

1 Cook orzo according to package directions. Meanwhile, in a small microwave-safe bowl, combine zucchini and water. Cover and cook on high for 1 minute or until crisp-tender; drain.

2 Drain orzo; place in a large bowl. Add the zucchini, feta cheese, oil, oregano, salt and pepper; toss to coat. Serve warm or chilled. **Yield:** 5 servings.

Breaded Eggplant Slices

These crisp, golden rounds are a fun and different way to serve eggplant. Even folks who aren't fond of this unique vegetable like it fixed this way.

—**Phyllis Schmalz, Kansas City, Kansas**

- 1 medium eggplant (about 1 pound)
- 1/2 cup dry bread crumbs
- 1/4 cup grated Parmesan cheese
- 1 bottle (8 ounces) fat-free Italian salad dressing

1 Cut eggplant into 1/2-in. slices. In a shallow bowl, combine bread crumbs and Parmesan. Place salad dressing in another bowl. Dip eggplant into salad dressing, then coat with crumb mixture.

2 Arrange in a single layer on baking sheets coated with cooking spray. Bake at 450° for 6-8 minutes on each side or until golden brown. **Yield:** 4 servings.

Noodles Florentine

With this recipe, you get noodles and a vegetable in one dish. It fills you up without breaking the bank.

—**Marcia Orlando, Boyertown, Pennsylvania**

- 5 cups uncooked medium egg noodles
- 2 tablespoons butter
- 2 tablespoons all-purpose flour
- 1 cup milk
- 1 package (10 ounces) frozen chopped spinach, thawed and squeezed dry
- 1/4 teaspoon ground nutmeg

Salt and pepper to taste
- 1 cup (4 ounces) shredded Swiss cheese

1 In a large saucepan, cook noodles according to package directions until tender. In another saucepan, melt butter; stir in flour until smooth. Gradually add milk. Bring to a boil; cook and stir for 2 minutes or until thickened. Stir in the spinach, nutmeg, salt and pepper. Drain noodles. Add to spinach mixture; toss gently to coat.

2 Transfer to a greased shallow 2-qt. baking dish; sprinkle with cheese. Cover and bake at 350° for 20 minutes or until heated through. **Yield:** 4 servings.

3 In a small nonstick skillet coated with cooking spray, cook onion over medium-high heat in remaining oil for 6 minutes. Stir in the sugar; cook 7-10 minutes longer or until onion is tender and lightly browned. Serve with cauliflower puree. **Yield:** 4 servings.

EDITOR'S NOTE: This recipe was tested in a 1,100-watt microwave.

Maple Baked Beans

Maple syrup and a dash of cinnamon jazz up canned beans for a unique taste twist. This sweet, saucy side dish is a snap to fix in the microwave, so it's handy to add to any menu.

—**Susan Baxter, Morgantown, Indiana**

- 2 cans (15-3/4 ounces *each*) pork and beans
- 1/2 cup ketchup
- 1/2 cup maple syrup
Dash ground cinnamon

1 In a large microwave-safe bowl, combine all ingredients. Microwave, uncovered, on high for 11-15 minutes or until mixture reaches desired thickness, stirring every 5 minutes. Let stand for 5 minutes before serving. **Yield:** 4-6 servings.

EDITOR'S NOTE: This recipe was tested in a 1,100-watt microwave.

Creamed Spinach

This delicious recipe is a lifesaver during the holidays, when time is short. With only three ingredients, it's also easy to make.

—**Sherri Hoover, Perth Road, Ontario**

- 2 packages (10 ounces *each*) frozen chopped spinach, thawed and squeezed dry
- 2 cups (16 ounces) sour cream
- 1 envelope onion soup mix

1 In a large bowl, combine all ingredients. Spoon into a greased 1-qt. baking dish. Cover and bake at 350° for 25-30 minutes or until heated through. **Yield:** 4 servings.

Cauliflower Puree with Onions

This cauliflower dish is creamy, tasty and has the appearance and texture of mashed potatoes. The onions on top are a sweet addition that contrasts well with the mildness of cauliflower.

—**Becky Oliver, Fairplay, Colorado**

- 1 package (16 ounces) frozen cauliflower
- 2 tablespoons water
- 4-1/2 teaspoons olive oil, *divided*
- 1/4 teaspoon salt
- 1/4 teaspoon pepper
- 1 large sweet onion, thinly sliced
- 2 tablespoons sugar

1 Place cauliflower and water in a microwave-safe bowl. Cover and cook on high for 6 minutes; stir. Cook 1-2 minutes longer or until tender. Cool slightly. Drain, reserving 2 tablespoons cooking liquid.

2 Place the cauliflower, reserved liquid, 1-1/2 teaspoons oil, salt and pepper in a food processor or blender; cover and process until blended. Keep warm.

Whipped Carrots with Cranberries

The buttery texture and sweetness of cranberries and brown sugar make this a great complement to Thanksgiving turkey.

—Margie Haen, Menomonee Falls, Wisconsin

- 1 pound sliced fresh carrots
- 3 tablespoons butter
- 1 tablespoon brown sugar
- 1/2 teaspoon ground ginger
- 1/4 teaspoon salt
- 1/4 cup dried cranberries

1 Place 2 in. of water in a small saucepan; add carrots. Bring to a boil. Reduce heat; cover and simmer for 15-20 minutes or until tender. Drain.

2 Place carrots in a food processor; add the butter, brown sugar, ginger and salt. Cover and process until smooth. Transfer to a serving bowl; stir in cranberries. **Yield:** 4 servings.

Pineapple Cabbage Saute

This dish from our home economists works best with thinly sliced cabbage, so it is best not to use a shredder. Pineapple adds a bit of sweetness.

—Taste of Home Test Kitchen

- 1   can (8 ounces) crushed pineapple
- 6   cups thinly sliced cabbage
- 1   tablespoon olive oil
- 2   tablespoons honey mustard salad dressing
- 1/8   teaspoon white pepper

1 Drain pineapple, reserving 1 tablespoon juice; set aside. In a large skillet, saute cabbage in oil for 5-8 minutes or until crisp-tender. Add the salad dressing, pepper and reserved pineapple and juice. Cook for 1 minute or until heated through. **Yield:** 6 servings.

Savory Lemon Limas

If you are a lima bean lover like me, this recipe just makes them even more delicious. If you simply tolerate the beans, like my husband does, you might actually find these quite tasty!

—Cathy Attig, Jacobus, Pennsylvania

- 1/2 cup water
- 1-1/2 cups frozen lima beans, thawed
- 1 tablespoon butter, melted
- 1 tablespoon lemon juice
- 1 teaspoon sugar
- 1/2 to 3/4 teaspoon ground mustard
- 1/4 teaspoon salt

1 In a small saucepan, bring water to a boil. Add lima beans; return to a boil. Reduce heat; cover and simmer for 8-10 minutes or until tender. Drain. Combine the butter, lemon juice, sugar, mustard and salt; pour over beans and toss to coat. **Yield:** 4 servings.

Crispy Potato Cubes

My mother used to serve these savory herb potatoes when I was growing up. She shared the recipe when I got married.

—Jenelle Piepmeier, Severna Park, Maryland

- 1/3 cup all-purpose flour
- 3/4 teaspoon salt
- 1/2 teaspoon dried thyme
- 1/2 teaspoon dried marjoram
- 1/8 teaspoon pepper
- 5 medium potatoes, peeled and cut into 1-inch cubes
- 1/4 cup butter, melted
- 1 garlic clove, minced
- 1 bay leaf

1 In a large resealable plastic bag, combine the flour, salt, thyme, marjoram and pepper. Add potatoes; seal bag and shake to coat. Pour butter into a 13-in. x 9-in. x 2-in. baking dish; stir in the garlic. Add potatoes and bay leaf.

2 Cover and bake at 450° for 20 minutes. Uncover and stir; bake 15-20 minutes longer or until potatoes are lightly browned and tender. Discard bay leaf. **Yield:** 4 servings.

Snappy Pea Pods

This side dish is great and really quick. Sesame oil enhances the pea pods' flavor.

—Trisha Kruse, Eagle, Idaho

- 1/2 pound sliced fresh mushrooms
- 1 small onion, thinly sliced
- 1 tablespoon sesame oil
- 3/4 pound fresh *or* frozen sugar snap peas
- 1/2 cup chicken broth
- 1/4 teaspoon salt
- 1/4 teaspoon pepper

1 In a large skillet, saute mushrooms and onion in oil until crisp-tender. Add the remaining ingredients. Bring to a boil; cover and simmer for 2-4 minutes or until peas are crisp-tender. Serve with a slotted spoon. **Yield:** 4 servings.

Corn Fritter Patties

These five-ingredient fritters are a thrifty way to enjoy a Southern staple without having to leave home.

—Megan Hamilton, Pineville, Missouri

- 1 cup pancake mix
- 1 egg, lightly beaten
- 1/4 cup plus 2 tablespoons milk
- 1 can (7 ounces) whole kernel corn, drained
- 2 cups vegetable oil

1 In a small bowl, combine the pancake mix, egg and milk just until moistened. Stir in the corn.

2 In an electric skillet or deep-fat fryer, heat 1/4 in. of oil to 375°. Drop batter by 1/4 cupfuls into oil; press lightly to flatten. Cook for 2 minutes on each side or until golden brown. **Yield:** 7 patties.

Beans 'n' Caramelized Onions

Brown sugar, bacon and cider vinegar season this simple side. I often make it for family and friends, and it never fails to please!

—Jill Heatwole, Pittsville, Maryland

- 4 bacon strips
- 2 large onions, cut lengthwise into 1/2-inch-thick wedges
- 2 pounds fresh green beans, trimmed
- 3 tablespoons cider vinegar
- 4-1/2 teaspoons brown sugar
- 1/4 teaspoon salt
- 1/4 teaspoon pepper

1 In a large skillet, cook bacon over medium heat until crisp. Remove to paper towels. Drain, reserving 2 tablespoons drippings. Crumble bacon and set aside. In the drippings, cook onions over medium-low heat until tender and golden brown, about 50 minutes.

2 Meanwhile, place the beans in a large saucepan and cover with water; bring to a boil. Cook, uncovered, for 8-10 minutes or until crisp-tender; drain. Stir the vinegar and brown sugar into onions; add beans. Cook, uncovered, over medium heat for 1 minute. Add bacon; toss gently. Season with salt and pepper. **Yield:** 9 servings.

Tex-Mex Rice

My grandmother gave me the recipe for this spiced rice. I sometimes add ground beef for a satisfying skillet meal.

—Kat Thompson, Prineville, Oregon

- 1 cup uncooked long grain rice
- 1 medium onion, chopped
- 2 tablespoons vegetable oil
- 2 cups boiling water
- 1 medium green pepper, chopped
- 1-1/2 teaspoons chili powder
- 1 teaspoon salt
- 1 can (14-1/2 ounces) diced tomatoes, drained

1 In a large skillet, saute rice and onion in oil until rice is browned and onion is tender. Stir in the water, green pepper, chili powder and salt. Bring to a boil. Reduce heat; cover and simmer for 15 minutes or until rice is tender. Stir in tomatoes; heat through. **Yield:** 6 servings.

Smashed Red Potatoes

Olive oil and parsley are a nice change from milk and butter in this potato dish.

—**Taste of Home Test Kitchen**

  2   pounds red potatoes, cut into small wedges
  1/4 cup minced fresh parsley
  2   tablespoons olive oil
  1   teaspoon salt
  1/2 teaspoon pepper

1 Place potatoes in a large saucepan and cover with water. Bring to a boil. Reduce heat to medium; cook, uncovered, for 15-20 minutes or until tender. Drain and place in a large bowl. Coarsely mash the potatoes, adding the parsley, oil, salt and pepper. **Yield:** 6 servings.

Savory Orange Dressing

This recipe was in my files for years before I finally tried it one Thanksgiving. My family loves the combination of orange and carrots.

—Dixie Terry, Marion, Illinois

1	cup sliced celery
1/2	cup chopped onion
1/3	cup butter
2	teaspoons chicken bouillon granules
2-1/2	cups boiling water
1	package (14 ounces) seasoned stuffing cubes
1/2	cup shredded carrot
1/4	cup orange juice
2	teaspoons grated orange peel

1 In a small skillet, saute celery and onion in butter until tender. In a large bowl, dissolve bouillon in boiling water. Stir in the stuffing cubes, carrot, orange juice, peel and the celery mixture.

2 Spoon into a greased 13-in. x 9-in. x 2-in. baking dish. Cover and bake at 350° for 20 minutes. Uncover; bake 15 minutes longer or until heated through. **Yield:** 10 servings.

Mixed Vegetables

Colorful carrot coins, broccoli and zucchini star in this appealing side dish. Simmered in Italian salad dressing, the veggies take on that zesty flavor.

—Taste of Home Test Kitchen

- 1   medium carrot, cut into 1/4-inch slices
- 1/2   cup water
- 1   cup broccoli florets
- 1   medium onion, cut into 16 wedges
- 1   medium zucchini, cut into 1/4-inch slices
- 1/4   cup Italian salad dressing
- 1/4   teaspoon dried oregano

1 In a nonstick skillet, bring carrot and water to a boil. Reduce heat; cover and simmer for 5 minutes. Add the broccoli, onion and zucchini; return to a boil. Reduce heat; cover and simmer for 2 minutes. Add salad dressing and oregano. Cook and stir over medium heat for 4 minutes or until vegetables are tender and liquid is reduced. **Yield:** 4 servings.

Sweet Potato Wedges

Quartered sweet potatoes bake in a mildly spiced butter sauce in this recipe. They're a better-for-you change from french fries.

—Donna Howard, Stoughton, Wisconsin

- 3   pounds sweet potatoes, peeled and quartered lengthwise (about 10 cups)
- 6   tablespoons butter, melted
- 6   tablespoons orange juice
- 3/4   teaspoon salt
- 3/4   teaspoon ground cinnamon

1 Arrange sweet potatoes in a greased 13-in. x 9-in. x 2-in. baking dish. Combine the butter, orange juice, salt and cinnamon; drizzle over sweet potatoes. Cover and bake at 350° for 55-60 minutes or until tender. **Yield:** 10 servings (8 cups).

Bacon Bean Stalks

You don't have to wait for the harvest to prepare these bean bundles. Make them whenever beans are available and get ready to rake in compliments!

—Taste of Home Test Kitchen

- 1   pound fresh wax or green beans
- 6   bacon strips
- 1/4   teaspoon onion powder

1 Place beans in a saucepan and cover with water; bring to a boil. Cook, uncovered, for 8 minutes or until crisp-tender.

2 Meanwhile, in a skillet or microwave, cook bacon until partially cooked, about 3 minutes; drain on paper towels. Drain beans; place about 12 beans on each bacon strip.

3 Position one end of beans so they are nearly even; cut about 1/4 in. from that end so stalks will stand when served. Wrap bacon strip around beans; secure with a toothpick. Lay stalks flat on an ungreased baking sheet. Sprinkle with onion powder. Bake, uncovered, at 400° for 10-15 minutes or until bacon is crisp. **Yield:** 6 servings.

Sunny Carrot Sticks

These carrots have a lightly sweet sauce with a delicate orange flavor. Kids of all ages will gobble up these great-tasting veggies!

—Wendy Masters, Grand Valley, Ontario

> 1   pound carrots, julienned
> 1   tablespoon brown sugar
> 1   teaspoon cornstarch
> 1/4 cup orange juice
> 2   tablespoons butter

1 Place 1 in. of water and carrots in a large saucepan; bring to a boil. Reduce heat; cover and simmer for 15-20 minutes or until tender.

2 Meanwhile, in another saucepan, combine brown sugar and cornstarch. Stir in orange juice until smooth. Bring to a boil; cook and stir for 2 minutes or until thickened and bubbly. Stir in butter. Drain carrots; drizzle with orange juice mixture. Toss to coat. **Yield:** 4 servings.

Baked Rice Pilaf

I'm always in search of inexpensive yet delicious dishes like this one to serve friends and family. The recipe can be doubled for a crowd.

—Sheree Feero, Golden, Colorado

> 1-3/4 cups water
> 1   cup shredded carrot
> 1   cup chopped celery
> 3/4 cup uncooked long grain rice
> 3   tablespoons minced fresh parsley
> 2   tablespoons finely chopped onion
> 2   tablespoons butter, melted
> 1   tablespoon chicken bouillon granules

1 Combine all ingredients in an ungreased 8-in. square baking dish. Cover and bake at 375° for 40-45 minutes or until rice is tender, stirring after 25 minutes. **Yield:** 4 servings.

TIP
Keeping Parsley Fresh

To keep fresh parsley in the refrigerator for several weeks, wash the entire bunch in warm water, shake off all excess moisture, wrap in paper towel and seal in a plastic bag.

Crunchy Celery Casserole

I first sampled this tempting treatment for celery when a friend brought it to a 4-H covered dish dinner. We could not believe how good it tastes or how fast it is to prepare in the microwave.

—Michelle Garretson, Newcomerstown, Ohio

> 10 celery ribs, thinly sliced
> 2   cans (10-3/4 ounces *each*) condensed cream of celery soup, undiluted
> 1   can (8 ounces) sliced water chestnuts, drained
> 1   can (2.8 ounces) French-fried onions

1 In a bowl, combine the celery, soup and water chestnuts. Pour into a greased microwave-safe 8-in. square dish. Cover and microwave on high for 20 minutes or until the celery is tender, stirring every 5 minutes. Sprinkle with onions. Microwave, uncovered, 3-1/2 minutes longer. **Yield:** 8 servings.

EDITOR'S NOTE: This recipe was tested in a 1,100-watt microwave.

Tomato Spinach Spirals

A great side dish or meatless main course, this pasta pleaser comes together in a snap. It is tasty, easy and affordable.

—Janet Montano, Temecula, California

    1   package (8 ounces) spiral pasta
    1   package (10 ounces) frozen creamed spinach
    1   can (14-1/2 ounces) diced tomatoes, undrained
    3   tablespoons grated Romano cheese, *divided*
    3   tablespoons grated Parmesan cheese, *divided*
    1/2 teaspoon salt

1 Cook pasta according to package directions. Meanwhile, prepare spinach according to package directions. Drain pasta; place in a large bowl. Add the spinach, tomatoes, 2 tablespoons of Romano cheese, 2 tablespoons of Parmesan cheese and salt; toss to coat. Sprinkle with the remaining cheese. **Yield:** 6 servings.

Home-Style Scalloped Potatoes

The secret to a good scalloped potato dish is to make sure it has plenty of creamy sauce. My husband and sons rate this simply delicious potato casserole the "best ever" and request it often.

—Christine Eilerts, Tulsa, Oklahoma

1/3	cup chopped onion
5	tablespoons butter
5	tablespoons all-purpose flour
1-1/4	teaspoons salt
1/2	teaspoon pepper
5	cups milk
6	cups thinly sliced potatoes

1 In a large saucepan, saute onion in butter until tender. Stir in the flour, salt and pepper until blended. Gradually add milk. Bring to a boil; cook and stir for 2 minutes or until sauce is thickened.

2 Place half of potatoes in a greased 3-qt. baking dish. Pour half of sauce over potatoes. Repeat layers. Bake, uncovered, at 350° for 60-70 minutes or until potatoes are tender and top is lightly browned. Serve immediately. **Yield:** 8 servings.

Vegetable Fried Rice

Our home economists stirred up this pleasing, low-fat combination of rice, vegetables and seasonings. Quick and easy to prepare, it makes great use of leftover rice.

—Taste of Home Test Kitchen

- 1/4 cup finely chopped onion
- 2 teaspoons vegetable oil
- 2 teaspoons minced fresh gingerroot
- 2 garlic cloves, minced
- 3 tablespoons teriyaki sauce
- 2 tablespoons lime juice
- 1 teaspoon brown sugar
- 1/4 teaspoon salt
- 1/4 teaspoon hot pepper sauce
- 3 cups cold cooked rice
- 2 cups frozen mixed vegetables, thawed

1 In a large nonstick skillet, saute onion in oil until tender. Add ginger and garlic; saute 1 minute longer or until garlic is tender. Add the teriyaki sauce, lime juice, brown sugar, salt and hot pepper sauce; bring to a boil. Reduce heat; cook and stir for 2 minutes. Add rice and mixed vegetables; cook and stir over medium heat until vegetables are tender. **Yield:** 6 serving.

Con Queso Spirals

Spicy Mexican cheese dip from the snack aisle creates a zippy coating for spiral pasta.

—JoAnne Palmer, Mechanicsville, Maryland

- 2-1/2 cups uncooked spiral pasta
- 1 tablespoon butter
- 1 cup salsa con queso dip

Sour cream

1 Cook pasta according to package directions; drain. Place in a bowl; stir in butter until melted. Stir in con queso dip. Serve with sour cream. **Yield:** 4 servings.

Curried Barley with Raisins

Besides being frugal, this side dish is fast. That's because it calls for quick-cooking barley, which only takes 10-12 minutes to prepare.

—Taste of Home Test Kitchen

- 1 cup chopped celery
- 1 cup chopped onion
- 1 teaspoon olive oil
- 1 teaspoon minced garlic
- 1/2 teaspoon curry powder
- 1-1/2 cups cooked barley
- 1/4 cup slivered almonds, toasted
- 1/4 cup raisins
- 1/4 cup minced fresh parsley
- 1/4 teaspoon salt
- 1/4 teaspoon pepper

1 In a large skillet, saute celery and onion in oil for 8-10 minutes or until crisp-tender. Add the garlic and curry; saute for 1 minute. Warm barley in the microwave; stir into skillet. Add the remaining ingredients; cook and stir until heated through. **Yield:** 4 servings.

Simple Sauteed Zucchini

Put your bumper crop of summer zucchini to good use! This simple vegetable side dish can be cooked up in just a few minutes.

—Christy Maestri, Ozark, Arkansas

12	cups thinly sliced zucchini (about 10 medium)
3/4	teaspoon dried thyme
3/4	teaspoon dried rosemary, crushed
1/2	teaspoon dill weed
3	tablespoons olive oil

Salt and pepper to taste

1 In a Dutch oven, saute the zucchini, thyme, rosemary and dill in oil until crisp-tender. Reduce heat to medium; cover and cook for 5-7 minutes or until tender, stirring occasionally. Season with salt and pepper. **Yield:** 10-12 servings.

Corn 'n' Broccoli Bake

This sweet, comforting side dish is a very creamy casserole that resembles corn pudding. I like that this bake doesn't require a lot of ingredients.

—Betty Sitzman, Wray, Colorado

1	can (16 ounces) cream-style corn
3	cups frozen chopped broccoli, thawed
1/2	cup crushed saltines, *divided*
1	egg, beaten
1	tablespoon dried minced onion

Dash pepper

2	tablespoons butter, melted

1 In a bowl, combine the corn, broccoli, 1/4 cup of saltine crumbs, egg, onion and pepper. Place in a greased 1-1/2-qt. baking dish. Combine butter and remaining saltine crumbs; sprinkle on top. Cover and bake at 350° for 45 minutes. **Yield:** 6 servings.

Bread 'n' Butter Dressing

This moist stuffing is a speedy way to stretch a meal. With yummy herb flavor from sage and thyme, it's tastier than the boxed stuffing mixes you buy at the store.

—Myra Innes, Auburn, Kansas

8	slices bread
6	tablespoons butter, *divided*
3/4	cup chicken broth
1/4	cup chopped onion
1/2	teaspoon rubbed sage
1/4	teaspoon dried thyme
1/4	teaspoon salt
1/4	teaspoon pepper

1 Toast bread and spread with 2 tablespoons of butter; cut into 3/4-in. cubes. Place in a 1-qt. microwave-safe dish; set aside.

2 Place remaining butter in a microwave-safe bowl; cover and microwave on high for 40-50 seconds. Stir in broth, onion and seasonings. Pour over the bread cubes and toss to coat. Microwave, uncovered, on high for 4-1/2 minutes, stirring once. **Yield:** 4 servings.

EDITOR'S NOTE: This recipe was tested in a 1,100-watt microwave.

Lemon Dill Couscous

I add a touch of lemon and a hint of dill to dress up couscous with flavorful results. This is a low-fat side to most any full-flavored meat entree.

—**Mary Jo Welch, Brandon, Manitoba**

   3/4   cup uncooked plain couscous
3-1/4   teaspoons lemon juice
   1/4   to 1/2 teaspoon dill weed

1 Follow couscous package directions for 2 servings, adding salt to the water and omitting the oil or butter from the first step. Stir in the couscous, lemon juice and dill. Cover and remove from the heat; let stand for 5 minutes. Fluff with a fork. **Yield:** 2 servings.

EDITOR'S NOTE: This recipe was tested with Near East plain couscous.

Four-Bean Supreme

This recipe has been in my family as long as anyone can remember. It's possible it came from Ireland with my great-great-grandparents.

—Jaki Allen, Irons, Michigan

- 1   can (16 ounces) kidney beans, rinsed and drained
- 1   can (16 ounces) pork and beans, undrained
- 1   can (15-1/2 ounces) great northern beans, rinsed and drained
- 1   can (15 ounces) black beans, rinsed and drained
- 1   medium onion, chopped
- 1/3   cup packed brown sugar
- 1   teaspoon sugar
- 1   teaspoon salt
- 1   teaspoon lemon juice
- 1/2   to 1 teaspoon hot pepper sauce
- 1/4   teaspoon *each* dried basil, dried oregano, ground cumin, garlic powder, onion powder and pepper
- 3   bacon strips, cut into 2-inch pieces

1 In a bowl, combine the beans. In another bowl, combine the onion, sugars, salt, lemon juice, hot pepper sauce and seasonings. Stir into beans.

2 Pour into a greased 2-qt. baking dish. Top with bacon pieces. Bake, uncovered, at 350° for 1 hour or until heated through. **Yield:** 8-10 servings.

Party Potatoes

Flavored with garlic salt and chives, these potatoes are rich, creamy and so yummy. A sprinkling of paprika gives them a festive look.

—Cyneli Fynaardt, Oskaloosa, Iowa

- 6   large potatoes, peeled and cubed
- 1   package (8 ounces) cream cheese, cubed
- 1   cup (8 ounces) sour cream
- 1/2   cup milk
- 1   teaspoon garlic salt
- 2   teaspoons minced chives
- 2   tablespoons butter, melted
- 1/2   teaspoon paprika

1 Place potatoes in a large saucepan and cover with water. Bring to a boil. Reduce heat; cover and cook for 15-20 minutes or until tender. Drain; mash potatoes. Beat in the cream cheese, sour cream, milk, garlic salt and chives until well blended.

2 Transfer to a greased shallow 3-qt. baking dish. Drizzle potatoes with butter and sprinkle with paprika. Bake, uncovered, at 350° for 30-35 minutes or until edges are bubbly and potatoes are heated through. **Yield:** 8 servings.

Brown Rice Casserole

This hearty dish even passes the test for my teenage boys. Brown rice really fills them up.

—Glenda Schwartz, Morden, Manitoba

2	quarts water
1-1/2	cups uncooked brown rice
1	cup dry split peas
1	cup chopped fresh mushrooms
2	celery ribs, chopped
2	medium carrots, grated
1	medium onion, chopped
2	garlic cloves, minced
1	tablespoon vegetable oil
1	can (14-1/2 ounces) diced tomatoes, undrained
1/2	to 1 teaspoon salt
1/2	to 1 teaspoon dried thyme
1/2	to 1 teaspoon dried oregano
1/2	to 1 teaspoon pepper
1	cup (4 ounces) shredded cheddar cheese

1 In a large saucepan, bring water, rice and peas to a boil. Reduce heat; cover and simmer for 20-25 minutes or until tender. Drain and set aside.

2 In a skillet, saute the mushrooms, celery, carrots, onion and garlic in oil until vegetables are tender. Combine the vegetables, rice mixture, tomatoes and seasonings.

3 Transfer to a greased 2-1/2-qt. baking dish. Cover and bake at 350° for 30 minutes. Uncover; sprinkle with cheese. Bake 5-10 minutes longer or until the cheese is melted. **Yield:** 9 servings.

Braised Brussels Sprouts

Bacon and caraway seeds add just the right touch to these brussels sprouts. The Old-World flavor pairs well with countless main courses.

—Yvonne Anderson, New Philadelphia, Ohio

2	pounds fresh brussels sprouts
2	bacon strips, diced
1	medium onion, chopped
1	cup chicken broth
1	teaspoon caraway seeds
1/4	teaspoon salt
1/8	teaspoon pepper

1 Trim brussels sprouts and cut an "X" in the core of each. In a large saucepan, bring 1/2 in. of water and brussels sprouts to a boil. Cook for 8-10 minutes or until crisp-tender.

2 Meanwhile, in a large skillet, cook bacon over medium heat until crisp. Using a slotted spoon, remove to paper towels to drain, reserving drippings.

3 In same skillet, saute onion in the drippings until tender. Stir in the broth, caraway seeds, salt and pepper. Bring to a boil. Reduce heat; simmer, uncovered, until liquid is almost evaporated. Drain sprouts. Add sprouts and bacon to onion mixture; toss to coat. **Yield:** 8 servings.

TIP
Preparing Brussels Sprouts

Remove any loose or yellowed outer leaves; trim stem end. Rinse sprouts. When cooking brussels sprouts whole, cut an "X" in the core end with a sharp knife.

TIP

Don't Have Half-and-Half?

If you don't have half-and-half cream on hand to make Cauliflower Casserole (at right), you can substitute 1-1/2 cups of evaporated milk.

Bacon Cheese Fries

These tempting potatoes are one finger food I can make a meal of. Quick to fix, they're a hit at parties and as a snack. Ranch dressing is a tasty alternative to sour cream.

—**Marilyn Dutkus, Laguna Beach, California**

- 1 package (32 ounces) frozen french-fried potatoes
- 1 cup (4 ounces) shredded cheddar cheese
- 1/2 cup thinly sliced green onions
- 1/4 cup crumbled cooked bacon

Ranch salad dressing

1 Cook French fries according to package directions. Place fries on a broiler-proof dish or platter. Sprinkle with cheese, onions and bacon. Broil for 1-2 minutes or until cheese is melted. Serve with ranch dressing. **Yield:** 8-10 servings.

Cauliflower Casserole

The addition of ham makes this side dish hearty and satisfying. It works well for family as well as guests.

—**Carolyn Martin, Brewster, New York**

- 4 ounces fully cooked ham, chopped
- 4 garlic cloves, minced
- 6 tablespoons butter
- 1 large head cauliflower, broken into florets and thinly sliced
- 2 tablespoons all-purpose flour
- 1-1/2 cups half-and-half cream
- 1/2 cup shredded Swiss cheese
- 1/3 cup minced fresh parsley

1 In a large skillet, saute the ham and garlic in butter for 2 minutes. Add the cauliflower; cook and stir for 2 minutes. Combine the flour and cream until smooth; gradually stir into skillet. Bring to a boil; cook and stir for 1-2 minutes or until thickened.

2 Transfer to a greased 8-in. square baking dish. Sprinkle with cheese and parsley. Bake, uncovered, at 350° for 35-40 minutes or until heated through. **Yield:** 6-8 servings.

Garlic Angel Hair Pasta

I add the garlic cloves to the noodles as they cook. It gives me flavorful results fast, which is especially nice on busy weeknights or when I have dinner guests.

—**Denise Baumert, Dalhart, Texas**

- 8 ounces uncooked angel hair pasta
- 2 garlic cloves, peeled and halved
- 1/4 cup butter, cubed
- 1/4 cup grated Parmesan cheese
- 1 teaspoon snipped fresh *or* dried chives
- 1/2 teaspoon garlic salt, optional

1 Cook pasta according to package directions, adding garlic to the water. Drain; discard garlic. Transfer pasta to a serving bowl; add butter. Toss gently until butter is melted. Add the Parmesan cheese, chives and garlic salt if desired; toss to coat. **Yield:** 8 servings.

Roasted Vegetables

Garlic and other seasonings give great flavor to this colorful medley of vegetables. The pretty side dish is tasty and inexpensive, too.

—Sally Domark, Orland Hills, Illinois

2	medium potatoes, peeled and cut into 1/2-inch cubes
2	medium carrots, cut into 1/2-inch slices
1	large zucchini, cut into 1/2-inch slices
1	large sweet red pepper, cut into 1-inch pieces
1	tablespoon olive oil
1	teaspoon *each* dried basil and oregano *or* 1 tablespoon minced fresh basil and oregano
1/2	teaspoon salt, optional
1/4	teaspoon pepper
2	garlic cloves, minced

1 In a large bowl, combine the potatoes, carrots, zucchini and red pepper. Combine the remaining ingredients; drizzle over vegetables. Stir to coat.

2 Transfer to an ungreased 13-in. x 9-in. x 2-in. baking dish. Bake, uncovered, at 375° for 30-35 minutes or until tender. **Yield:** 6 servings.

Dilly Corn

Frozen corn enhanced with dill weed and a little garlic powder complements almost any dish.

—Bernadette Bennett, Waco, Texas

1 cup water
1 teaspoon beef bouillon granules
2-1/4 cups frozen corn
3 teaspoons dill weed
1 teaspoon garlic powder

1 In a small saucepan, bring water and bouillon to a boil. Stir in corn, dill and garlic powder. Return to a boil. Reduce heat; cover and simmer for 3-4 minutes or until corn is tender. Drain. **Yield:** 3 servings.

Parmesan Bow Ties

This fuss-free side dish calls for just four ingredients you can easily keep in your pantry and refrigerator. Serve it on special occasions as well as for everyday dinners.

—Taste of Home Test Kitchen

2 cups uncooked bow tie pasta
1/4 cup zesty Italian salad dressing
1/4 cup shredded Parmesan cheese
1 tablespoon minced fresh parsley

1 Cook pasta according to package directions. Drain pasta and rinse in cold water. Transfer to a serving bowl. Add the remaining ingredients; toss to coat. **Yield:** 4 servings.

Noodle Rice Pilaf

By adding a few fine egg noodles to a rice pilaf, you can have a deliciously different side dish. Terrific with fish, this also goes well with meat or poultry.

—**Kathy Schrecengost, Oswego, New York**

- 1/4 cup butter, cubed
- 1 cup uncooked long grain rice
- 1/2 cup uncooked fine egg noodles *or* vermicelli
- 2-3/4 cups chicken broth
- 2 tablespoons minced fresh parsley

1 In a large saucepan, cook and stir the rice and noodles in butter for 3-4 minutes or until lightly browned. Stir in broth; bring to a boil. Reduce heat; cover and simmer for 20-25 minutes or until broth is absorbed and rice is tender. Stir in parsley. **Yield:** 4 servings.

Baked Onion Rings

These crispy, lightly browned rings are a healthy alternative to the deep-fried version. Thyme and paprika enhance the flavor of the tender onions.

—**Della Stamp, Long Beach, California**

- 1 pound sweet onions
- 3 egg whites
- 1 cup dry bread crumbs
- 2 teaspoons dried thyme
- 1 teaspoon salt
- 1 teaspoon paprika
- 1/4 teaspoon pepper

1 Cut onions into 1/2-in. slices; separate into rings and place in a bowl. Cover with ice water; soak for 30 minutes. Drain.

2 In a small bowl, beat egg whites until foamy. In another bowl, combine the bread crumbs, thyme, salt, paprika and pepper. Divide the crumb mixture among three large resealable plastic bags. Dip a third of the onions in the egg whites; add a few rings at a time to crumb mixture and shake to coat. Place on a baking sheet coated with cooking spray.

3 Repeat with remaining onions and crumb mixture. Bake at 400° for 20 minutes or until lightly browned and crisp. **Yield:** 4 servings.

TIP
Sweet on Onions
Use sweet onions (like Vidalia, Walla Walla or Bermuda) when making Baked Onion Rings. Wrap individually in foil and store in the refrigerator crisper drawer. Use within several weeks of purchase.

Corn Bread Casserole

Since my husband likes spicy foods, I frequently sprinkle chopped jalapeno peppers over half of this casserole just for him.

—Carrina Cooper, McAlpin, Florida

1	can (15-1/4 ounces) whole kernel corn, drained
1	can (14-3/4 ounces) cream-style corn
1	package (8-1/2 ounces) corn bread/muffin mix
1	egg
2	tablespoons butter, melted
1/4	teaspoon garlic powder
1/4	teaspoon paprika

1 In a large bowl, combine all ingredients. Pour into a greased 11-in. x 7-in. x 2-in. baking dish. Bake, uncovered, at 400° for 25-30 minutes or until the top and edges are golden brown. **Yield:** 4-6 servings.

Pleasing Peas And Asparagus

Guests won't be able to resist the fresh flavor and color of this springtime vegetable combination.

—Nina Hall, Spokane, Washington

1/2	cup water
2	packages (10 ounces each) frozen peas
3/4	pound fresh asparagus, cut into 1-inch pieces or frozen asparagus tips
3	tablespoons butter
1	tablespoon minced fresh parsley
3/4	teaspoon garlic salt, optional

Dash pepper

1 In a large saucepan, bring water to a boil. Add peas, asparagus, butter, parsley, garlic salt if desired and pepper. Return to a boil.

2 Reduce heat; cover and simmer until asparagus is crisp-tender, about 10 minutes. Drain; serve immediately. **Yield:** 6 servings.

Apricot Rice Stuffing

This fruit rice stuffing can accompany any weekday or special-occasion entree.

—Katrina Forar, Lakewood, Colorado

1/2	cup finely chopped onion
1/2	cup finely chopped celery
1/4	cup butter
3	cups cooked rice
3/4	cup chopped dried apricots
1/4	cup minced fresh parsley
1/2	teaspoon salt
1/4	teaspoon pepper
1/4	teaspoon dried thyme
1/4	teaspoon ground nutmeg
1/8	teaspoon ground cloves

1 In a large skillet, saute onion and celery in butter until tender. Stir in the rice, apricots, parsley and seasonings. Transfer to a greased 1-qt. baking dish. Cover and bake at 350° for 30 minutes. Uncover; bake 5-10 minutes longer or until heated through. **Yield:** 4 servings.

Soups
& Salads

Chicken Noodle Soup

I cook most of the weekend meals and share weekday cooking duties with my wife. I also like to take food to neighbors, coworkers and our parents. And I try to send things like this hearty soup to people I know are sick.

—Terry Kuehn, Waunakee, Wisconsin

- 1 stewing chicken (about 4 pounds), cut up
- 3 quarts water
- 2 cans (14-1/2 ounces *each*) chicken broth
- 5 celery ribs, coarsely chopped, *divided*
- 4 medium carrots, coarsely chopped, *divided*
- 2 medium onions, quartered, *divided*
- 2/3 cup coarsely chopped green pepper, *divided*
- 1-1/4 teaspoons pepper, *divided*
- 1 bay leaf
- 2 teaspoons salt
- 8 ounces uncooked medium egg noodles

1 In a large kettle, combine the chicken, water, broth, half of the celery, carrots, onions and green pepper, 1/2 teaspoon pepper and the bay leaf. Bring to a boil. Reduce heat; cover and simmer for 2-1/2 hours or until chicken is tender. Chop the remaining onion; set aside.

2 Remove chicken from broth. When cool enough to handle, remove meat from bones and cut into bite-size pieces; set aside. Discard bones and skin.

3 Strain broth and skim fat; return broth to kettle. Add the salt, chopped onion and remaining celery, carrots, green pepper and pepper. Bring to a boil. Reduce heat; cover and simmer for 10-12 minutes or until vegetables are crisp-tender. Remove and discard bay leaf. Add noodles and chicken. Cover and simmer for 12-15 minutes or until noodles are tender. **Yield:** 16 servings (4 quarts).

Marshmallow Fruit Bowl

I dress up canned fruit with marshmallows and a home-cooked, pudding-like dressing to make this light and refreshing salad. It's an economical addition to most any meal.

—Patricia Staudt, Marble Rock, Iowa

- 1 can (20 ounces) pineapple tidbits
- 1 can (15 ounces) chunky mixed fruit
- 1/4 cup sugar
- 2 tablespoons all-purpose flour
- 1/4 cup lemon juice
- 2 eggs, lightly beaten
- 1/2 cup whipped topping
- 1 cup miniature marshmallows

1 Drain pineapple and mixed fruit, reserve 1 cup of juice. Set fruit aside.

2 In a large saucepan, combine sugar and flour. Stir in lemon juice and reserved fruit juices until smooth. Cook and stir over medium-high heat until thickened and bubbly. Reduce heat to low; cook and stir 2 minutes longer. Remove from the heat. Stir a small amount of hot filling into eggs. Return all to the pan, stirring constantly. Bring to a gentle boil; cook and stir for 2 minutes. Remove from the heat. Cool completely.

3 Fold in the whipped topping, marshmallows, pineapple and mixed fruit. Transfer to a serving bowl. **Yield:** 10 servings.

Classic Macaroni Salad

This medley is a tasty take on an all-time favorite. It goes great with a simple grilled meat, such as burgers or chicken.

—Dorothy Bayes, Sardis, Ohio

- 2 cups uncooked elbow macaroni
- 1 cup mayonnaise
- 2 tablespoons sweet pickle relish
- 2 teaspoons sugar
- 3/4 teaspoon ground mustard
- 1/4 teaspoon salt
- 1/8 teaspoon pepper
- 1/2 cup chopped celery
- 1/3 cup chopped carrot
- 1/4 cup chopped onion
- 1 hard-cooked egg, sliced

Dash paprika

1 Cook macaroni according to package directions; drain and rinse with cold water. Cool completely.

2 For dressing, in a small bowl, combine the mayonnaise, pickle relish, sugar, mustard, salt and pepper. In a large bowl, combine the macaroni, celery, carrot and onion. Add dressing and toss gently to coat.

3 Refrigerate until serving. Garnish with egg and paprika. **Yield:** 8 servings.

Tarragon Beef Salad

This main-dish salad features grilled steak with a tarragon-flavored dressing.

—Phyllis Townsend, Vienna, Virginia

2	pounds beef round steak (1 inch thick)
1	cup olive oil
1/3	cup red wine vinegar
1	tablespoon dried tarragon
1	teaspoon salt
3/4	teaspoon sugar
1/2	teaspoon ground mustard
1/2	teaspoon pepper
1/4	teaspoon garlic powder
1	large red onion, sliced and separated into rings
1/2	pound fresh mushrooms, sliced
1	large bunch romaine
1/2	cup minced fresh parsley

1 Broil steak 6 in. from the heat for 7 minutes on each side or until meat reaches desired doneness (for medium-rare, a meat thermometer should read 145°; medium, 160°; well-done, 170°). Cool slightly. Cut steak into very thin strips.

2 In a large bowl, combine the oil, vinegar, tarragon, salt, sugar, mustard, pepper and garlic powder. Add the steak, onion and mushrooms; toss to coat. Cover and refrigerate for at least 4 hours.

3 Just before serving, place romaine on plates. Using a slotted spoon, arrange beef mixture over romaine. Garnish with parsley. **Yield:** 8 servings.

Quick Corn Chowder

When my husband and I decided I'd stay home with our new baby, his salary had to be stretched pretty thin. I became an expert at preparing meals with more "sense" than dollars. This tasty, filling chowder is a budget saver.

—Diane Brewster, Highland, New York

1	bacon strip, diced
1	medium onion, diced
1	can (14-1/2 ounces) chicken broth
2	cups water
2	large potatoes, peeled and diced
1	can (15 ounces) whole kernel corn, drained
1	cup milk, *divided*
1/2	teaspoon salt
1/4	teaspoon pepper
1/4	cup all-purpose flour

Chopped fresh parsley, optional

1 In a large saucepan, cook bacon over medium heat until crisp. Using a slotted spoon, remove to paper towel to drain. Saute onion in drippings until tender. Add the broth, water and potatoes; bring to a boil. Reduce heat; cover and simmer for 15 minutes or until potatoes are tender.

2 Stir in the corn, 3/4 cup milk, salt and pepper. Combine flour and remaining milk until smooth; gradually add to soup. Bring to a boil; cook and stir for 2 minutes or until thickened. Garnish with bacon and parsley if desired. **Yield:** 6 servings.

Ham and Lentil Soup

This delicious soup is a great way to use up leftover cooked ham. Its robust broth makes this dish perfect for a cold day. Just serve with fresh crusty bread and butter.

—Connie Jones Pixley, Roxboro, North Carolina

- 1   cup chopped celery
- 1   cup chopped carrots
- 1/2 cup chopped onion
- 1   tablespoon butter
- 8   cups water
- 2   cups dried lentils, rinsed
- 1   cup cubed fully cooked ham
- 2   teaspoons salt
- 1   teaspoon dried marjoram
- 1/2 teaspoon pepper

1 In a large skillet, saute the celery, carrots and onion in butter for 3-4 minutes or until crisp-tender.

2 In a 5-qt. slow cooker, combine the water, lentils, ham, salt, marjoram and pepper. Stir in the celery mixture. Cover and cook on low for 4 hours or until lentils are tender. **Yield:** 11 servings (2-3/4 quarts).

Five-Can Chili

Who says a thick chili has to simmer all day on the stove. With five canned goods and zero prep time, a warm pot of this zesty specialty is a snap to whip up even on a busy weeknight.

—Jo Mann, Westover, Alabama

- 1   can (15 ounces) chili with beans
- 1   can (15 ounces) mixed vegetables, drained
- 1   can (11 ounces) whole kernel corn, drained
- 1   can (10-3/4 ounces) condensed tomato soup, undiluted
- 1   can (10 ounces) diced tomatoes and green chilies

1 In a large saucepan, combine all ingredients; heat through. **Yield:** 6 servings.

Creamy Tomato Soup

This soup uses only a handful of ingredients and is ready in minutes. My husband really enjoys it, so I like to pack it in his lunch.

—Sue Gronholz, Beaver Dam, Wisconsin

- 2   tablespoons all-purpose flour
- 1   tablespoon sugar
- 2   cups milk, *divided*
- 4   cups tomato juice, heated

Chopped fresh parsley

1 In a large saucepan, combine the flour, sugar and 1/4 cup milk; stir until smooth. Add remaining milk. Bring to a boil over medium heat, stirring constantly. Cook and stir for 2 minutes or until thickened. Slowly stir in hot tomato juice until blended. Sprinkle with parsley. **Yield:** 4 servings.

Louisiana-Style Taco Soup

This is one of my family's favorite quick and easy soups on a cold winter's day. With just a few ingredients and your favorite garnish, it's ready in no time.

—Julie Whitlow, Alexandria, Indiana

- 1 package (8 ounces) red beans and rice mix
- 1 package (9 ounces) tortilla soup mix
- 1 pound ground beef
- 1 cup salsa
- 1/4 cup sour cream

1 Prepare mixes according to package directions. Meanwhile, in a Dutch oven, cook beef over medium heat until no longer pink; drain. Stir in salsa and the prepared rice and soup. Cook, uncovered, for 5 minutes or until heated through. Garnish with sour cream. **Yield:** 13 servings (3 quarts).

Low-Fat Broccoli Soup

This delicious soup is a great way to eat a nutritious vegetable. It has a wonderful, fresh flavor.

—Kay Fairley, Charleston, Illinois

- 2 cups chopped fresh *or* frozen broccoli
- 1/2 cup chopped onion
- 1 can (14-1/2 ounces) reduced-sodium chicken broth
- 2 tablespoons cornstarch
- 1 can (12 ounces) fat-free evaporated milk

1 In a large saucepan, combine the broccoli, onion and broth; bring to a boil. Reduce heat; simmer, uncovered, for 10-15 minutes or until vegetables are tender. Cool slightly. Puree half of the mixture in a blender; return to the saucepan.

2 In a small bowl, combine the cornstarch and 3 tablespoons of milk until smooth. Gradually add remaining milk. Stir into the broccoli mixture. Bring to a boil; cook and stir for 2 minutes or until thickened. **Yield:** 4 servings.

Snap Salad

It's so simple to fix a batch of this colorful, refreshing salad. It goes great with any meal and is a deliciously different combination.

—Rick Leeser, Medford, Oregon

- 2 medium cucumbers, halved and thinly sliced
- 2 medium carrots, julienned
- 1/4 cup diced onion
- 2 tablespoons raisins
- 3/4 cup water
- 1/4 cup white vinegar
- 2 tablespoons sugar
- 1/2 teaspoon salt
- 1/4 teaspoon paprika
- 1/4 teaspoon pepper

1 In a large bowl, combine the cucumbers, carrots, onion and raisins. Combine the vinegar, sugar, salt, paprika and pepper. Pour over the cucumber mixture; toss to coat. Cover and refrigerate for at least 6 hours. Serve with a slotted spoon. **Yield:** 6 servings.

TIP

Save the Stalks

Don't throw out those broccoli stalks when making Low-Fat Broccoli Soup. Use a vegetable peeler to remove the tough outer layer. Chop the peeled stalks and florets; cook as directed.

Sausage Mushroom Soup

After trying this soup in a restaurant, I went home and made it myself. Now I can have it whenever I want.

—Twila Maxwell, Hermitage, Pennsylvania

- 1 pound bulk Italian sausage
- 2 cans (14-1/2 ounces *each*) beef broth
- 2 jars (4-1/2 ounces *each*) sliced mushrooms
- 1 cup finely chopped celery
- 1/2 cup quick-cooking barley
- 1/3 cup shredded carrot

1 In a large saucepan, cook sausage over medium heat until no longer pink; drain.

2 Add the broth, mushrooms, celery, barley and carrot. Bring to a boil. Reduce heat; cover and simmer for 10 minutes or until vegetables and barley are tender. **Yield:** 6 servings.

Cucumbers with Dressing

Just a few simple ingredients—mayonnaise, sugar, vinegar and salt—dress up slices of this crisp garden vegetable.

—Michelle Beran, Claflin, Kansas

- 1 cup mayonnaise
- 1/4 cup sugar
- 1/4 cup vinegar
- 1/4 teaspoon salt
- 4 cups sliced cucumbers

1 In a large bowl, combine the mayonnaise, sugar, vinegar and salt. Add cucumbers; toss to coat. Cover and refrigerate for 2 hours. **Yield:** 6-8 servings.

Sunflower Broccoli Salad

The unique crunch of sunflower kernels and bold flavor from a sesame oil dressing turn basic broccoli into a sensational salad.

—Rick and Sheila Ellison, Prattville, Alabama

- 2 quarts water
- 6 cups fresh broccoli florets
- 3 tablespoons rice vinegar
- 3 tablespoons reduced-sodium soy sauce
- 3 tablespoons sesame oil

Sugar substitute equivalent to 1 tablespoon sugar
- 1/4 cup unsalted sunflower kernels

1 In a large kettle, bring water to a boil. Add the broccoli; cover and cook for 3 minutes. Drain and immediately place broccoli in ice water. Drain and pat dry.

2 In a small bowl, whisk the vinegar, soy sauce, oil and sugar substitute. Pour over broccoli; toss to coat. Cover and refrigerate for at least 1 hour, stirring several times. Just before serving, stir in sunflower kernels. **Yield:** 6 servings.

EDITOR'S NOTE: This recipe was tested with Splenda sugar blend.

Onion Soup with Sausage

With a yummy slice of mozzarella cheese bread on top, this hearty broth makes an impressive luncheon entree or light supper. It looks great and tastes simply wonderful.

—Sundra Hauck, Bogalusa, Louisiana

- 1/2 pound pork sausage links, cut into 1/2-inch pieces
- 1 pound sliced fresh mushrooms
- 1 cup sliced onion
- 2 cans (14-1/2 ounces each) beef broth
- 4 slices Italian bread
- 1/2 cup shredded part-skim mozzarella cheese

1 In a large saucepan, cook sausage over medium heat until no longer pink; drain. Add mushrooms and onion; cook for 4-6 minutes or until tender. Stir in the broth. Bring to a boil. Reduce heat; simmer, uncovered, for 4-6 minutes or until heated through.

2 Ladle into four 2-cup ovenproof bowls. Top each with a slice of bread; sprinkle with cheese. Broil until cheese is melted. **Yield:** 4 servings.

Black Bean Taco Salad

Twenty minutes is all it takes to make this pleasing, Southwest-inspired salad. If your family likes a little zip, add some cumin or chili powder to the beef as it is being browned.

—Taste of Home Test Kitchen

- 1 pound ground beef
- 4 cups torn leaf lettuce
- 1 large tomato, chopped
- 1 cup canned black beans, rinsed and drained
- 1/2 cup Catalina salad dressing
- 4 cups nacho tortilla chips

1 In a large skillet, cook beef over medium heat until no longer pink; drain. In a bowl, combine the lettuce, tomato, beans and beef. Drizzle with dressing and toss to coat. Arrange tortilla chips on a serving plate; top with beef. **Yield:** 4 servings.

Rock 'n' Roast 'n' Chili

I got the basics of this recipe from a friend at a Super Bowl party and tweaked it. I have to tone it down a bit for my wife, and my mom once asked if I was trying to get my inheritance early! People who like spicy food really go for it.

—Rob Via, Charlotte, North Carolina

- 2 pounds beef stew meat, cut into 3/4-inch cubes
- 1 medium onion, chopped
- 2 to 3 garlic cloves, minced
- 2 tablespoons vegetable oil
- 1 jar (16 ounces) hot banana peppers
- 2 cans (14-1/2 ounces each) diced tomatoes, undrained
- 1 can (10 ounces) diced tomatoes and green chilies, undrained
- 1 can (6 ounces) tomato paste
- 1 can (16 ounces) kidney beans, rinsed and drained
- 1 can (4 ounces) chopped green chilies
- 1 jalapeno pepper, seeded and chopped
- 2 tablespoons chili powder
- 1 to 2 tablespoons hot pepper sauce
- 1 teaspoon salt
- 1/8 teaspoon ground cumin

Additional banana peppers, optional

1 In a large saucepan, cook the beef, onion and the garlic in oil over medium heat until meat is no longer pink; drain. Seed and chop 10 hot banana peppers (refrigerate remaining peppers for another use). Add the hot peppers, tomatoes, tomato paste, beans, chilies, jalapeno and seasonings to beef mixture.

2 Bring to a boil. Reduce heat; cover and simmer for 2 hours or until meat is tender. Uncover; simmer until chili reaches desired thickness. Garnish with additional banana peppers if desired. **Yield:** 8 servings.

EDITOR'S NOTE: When cutting hot peppers, disposable gloves are recommended. Avoid touching your face.

Supreme Spaghetti Salad

Bottled Italian salad dressing really perks up pasta and fresh vegetables in this swift salad. It's a delicious addition to any meal or picnic.

—Wendy Byrd, Salem, Virginia

- 1   package (1 pound) spaghetti, broken into 4-inch pieces
- 1   bottle (16 ounces) zesty Italian salad dressing
- 1   large cucumber, diced
- 1   large tomato, seeded and diced
- 1-1/2   cups fresh broccoli florets
- 2   tablespoons shredded Parmesan cheese
- 2   teaspoons Salad Supreme Seasoning

1 Cook spaghetti according to package directions. Drain and rinse in cold water.

2 Place spaghetti in a large serving bowl. Add the salad dressing, cucumber, tomato, broccoli, Parmesan cheese and seasoning; toss to coat. Cover and refrigerate for at least 45 minutes. **Yield:** 12 servings.

EDITOR'S NOTE: This recipe was tested with McCormick's Salad Supreme Seasoning. Look for it in the spice aisle.

Roasted Potato Salad

I pack this potato salad in a cooler to dish up cold at picnics or transfer it to a slow cooker to serve it warm for church potlucks.

—Terri Adams, Kansas City, Kansas

- 1 large whole garlic bulb
- 2 pounds small red potatoes, quartered
- 1/4 cup chicken broth
- 2 medium green peppers, cut into large chunks
- 2 cups frozen cut green beans, thawed
- 2 green onions, sliced
- 1/4 cup white wine vinegar
- 2 tablespoons olive oil
- 2 teaspoons sugar
- 1/2 teaspoon salt
- 1/4 teaspoon dried rosemary, crushed

1 Remove papery outer skin from garlic (do not peel or separate cloves). Cut top off garlic bulb. Place cut side up in a greased 15-in. x 10-in. x 1-in. baking pan. Add potatoes; drizzle with broth. Bake, uncovered, at 400° for 30-40 minutes or until garlic is softened.

2 Remove garlic; set aside. Add green peppers, green beans and onions to pan. Bake 30-35 minutes longer or until tender. Cool for 10-15 minutes.

3 Squeeze softened garlic into a large bowl. Stir in the vinegar, oil, sugar, salt and rosemary. Add vegetables; toss to coat. Serve warm or cold. **Yield:** 9 servings.

Chunky Potato Soup

The first time I made this creamy, satisfying soup, it instantly became our family's favorite. It is perfect on chilly days. Even those who don't normally like Swiss cheese savor this soup.

—Stephanie Moon-Martin, Silverdale, Washington

- 4 medium potatoes (about 2 pounds), peeled and cubed
- 3/4 cup chopped onion
- 1 small carrot, chopped
- 1/4 cup chopped celery
- 1-1/2 cups chicken broth
- 3 tablespoons butter, cubed
- 3 tablespoons all-purpose flour
- 2-1/2 cups milk
- 1 tablespoon minced fresh parsley
- 3/4 teaspoon salt
- 1/2 teaspoon pepper
- 1 cup (4 ounces) shredded Swiss cheese

1 In a large saucepan, combine the potatoes, onion, carrot, celery and broth. Bring to a boil. Reduce heat; cover and simmer for 12-15 minutes or until vegetables are tender; lightly mash.

2 Meanwhile, in a small saucepan, melt butter; stir in flour until smooth. Gradually stir in milk. Bring to a boil; cook and stir for 2 minutes or until thickened. Stir into the potato mixture. Cook and stir until thickened and bubbly. Add parsley, salt and pepper. Remove from the heat. Add cheese and stir until melted. **Yield:** 7 servings.

Southwestern Bean and Rice Salad

We enjoy fajitas and tacos, but finding a good side dish to go with them wasn't easy...until this recipe came along.

—Stephanie Liston, Ankeny, Iowa

- 3 cups cooked long grain rice, cooled
- 1 can (16 ounces) kidney beans, rinsed and drained
- 1 medium green pepper, diced
- 1 can (2-1/4 ounces) sliced ripe olives, drained
- 1/3 cup lime juice
- 1/4 cup chopped green onions
- 2 tablespoons vegetable oil
- 1 tablespoon minced fresh cilantro
- 2 garlic cloves, minced
- 1/2 teaspoon salt
- 1/2 teaspoon ground cumin

1 In a large bowl, combine the rice, beans, green pepper and olives. In a jar with a tight-fitting lid, combine the lime juice, onions, oil, cilantro, garlic, salt and cumin; shake well. Pour over rice mixture; toss to coat. Cover and refrigerate for 1 hour or until chilled. Toss before serving. **Yield:** 8 servings.

1 In a large saucepan, combine the beans, corn, broth, peppers and garlic salt. Bring to a boil. Reduce heat; simmer, uncovered, for 20 minutes or until heated through. **Yield:** 6 servings.

EDITOR'S NOTE: When cutting hot peppers, disposable gloves are recommended. Avoid touching your face.

Pork 'n' Bean Soup

I love to cook, but rarely use a recipe. I enjoy creating my own dishes to suit our tastes. Starting with canned pork and beans, I made this comforting soup.

—Kelly Olson, Moab, Utah

- 2 cans (11 ounces *each*) pork and beans
- 1 can (15-1/2 ounces) great northern beans, rinsed and drained
- 1 package (16 ounces) frozen corn, thawed
- 4 cups chicken broth
- 3 pickled jalapeno peppers, seeded and chopped
- 1 teaspoon garlic salt

Corny Coleslaw

Corn and cabbage make a different combo in this creamy coleslaw sprinkled with peanuts. It's especially tasty when I use homegrown corn I've cut off the cob. Thawed frozen corn works well, too.

—Patrice Ehrlich, Merced, California

- 5 cups shredded cabbage
- 1-1/2 cups whole kernel corn
- 2 tablespoons finely chopped onion
- 1/2 cup sour cream
- 1/2 cup mayonnaise
- 2 tablespoons sugar
- 2 tablespoons lemon juice
- 1 teaspoon prepared mustard
- 1/2 teaspoon salt
- 1/2 cup chopped salted peanuts

1 In a large bowl, combine the cabbage, corn and onion. In a small bowl, combine the sour cream, mayonnaise, sugar, lemon juice, mustard and salt. Pour over cabbage mixture; toss to coat.

2 Cover and refrigerate for 1 hour. Stir in peanuts just before serving. **Yield:** 6 servings.

Cabbage Chicken Salad

We were on a tight budget when I was little, so my mother often made this delightful salad, which fit our pocketbook as well as our taste buds. It can be a light supper or a crunchy complement to sandwiches.

—Heather Myrick, Southaven, Mississippi

- 1 package (3 ounces) chicken ramen noodles
- 2 cups shredded cabbage
- 1 cup cubed cooked chicken
- 1/4 cup sliced green onions
- 3 tablespoons sesame seeds, toasted
- 1/3 cup white vinegar
- 2 tablespoons sugar
- 2 tablespoons water
- 4 teaspoons vegetable oil
- 1/4 teaspoon salt
- 1/8 teaspoon pepper

1 Set seasoning packet from noodles aside. Crumble the noodles into a large bowl; add the cabbage, chicken, onions and sesame seeds. In a jar with a tight-fitting lid, combine the vinegar, sugar, water, oil, salt, pepper and contents of seasoning packets; shake well. Pour over cabbage mixture and toss to coat. Cover and refrigerate for 8 hours or overnight. **Yield:** 4 servings.

Frosty Pineapple Salad

I serve this cool pineapple treat as a salad or dessert. The frozen fluff calls for only four ingredients, and it's particularly refreshing on a summer day.

—Lillian Volf, Moncks Corner, South Carolina

- 1-1/2 cups buttermilk
- 3/4 cup sugar
- 1 can (20 ounces) unsweetened crushed pineapple, drained
- 1 carton (8 ounces) frozen whipped topping, thawed

1 In a bowl, combine the buttermilk, sugar and pineapple; mix well. Fold in the whipped topping. Transfer to a 13-in. x 9-in. x 2-in. dish. Freeze for 4 hours or until firm. Remove from the freezer 20 minutes before serving. **Yield:** 12 servings.

Sweet-Sour Spinach Salad

Quick and easy is often on my mealtime agenda, so this salad is perfect. You can use raisins for the dried cranberries.

—Judith Priglmeier, Aitkin, Minnesota

- 1 package (9 ounces) fresh spinach, torn
- 1/4 cup dried cranberries
- 1/4 cup chopped green onions
- 1/2 cup vegetable oil
- 1/4 cup sugar
- 3 tablespoons cider vinegar
- 1/2 teaspoon ground mustard
- 1/8 to 1/4 teaspoon celery seed

1 In a large salad bowl, combine the spinach, cranberries and onions. In a jar with a tight-fitting lid, combine the oil, sugar, vinegar, mustard and celery seed; shake well. Drizzle over salad and toss to coat. Serve immediately. **Yield:** 4 servings.

Lemon Vinaigrette on Greens

The refreshing flavor of this vinaigrette is also great on fresh spinach.

—Susan Garoutte, Georgetown, Texas

1/4	cup lemon juice
1/4	cup vegetable oil
1/4	cup olive oil
2	green onions, finely chopped
1	tablespoon minced fresh parsley
1-1/2	teaspoons sugar
1/2	teaspoon ground mustard
1/4	teaspoon salt
1/8	teaspoon pepper
4	cups torn romaine

1 In a jar with a tight-fitting lid, combine the lemon juice, oils, onions, parsley, sugar, mustard, salt and pepper; shake well. Place romaine in a salad bowl. Drizzle with the dressing; toss to coat. **Yield:** 4 servings.

Minestrone Macaroni

This is by far the easiest budget-friendly recipe that I've found. My family thinks it's even better as a leftover.

—Diane Varner, Elizabeth, Colorado

1	pound ground beef
2	cans (14-1/2 ounces *each*) Italian diced tomatoes, undrained
2-1/4	cups water
1-1/2	cups uncooked elbow macaroni
2	beef bouillon cubes
1	can (16 ounces) kidney beans, rinsed and drained
1	can (15 ounces) garbanzo beans, rinsed and drained
1	can (14-1/2 ounces) cut green beans, rinsed and drained

1 In a large skillet, cook beef over medium heat until no longer pink; drain. Add the tomatoes, water, macaroni and bouillon; bring to a boil. Reduce heat; cover and simmer for 12-15 minutes or until macaroni is tender. Stir in beans and cook until heated through. **Yield:** 6 servings.

Walnut Romaine Salad

This nutty tossed salad offers plenty of crunch and has a zippy vinegar-and-oil dressing.

—Harriet Stichter, Milford, Indiana

1	small bunch romaine, torn
1	small zucchini, chopped
1	cup seasoned salad croutons
1/4	cup chopped walnuts
6	tablespoons olive *or* vegetable oil
2	tablespoons red wine vinegar *or* cider vinegar
2	tablespoons Dijon mustard
2	tablespoons honey
1	garlic clove, minced

Dash pepper

1 In a large bowl, toss the romaine, zucchini, croutons and walnuts. In a small bowl, whisk the oil, vinegar, mustard, honey, garlic and pepper until smooth. Serve with the salad. **Yield:** 12 servings.

Curried Squash Soup

Growing up on a farm, I helped in the kitchen and had three brothers who liked to eat! My love of cooking continues to this day.

—Dianne Conway, London, Ontario

4	pounds butternut squash
1	large onion, diced
1	medium apple, peeled and diced
1	garlic clove, minced
1/4	cup butter
2	teaspoons curry powder
1/2	teaspoon ground ginger
3	cups chicken broth
1/2	cup heavy whipping cream
1/2	teaspoon salt
1/4	teaspoon pepper
1/8	teaspoon cayenne pepper, optional

1 Cut squash in half; discard seeds. Place squash cut side down in a 15-in. x 10-in. x 1-in. baking pan. Add 1/2 in. of hot water to pan. Bake, uncovered, at 350° for 40 minutes. Drain water from pan; turn squash cut side up. Bake 20-30 minutes longer or until tender. Cool slightly.

2 Carefully scoop out squash and place in a blender or food processor; cover and process until smooth. Set aside.

3 In a large saucepan, saute the onion, apple and garlic in butter until tender. Stir in curry powder and ginger; cook and stir for 1 minute. Stir in broth and pureed squash. Bring to a boil. Reduce heat; simmer, uncovered, for 15 minutes.

4 Reduce heat to low. Add the cream, salt, pepper and cayenne if desired; heat through (do not boil). **Yield:** 8 servings (2 quarts).

Turkey Bean Soup

Substitute your favorite beans in this nourishing soup if cannellini and lima beans are not your family's favorites.

—Taste of Home Test Kitchen

- 1 pound ground turkey
- 1 cup chopped onion
- 1 cup chopped celery
- 1 tablespoon olive oil
- 1 can (49-1/2 ounces) chicken broth
- 2 cups frozen corn
- 1 can (15 ounces) cannellini *or* white kidney beans, rinsed and drained
- 1 cup frozen lima beans
- 1 can (4 ounces) chopped green chilies
- 1 teaspoon dried oregano
- 1 teaspoon ground cumin
- 1 teaspoon chili powder
- 1/2 teaspoon salt

Shredded cheddar cheese, optional

1 In a Dutch oven, cook the turkey, onion and celery in oil over medium heat until meat is no longer pink.

2 Add the broth, corn, beans, chilies, oregano, cumin, chili powder and salt. Bring to a boil. Reduce heat; cover and simmer for 30 minutes or until heated through. Serve with cheese if desired. **Yield:** 8 servings (2 quarts).

Fruited Chicken Salad

Pineapple, dates and golden raisins sweeten this fresh-tasting chicken salad. I often serve it on lettuce, but you could stuff it into a pita bread, too.

—Audrey Moser, Drummond Island, Michigan

- 4 cups cubed cooked chicken breast
- 1 can (8 ounces) unsweetened crushed pineapple, drained
- 1/2 cup diced celery
- 1/2 cup diced red onion
- 1/2 cup golden raisins
- 1/2 cup chopped dates

DRESSING:

- 3/4 cup salad dressing
- 1/2 cup sour cream
- 2 teaspoons lemon juice
- 1 teaspoon ground mustard
- 1/4 teaspoon garlic powder
- 1/8 teaspoon pepper
- 6 lettuce leaves

1 In a large bowl, combine the chicken, pineapple, celery, onion, raisins and dates. In another bowl, combine the salad dressing, sour cream, lemon juice, mustard, garlic powder and pepper. Pour over chicken mixture; toss to coat. Serve on a lettuce leaf. **Yield:** 6 servings.

Egg Drop Soup

This soup is the perfect way to start an Asian meal. Spinach and green onions add great color.

—Mary Kelley, Minneapolis, Minnesota

- 5 cups chicken broth
- 1/2 teaspoon sugar
- 1 egg, lightly beaten
- 1/3 cup sliced fresh spinach
- 2 green onions, sliced

1 In a large saucepan, bring the broth and sugar to a boil over medium heat. Reduce heat to low. Drizzle beaten egg into hot broth. Remove from the heat; stir in spinach and onions. **Yield:** 4 servings.

Curried Bean Salad

Cumin and curry powder give this chilled three-bean salad terrific zip. I get a lot of compliments on this easy-to-make dish.

—Howie Wiener, Spring Hill, Florida

- 1 can (16 ounces) kidney beans, rinsed and drained
- 1 can (15 ounces) pinto beans, rinsed and drained
- 1 can (15 ounces) garbanzo beans or chickpeas, rinsed and drained
- 1 can (15-1/4 ounces) whole kernel corn, drained
- 3 celery ribs, chopped
- 1/2 cup chopped green onions
- 1/2 cup cider vinegar
- 1/4 cup vegetable oil
- 4 garlic cloves, minced
- 2 teaspoons dried oregano
- 1 teaspoon pepper
- 1/2 teaspoon ground cumin
- 1/2 teaspoon curry powder

1 In a bowl, combine the beans, corn, celery and onions. In a jar with a tight-fitting lid, combine the remaining ingredients; shake well. Drizzle over bean mixture and toss gently to coat. Cover and refrigerate overnight. Serve with a slotted spoon. **Yield:** 6 servings.

Amish Chicken Corn Soup

Cream corn and butter add richness to this homey chicken noodle soup. It makes a big batch, but it freezes well for future meals. That is one reason why soups are my favorite thing to make.

—Beverly Hoffman, Sandy Lake, Pennsylvania

- 12 cups water
- 2 pounds boneless skinless chicken breasts, cubed
- 1 cup chopped onion
- 1 cup chopped celery
- 1 cup shredded carrots
- 3 chicken bouillon cubes
- 2 cans (14-3/4 ounces *each*) cream-style corn
- 2 cups uncooked egg noodles
- 1/4 cup butter
- 1 teaspoon salt
- 1/4 teaspoon pepper

1 In a Dutch oven, combine the water, chicken, onion, celery, carrots and bouillon. Bring to a boil. Reduce heat; simmer, uncovered, for 30 minutes or until chicken is no longer pink and vegetables are tender.

2 Stir in the corn, noodles and butter; cook 10 minutes longer or until noodles are tender. Season with salt and pepper. **Yield:** 16 servings (about 4 quarts).

Tuna Pasta Salad

Mustard and dill really provide wonderful flair to the flavor of this simple salad. It's very inexpensive to serve.

—Pat Kordas, Nutley, New Jersey

- 1 package (7 ounces) small pasta shells, cooked and drained
- 1 can (6 ounces) tuna, drained and flaked
- 1 large carrot, shredded
- 1/4 cup chopped onion
- 3/4 cup mayonnaise
- 1/4 cup milk
- 1 tablespoon lemon juice
- 2 teaspoons prepared mustard
- 1 teaspoon dill weed
- 1/2 teaspoon salt
- 1/8 teaspoon pepper

1 In a large salad bowl, combine the pasta, tuna, carrot and onion. Combine remaining ingredients; whisk until smooth. Pour over pasta mixture; toss to coat. Cover and refrigerate for 1-2 hours. **Yield:** 4 servings.

TIP
Using Your Noodle

When pasta is cooked in soup, it absorbs liquid and gives off starch. This can make the noodles mushy and the soup broth very thick, especially when stored in the refrigerator.

To avoid this, cook the pasta separately, then add to individual servings of warm soup.

Bean Counter Chowder

This nicely seasoned chowder makes a hearty meal. I like to serve it with rolls or breadsticks.

—Vivian Haen, Menomonee Falls, Wisconsin

1/2	cup chopped onion
2	garlic cloves, minced
1	tablespoon vegetable oil
1	medium tomato, chopped
2	cans (14-1/2 ounces *each*) chicken *or* vegetable broth
1-3/4	cups water
1/2	teaspoon *each* dried basil, oregano and celery flakes
1/4	teaspoon pepper
3	cans (15-1/2 ounces *each*) great northern beans, rinsed and drained
1	cup uncooked elbow macaroni
1	tablespoon minced parsley

1 In a large saucepan, saute onion and garlic in oil until tender. Add the tomato; simmer for 5 minutes. Add the broth, water and seasonings. Bring to a boil; cook for 5 minutes.

2 Add beans and macaroni; return to a boil. Reduce heat; simmer, uncovered, for 15 minutes or until macaroni is tender. Sprinkle with parsley. **Yield:** 8 servings (2 quarts).

TIP

Dressing Your Salad

Select the right salad greens for the dressing. A sturdy lettuce like iceberg or romaine can hold a creamy dressing. For a light vinaigrette, Bibb or Boston lettuce is suitable.

Greens with Creamy Herbed Salad Dressing

If you're looking for a way to spice up everyday greens, try this thick, creamy salad dressing. It also makes a delectable veggie dip.

—Janet Les, Chilliwack, British Columbia

- 1/2 cup mayonnaise
- 2 tablespoons plus 2 teaspoons milk
- 4 teaspoons white vinegar
- 1 teaspoon dried oregano
- 1/2 teaspoon dried basil
- 1/4 teaspoon sugar
- 1/4 teaspoon salt
- 1/4 garlic powder
- 1/4 teaspoon pepper
- 5 cups mixed salad greens

1 In a small bowl, whisk the mayonnaise, milk and vinegar until combined. Whisk in the oregano, basil, sugar, salt, garlic powder and pepper. Serve with salad greens. **Yield:** 5 servings.

Italian Vegetable Soup

With macaroni, kidney beans, tomatoes, zucchini and lots of other veggies, this flavorful soup is hearty enough for dinner with corn bread or rolls.

—Phyllis Schmalz, Kansas City, Kansas

- 2 medium carrots, diced
- 1 small onion, chopped
- 2 garlic cloves, minced
- 1 tablespoon olive oil

- 2 cans (14-1/2 ounces *each*) beef broth
- 1 can (14-1/2 ounces) diced tomatoes, undrained
- 2 cups water
- 1 small zucchini, diced
- 1 teaspoon dried basil
- 1 teaspoon salt
- 1/2 teaspoon dried oregano
- 1/4 teaspoon pepper
- 2 to 3 drops hot pepper sauce
- 1 can (16 ounces) kidney beans, rinsed and drained
- 1 cup chopped fresh spinach
- 3/4 cup uncooked elbow macaroni
- 2 tablespoons minced fresh parsley
- 1/2 cup shredded Parmesan cheese

1 In a Dutch oven or large saucepan, saute the carrots, onion and garlic in oil until tender. Stir in the broth, tomatoes, water, zucchini, basil, salt, oregano, pepper and hot pepper sauce. Bring to a boil. Reduce heat; cover and simmer for 15 minutes.

2 Stir in the kidney beans, spinach, macaroni and parsley. Cover and cook 15 minutes longer or until macaroni is tender. Garnish with Parmesan cheese. **Yield:** 6-8 servings.

Breads

Simple White Bread

These tasty, tall loaves are a terrific way to round out a hearty, penny-pinching meal. Serve one loaf and freeze the other one for later.

—Ruth VonLienen, Marengo, Iowa

- 2 packages (1/4 ounce *each*) active dry yeast
- 2-1/2 cups warm water (110° to 115°)
- 1/2 cup nonfat dry milk powder
- 1/2 cup vegetable oil
- 2 tablespoons sugar
- 1 tablespoon salt
- 8-1/2 to 9 cups all-purpose flour
- 1 tablespoon butter, melted

1 In a large bowl, dissolve yeast in 1/2 cup of water. Add the remaining water, dry milk powder, oil, sugar, salt and 3 cups of flour. Beat on medium speed for 3 minutes or until smooth. Stir in enough remaining flour to form a soft dough.

2 Turn onto a floured surface and knead until smooth and elastic, about 6-8 minutes. Place in a greased bowl, turning once to grease top. Cover and let rise in a warm place until doubled, about 1 hour.

3 Punch the dough down. Divide in half; shape into loaves. Place in two greased 9-in. x 5-in. x 3-in. loaf pans. Cover and let rise until doubled, about 1 hour.

4 Bake at 375° for 35 minutes or until golden brown. Remove from pans to cool on wire racks. Brush with butter. **Yield:** 2 loaves (16 slices each).

Herb Quick Bread

This simple loaf is especially good with soups and stews, but slices are also tasty alongside fresh green salads. The herbs make it a flavorful treat any time of the year.

—Donna Roberts, Shumway, Illinois

- 3 cups all-purpose flour
- 3 tablespoons sugar
- 1 tablespoon baking powder
- 1 tablespoon caraway seeds
- 1/2 teaspoon salt
- 1/2 teaspoon dried thyme
- 1/2 teaspoon ground nutmeg
- 1 egg
- 1 cup milk
- 1/3 cup vegetable oil

1 In a large bowl, combine the flour, sugar, baking powder, caraway seeds, salt, thyme and nutmeg. In a small bowl, whisk the egg, milk and oil; stir into dry ingredients just until moistened.

2 Transfer to a 9-in. x 5-in. x 3-in. loaf pan coated with cooking spray. Bake at 350° for 40-50 minutes or until a toothpick inserted near the center comes out clean. Cool for 10 minutes before removing from pan to a wire rack to cool completely. **Yield:** 1 loaf (14 slices).

TIP
Keep Homemade Bread Fresh

It's best to store bread at room temperature in a cool, dry place for up to 2-3 days. To keep it soft, store in an airtight plastic bag.

For longer storage, freeze bread for up to 3 months. Slice it before freezing and just take out the number of slices needed.

Cheddar Corn Bread

This corn bread pleases a crowd with its moist texture and big corn flavor. It's perfect with a steaming bowl of chili.

—Terri Adrian, Lake City, Florida

- 2 packages (8-1/2 ounces *each*) corn bread/muffin mix
- 2 eggs, lightly beaten
- 1/2 cup milk
- 1/2 cup plain yogurt
- 1 can (14-3/4 ounces) cream-style corn
- 1/2 cup shredded cheddar cheese

1 In a large bowl, combine the corn bread mix, eggs, milk and yogurt until blended. Stir in corn and cheese. Pour into a greased 13-in. x 9-in. x 2-in. baking dish.

2 Bake at 400° for 18-22 minutes or until a toothpick inserted near the center comes out clean. Cut into squares. Serve warm. **Yield:** 12 servings.

Onion French Bread

I often make homemade French bread to serve with soup for my family. Since I love variety in my cooking, I tried adding dried minced onion to my usual recipe in an attempt to copy a bread I had tasted, creating these two tasty loaves. Using the bread machine on the dough setting is a great time-saver.

—Ruth Fueller, Barmstedt, Germany

- 1 cup water (70° to 80°)
- 1/2 cup dried minced onion
- 1 tablespoon sugar
- 2 teaspoons salt
- 3 cups bread flour
- 2-1/4 teaspoons active dry yeast
- 1 tablespoon cornmeal
- 1 egg yolk, beaten

1 In bread machine pan, place the first six ingredients in order suggested by manufacturer. Select dough setting (check dough after 5 minutes of mixing; add 1-2 tablespoons of water or flour if needed).

2 When cycle is complete, turn dough onto a lightly floured surface. Cover and let rest for 15 minutes. Divide dough in half. Roll each portion into a 15-in. x 10-in. rectangle. Roll up jelly-roll style, starting with a long side; pinch seams to seal. Pinch ends to seal and tuck under.

3 Sprinkle the cornmeal onto a greased baking sheet. Place loaves on pan. Cover and let rise in a warm place until doubled, about 30 minutes. Brush with egg yolk. Make 1/4-in.-deep cuts 2 in. apart in each loaf. Bake at 375° for 20-25 minutes or until golden brown. Remove from pan to a wire rack. **Yield:** 2 loaves (about 3/4 pound each).

Orange Ginger Scones

A sprinkling of sugar tops off these tender treats with a touch of sweetness. I like to serve them hot with butter and jam.

—Edna Hoffman, Hebron, Indiana

2	cups all-purpose flour
4	tablespoons sugar, *divided*
2	teaspoons baking powder
2	teaspoons ground ginger
1/2	teaspoon salt
1/4	teaspoon baking soda
1/2	cup cold butter, cubed
3/4	cup sour cream
1	egg
1-1/2	teaspoons grated orange peel

1 In a large bowl, combine the flour, 2 tablespoons sugar, baking powder, ginger, salt and baking soda. Cut in butter until mixture resembles coarse crumbs. Whisk sour cream and egg; add to dry ingredients just until moistened. Stir in orange peel.

2 Turn onto a floured surface; knead 8-10 times. Divide dough in half. Pat each portion into a 7-in. circle; cut each into six wedges.

3 Separate wedges and place 1 in. apart on ungreased baking sheets. Sprinkle with remaining sugar. Bake at 400° for 10-12 minutes or until lightly browned. Serve warm. **Yield:** 1 dozen.

Whole Wheat Rolls

These good-for-you rolls rise high. They're a light, fluffy and change-of-pace accompaniment to any meal.

—Jennifer Martin, East Sebago, Maine

1-1/2	cups whole wheat flour
1/4	cup plus 2 tablespoons sugar
1	package (1/4 ounce) active dry yeast
1	teaspoon salt
1/2	cup milk
1/2	cup water
1/4	cup butter, cubed
1	egg
2	to 2-1/4 cups all-purpose flour

Vegetable oil, optional

1 In a large bowl, combine the whole wheat flour, sugar, yeast and salt; set aside. In a large saucepan, heat milk, water and butter to 120°-130°. Add to dry ingredients; beat just until moistened. Add egg; beat until smooth. Stir in enough all-purpose flour to form a soft dough.

2 Turn onto a floured surface and knead until smooth and elastic, about 6-8 minutes. Place in a greased bowl; turn once to grease top. Cover and let rise in a warm place until doubled, about 1 hour.

3 Punch dough down; shape into 12 balls. Place in a greased 9-in. square baking pan. Cover and let rise until doubled, about 1 hour. Brush the tops with oil if desired.

4 Bake at 400° for 15-20 minutes or until golden brown. Cover loosely with foil if tops brown too quickly. Remove from pan to a wire rack to cool. **Yield:** 1 dozen.

Jumbo Banana-Carrot Muffins

People are always surprised to hear these muffins contain both bananas and carrots. But they're also delighted with the delicious flavor!

—Julye Byrd, Azle, Texas

1-1/2	cups all-purpose flour
3/4	cup sugar
1	teaspoon baking powder
1	teaspoon baking soda
1/2	teaspoon salt
1/2	teaspoon ground cinnamon
1/4	teaspoon ground nutmeg
2	eggs, *separated*
1	tablespoon honey
1/4	teaspoon grated orange peel
2	medium ripe bananas, mashed
1	cup shredded carrots
1/2	cup unsweetened applesauce

1 In a large bowl, combine the first seven ingredients. In another bowl, beat egg yolks until light and lemon-colored. Beat in honey and orange peel. Stir into dry ingredients just until moistened. Fold in the bananas, carrots and applesauce.

2 In a small bowl, beat egg whites on high speed until stiff peaks form; fold into batter a third at a time.

3 Fill greased or paper-lined muffin cups two-thirds full. Bake at 350° for 25-30 minutes or until a toothpick comes out clean. Cool for 5 minutes before removing from pan to a wire rack. **Yield:** 9 jumbo muffins.

Oatmeal Wheat Bread

My mother taught me to make this bread when I was 10 years old. It tastes marvelous and it's good for you.

—Jackie Gavin, Essex Junction, Vermont

- 1-3/4   cups boiling water
- 1   cup quick-cooking oats
- 1/2   cup molasses
- 1/4   cup shortening
- 1-1/2   teaspoons salt
- 2   packages (1/4 ounce *each*) active dry yeast
- 1/2   cup warm water (110° to 115°)
- 1/4   cup orange juice
- 2-1/2   cups whole wheat flour
- 3   to 3-1/2 cups all-purpose flour

Melted butter

1 In a large bowl, pour boiling water over oats. Add the molasses, shortening and salt. Let stand until warm (110°-115°), stirring occasionally.

2 In a small bowl, dissolve yeast in warm water. Add the orange juice, oat mixture and whole wheat flour. Beat until smooth. Stir in enough remaining all-purpose flour to form a soft dough.

3 Turn onto a floured surface; knead until smooth and elastic, about 6-8 minutes. Place in a greased bowl, turning once to grease top. Cover and let rise in a warm place until doubled, about 1 hour.

4 Punch dough down. Shape into two loaves; place in greased 8-in. x 4-in. x 2-in. loaf pans. Cover and let rise until doubled, about 45 minutes.

5 Bake at 350° for 40 minutes. Remove from pans to cool on wire racks; brush with butter. **Yield:** 2 loaves (12 slices each).

Buttermilk Rolls

You don't have to break the bank to enjoy great, homemade baked goods. I use simple, everyday ingredients to make these lovely rolls.

—Bernice Morris, Marshfield, Missouri

- 1   package (1/4 ounce) active dry yeast
- 1/4   cup warm water (110° to 115°)
- 1-1/2   cups warm buttermilk (110° to 115°)
- 1/2   cup vegetable oil
- 3   tablespoons sugar
- 1   teaspoon salt
- 1/2   teaspoon baking soda
- 4-1/2   cups all-purpose flour

1 In a large bowl, dissolve yeast in water. Beat in the buttermilk, oil, sugar, salt, baking soda and 2 cups of flour until smooth. Stir in enough remaining flour to form a soft dough.

2 Turn onto a floured surface; knead until smooth and elastic, about 6-8 minutes. Place in a greased bowl, turning once to grease top. Cover and let rise in a warm place until doubled, about 1-1/2 hours.

3 Punch dough down. Divide into 18 pieces; roll into balls. Place on greased baking sheets. Cover and let rise until doubled, about 30 minutes.

4 Bake at 400° for 15-20 minutes or until golden brown. Cool on wire racks. **Yield:** 1-1/2 dozen.

EDITOR'S NOTE: Warmed buttermilk will appear curdled.

Honey-Oat Casserole Bread

This loaf is tender and moist. Slather slices with butter or use to make sandwiches.

—Beverly Sterling, Gasport, New York

1	cup boiling water
1	cup quick-cooking oats
1/4	cup butter, softened
1/4	cup honey
1	teaspoon salt
1	package (1/4 ounce) active dry yeast
1/4	cup warm water (110° to 115°)
2	eggs
3-1/2	cups all-purpose flour

1 In a large bowl, pour boiling water over oats. Add the butter, honey and salt. Let stand until mixture cools to 110°-115°, stirring occasionally.

2 In a large bowl, dissolve yeast in warm water. Add the eggs, oat mixture and 2 cups flour. Beat on medium speed for 2 minutes. Stir in enough remaining flour to form a soft dough (dough will be sticky). Cover and let rise in a warm place until doubled, about 55 minutes.

3 Punch dough down. Transfer to a greased 1-1/2-qt. round baking dish. Cover and let rise in a warm place until doubled, about 30 minutes.

4 Bake at 375° for 35-40 minutes or until golden brown. Cool for 10 minutes before removing from baking dish to a wire rack to cool. Cut into wedges. **Yield:** 1 loaf (12 wedges).

Soft Onion Breadsticks

The subtle onion flavor of these breadsticks pairs well with a variety of entrees. They're golden brown and delicious!

—Maryellen Hays, Wolcottville, Indiana

3/4	cup chopped onion
1	tablespoon vegetable oil
2-1/4	teaspoons active dry yeast
1/2	cup warm water (110° to 115°)
1/2	cup warm milk (110° to 115°)
1/4	cup butter, softened
2	eggs
1	tablespoon sugar
1-1/2	teaspoons salt
3-1/2	to 4 cups all-purpose flour
2	tablespoons cold water
2	tablespoons sesame seeds
1	tablespoon poppy seeds

1 In a small skillet, saute onion in oil until tender; cool. In a large bowl, dissolve yeast in warm water. Add the milk, butter, 1 egg, sugar, salt and 1 cup flour. Beat on medium speed for 2 minutes. Stir in onion and enough remaining flour to form a soft dough.

2 Turn onto a floured surface; knead until smooth and elastic, 6-8 minutes. Place in a greased bowl, turning once to grease top. Cover and let rise in a warm place until doubled, about 1 hour.

3 Punch dough down. Let stand for 10 minutes. Turn onto a lightly floured surface; divide into 32 pieces. Shape each piece into an 8-in. rope. Place 2 in. apart on greased baking sheets. Cover and let rise for 15 minutes.

4 Beat cold water and remaining egg; brush over breadsticks. Sprinkle half with sesame seeds and half with poppy seeds. Bake at 350° for 16-22 minutes or until golden brown. Remove to wire racks. **Yield:** 2 dozen.

Honey-Glazed Drop Biscuits

A handful of ingredients is all you'll need for these moist biscuits brushed with a sweet glaze. I make them for my church and by special request. I use a small ice cream scoop to drop the batter onto pans.

—Diane Patton, Toledo, Ohio

- 3-1/4   cups self-rising flour
- 1   cup milk
- 1/2   cup mayonnaise
- 1/2   cup honey
- 1/2   cup butter, melted

1 In a large bowl, combine the flour, milk and mayonnaise just until moistened. Turn onto a lightly floured surface; knead 8-10 times. Drop by tablespoonfuls 2 in. apart onto a greased baking sheet.

2 Bake at 425° for 10-14 minutes or until golden brown. Combine honey and butter; brush 1/2 cup over hot biscuits. Serve warm with remaining honey butter. **Yield:** 16 biscuits.

EDITOR'S NOTE: As a substitute for 3-1/4 cups self-rising flour, place 4-3/4 teaspoons baking powder and 1-1/2 teaspoons salt in a measuring cup. Add all-purpose flour to measure 1 cup. Combine with an additional 2-1/4 cups all-purpose flour.

Onion Crescent Rolls

These soft, buttery crescent rolls are a nice complement to any supper. They'll fill your home with that wonderful bread-baking aroma, and they're easy to make, too. I even serve them for special occasions like Easter and Christmas.

—Mary Maxeiner, Lakewood, Colorado

- 1/2   cup plus 2 tablespoons butter, softened, *divided*
- 1/2   cup sugar
- 2   eggs
- 1   package (1/4 ounce) active dry yeast
- 1   cup warm milk (110° to 115°)
- 1   cup diced onion
- 1/2   teaspoon salt
- 3-1/2   to 4-1/2 cups all-purpose flour

1 In a large bowl, cream 1/2 cup butter and sugar. Add eggs, one at a time, beating well after each addition. Dissolve yeast in warm milk; add to creamed mixture. Add the onion, salt and 1 cup flour; beat until blended. Stir in enough remaining flour to form a soft dough.

2 Turn onto a floured surface; knead until smooth and elastic, about 6-8 minutes. Place in a greased bowl, turning once to grease top. Cover and let rise in a warm place until doubled, about 1 hour.

3 Punch dough down. Turn onto a lightly floured surface; divide in half. Roll each portion into a 12-in. circle; cut each circle into 12 wedges. Roll up wedges from the wide end and place point side down 2 in. apart on greased baking sheets. Curve ends down to form crescents. Cover and let rise in a warm place until doubled, about 30 minutes.

4 Bake at 400° for 9-11 minutes or until lightly browned. Remove from pans to wire racks. Melt remaining butter; brush over warm rolls. **Yield:** 2 dozen.

Desserts

Boston Cream Angel Cake

Our home economists assure you can prepare this delectable dessert in no time. To change this cake to your family's liking, try different flavors of instant pudding or other ice cream toppings.

—Taste of Home Test Kitchen

- 2 cups plus 1 tablespoon cold milk, *divided*
- 1 package (3.4 ounces) instant French vanilla pudding mix
- 1 prepared angel food cake (16 ounces)
- 1 cup hot fudge ice cream topping

1 In a large bowl, whisk 2 cups milk and pudding mix for 2 minutes. Let stand for 2 minutes or until soft-set. Split cake into three horizontal layers; place bottom layer on a serving plate. Spread with half of the pudding. Repeat layers. Replace cake top. Cover and refrigerate until serving.

2 In a small microwave-safe bowl, heat hot fudge topping; stir in remaining milk. Drizzle over cake, allowing it to drip down the sides. Refrigerate leftovers. **Yield:** 8 servings.

Shortbread Meltaways

Although they don't cost much, these rich, bite-size cookies will definitely melt in your mouth.

—Ruth Whittaker, Wayne, Pennsylvania

- 1 cup butter, softened
- 1/2 cup confectioners' sugar
- 1 teaspoon vanilla extract
- 1 cup all-purpose flour
- 2/3 cup cornstarch

1 In a small mixing bowl, cream the butter and confectioners' sugar until light and fluffy. Beat in vanilla. Combine the flour and cornstarch; gradually add to creamed mixture.

2 Drop by 1/2 teaspoonfuls onto ungreased baking sheets. Bake at 350° for 11-13 minutes or until bottoms are lightly browned. Cool for 5 minutes before removing from pans to wire racks. **Yield:** 7 dozen.

Spice Puffs

Four ingredients are all I need to bake up a batch of these lovely, light-as-air muffins that make a sweet breakfast treat. They're my son's favorite and so simple to make.

—Sally Geipel, Franklin, Wisconsin

- 1 package (18-1/4 ounces) spice cake mix
- 1/2 cup butter, melted
- 1/2 cup sugar
- 1 teaspoon ground cinnamon

1 Prepare cake batter according to package directions. Fill 24 greased or paper-lined muffin cups two-thirds full. Bake at 350° for 20-25 minutes or until a toothpick comes out clean. Remove to wire racks. Cool for 5 minutes.

2 Place butter in a shallow bowl. In another shallow bowl, combine sugar and cinnamon. Dip top of warm puffs in butter, then in cinnamon-sugar. Serve warm. **Yield:** 2 dozen.

Chocolate Mint Parfaits

It takes just minutes to make this creamy, chocolate-mint delight. It's one of my family's favorite desserts.

—Karalee Reinke, Omaha, Nebraska

- 2 cups plus 1 tablespoon cold milk, *divided*
- 1 package (3.9 ounces) instant chocolate pudding mix
- 4 ounces cream cheese, softened
- 1 tablespoon sugar
- 1/4 teaspoon peppermint extract
- 1 cup whipped topping
- 4 to 6 mint Andes candies, optional

1 In a bowl, whisk 2 cups milk and pudding mix for 2 minutes; set aside. In a small bowl, beat cream cheese, sugar, extract and remaining milk. Fold in whipped topping. In parfait or dessert glasses, layer the pudding and cream cheese mixtures. Garnish with the mint candies if desired. **Yield:** 4-6 servings.

Icy Summer Treats

Kids not only love eating these cool and refreshing treats, they have fun making them as well!

—**Darlene Brenden, Salem, Oregon**

- 1 cup sugar
- 1 package (3 ounces) berry blue gelatin
- 1 package (.13 ounce) unsweetened berry blue soft drink mix
- 2 cups boiling water
- 2 cups cold water
- 10 disposable plastic cups (5 ounces)
  Heavy-duty aluminum foil
- 10 Popsicle sticks

1 In a bowl, combine the sugar, gelatin and soft drink mix in boiling water until dissolved. Add cold water. Pour into cups. Cover each cup with foil; insert sticks through the foil (the foil will hold sticks upright). Place cups in a 13-in. x 9-in. x 2-in. pan; freeze. To serve, remove foil and plastic cups. **Yield:** 10 servings.

Three-Fruit Dump Cake

This down-home dessert is perfect served warm with vanilla ice cream. Just "dump" the peaches, pears and apple pie filling into a dish, top with cake mix and bake until golden.

—**Wendy Crochet, Houma, Louisiana**

- 1 can (21 ounces) apple pie filling
- 1 can (15-1/4 ounces) sliced pears, drained
- 1 can (15-1/4 ounces) sliced peaches, drained
- 1 package (9 ounces) yellow cake mix
- 1/4 cup butter, cut into 1/8-inch pieces

1 In a large bowl, combine the pie filling, pears and peaches; spoon into a greased 8-in. square baking dish. Sprinkle with cake mix; dot with butter.

2 Bake at 350° for 45-50 minutes or until golden brown. Serve warm. **Yield:** 6-8 servings.

Rich Cheesecake Bars

I take turns with some of the ladies at church to provide coffee-time snacks for adult Bible class and Sunday school. These gooey bars, a traditional St. Louis dessert, are a favorite.

—**Tammy Helle, St. Louis, Missouri**

- 1 package (9 ounces) yellow cake mix
- 3 tablespoons butter, softened
- 1 egg

TOPPING:

- 1 package (3 ounces) cream cheese, softened
- 2 cups confectioners' sugar
- 1 egg

1 In a large bowl, combine the cake mix, butter and egg until well blended. Spread into a greased 9-in. square baking pan.

2 In a small bowl, beat the cream cheese, confectioners' sugar and egg until smooth; spread evenly over the batter.

3 Bake at 350° for 30-35 minutes or until a toothpick inserted near the center comes out clean. Cool on a wire rack. Store in the refrigerator. **Yield:** 2 dozen.

Sweet Potato Custard Pie

I enjoy baking and experimenting with ingredients. I came up with a hit when I developed this deliciously different pie.

—**Kathy Roberts, New Hebron, Mississippi**

2	small sweet potatoes, peeled and chopped
3/4	cup marshmallow creme
1/2	cup butter, cubed
1	can (5 ounces) evaporated milk
3	eggs
1	teaspoon vanilla extract
1/4	teaspoon almond extract
3/4	cup sugar
1/4	cup packed brown sugar
1	tablespoon all-purpose flour
1/8	teaspoon ground cinnamon
1/8	teaspoon ground nutmeg
1	unbaked pastry shell (9 inches)
1/2	cup whipping topping

1 Place sweet potatoes in a large saucepan and cover with water. Bring to a boil. Reduce heat; cover and simmer for 10 minutes or until tender. Drain potatoes and place in large bowl; mash. Add marshmallow creme and butter; beat until smooth. Add the milk, eggs and extracts; mix well.

2 Combine the sugars, flour, cinnamon and nutmeg; gradually beat into potato mixture until well blended. Pour into pastry shell.

3 Bake at 350° for 45-50 minutes or until a knife inserted near the center comes out clean. Cool on a wire rack. Serve with whipped topping. Refrigerate leftovers. **Yield:** 8 servings.

Cran-Apple Cobbler

I developed this economical recipe when I wanted a quick but special treat for my hungry husband. The yummy results can't be beat!

—Joan Gocking, Moundsville, West Virginia

- 1 can (21 ounces) apple pie filling
- 1/2 cup dried cranberries
- 1 package (7-3/4 ounces) cinnamon swirl biscuit mix
- 1/2 cup water

1 In an ungreased 9-in. pie plate, combine the pie filling and cranberries. In a small bowl, combine biscuit mix and water; drop by tablespoonfuls over filling.

2 Bake at 450° for 10-12 minutes or until lightly browned. Cover and bake 10-12 minutes longer or until topping is golden brown and a toothpick inserted in a biscuit comes out clean. Serve warm. **Yield:** 6 servings.

Cherry Enchiladas

This easy dessert reminds me of French crepes. It's the perfect meal-ending treat for those Tex-Mex brunches we have so often here.

—Mary Lou Chambers, Houston, Texas

- 2/3 cup cherry pie filling *or* pie filling of your choice
- 2 flour tortillas (6 inches), warmed
- 3 tablespoons sugar
- 3 tablespoons butter
- 3 tablespoons water

1 Spoon pie filling off center on each tortilla; roll up. Place seam side down in a greased 8-in. square baking dish; set aside. In a small saucepan bring the sugar, butter and water to a boil over medium heat; pour over enchiladas.

2 Bake, uncovered, at 350° for 20-25 minutes or until lightly browned. Serve immediately. **Yield:** 2 servings.

Butterscotch Fudge Bars

You can't go wrong with easy-to-make chocolate bars. I guarantee everyone will savor these effortless goodies.

—Edna Hoffman, Hebron, Indiana

- 1/2 cup butter, cubed
- 1 square (1 ounce) unsweetened chocolate
- 2/3 cup packed brown sugar
- 1 egg
- 1 teaspoon vanilla extract
- 1 cup all-purpose flour
- 1 teaspoon baking powder

Dash salt

- 1 cup butterscotch chips

1 In a microwave, melt butter and chocolate; stir until melted. Stir in brown sugar until dissolved. Cool to lukewarm. Stir in egg and vanilla. Combine the flour, baking powder and salt; stir into chocolate mixture until blended. Stir in chips.

2 Spread into a greased 9-in. square baking pan. Bake at 350° for 22-27 minutes or until a toothpick comes out with moist crumbs. Cool on a wire rack. Cut and serve. **Yield:** 1 dozen.

Delicate Chocolate Cake

A special friend gave me this recipe more than 20 years ago. The cake has a light cocoa flavor, and the frosting is rich and delicious.

—Annette Foster, Taylors, South Carolina

- 1/4 cup baking cocoa
- 1 cup water
- 1 cup vegetable oil
- 1/2 cup butter, cubed
- 2 cups self-rising flour
- 2 cups sugar
- 1/2 cup buttermilk
- 2 eggs

FROSTING (for the layer cake):

- 1/2 cup butter, cubed
- 1/4 cup baking cocoa
- 1/4 cup milk
- 4 to 4-1/2 cups confectioners' sugar
- 1 teaspoon vanilla extract

1 In a small saucepan over medium heat, combine cocoa and water until smooth; add the oil and butter. Bring to a boil; cook and stir for 1 minute. Remove from the heat.

2 In a large mixing bowl, combine flour and sugar; gradually add cocoa mixture, beating well. Add buttermilk and eggs; mix well. Pour into a greased 15-in. x 10-in. x 1-in. baking pan.

3 Bake at 350° for 28-30 minutes or until a toothpick inserted near the center comes out clean. Cool on a wire rack. Cut cake into four 7-1/2-in. x 5-in. rectangles. Wrap two of the rectangles separately in foil; refrigerate or freeze. Set the other two rectangles aside.

4 For frosting, combine the butter, cocoa and milk in a saucepan. Bring to a boil; cook and stir for 1 minute (the mixture will appear curdled). Pour into a large mixing bowl. Gradually add confectioners' sugar and vanilla; beat until frosting achieves spreading consistency. Frost the top of one cake rectangle; top with the second rectangle. Frost top and sides of cake. **Yield:** 1 two-layer cake (6-8 servings) plus 2 plain cake portions.

EDITOR'S NOTE: As a substitute for each cup of self-rising flour, place 1-1/2 teaspoons baking powder and 1/2 teaspoon salt in a measuring cup. Add all-purpose flour to measure 1 cup.

Hoosier Cream Pie

With its meringue topping, this traditional dessert is so pretty to look at and cuts nicely, too. My grandmother also used her recipe to make coconut pie and butterscotch pie.

—Edna Hoffman, Hebron, Indiana

3/4	cup sugar
1/4	cup cornstarch
1/4	teaspoon salt
2-1/2	cups milk
3	egg yolks, lightly beaten
2	tablespoons butter
1-1/2	teaspoons vanilla extract
3	medium firm bananas
1	pastry shell (9 inches), baked

MERINGUE:

3	egg whites
1/4	teaspoon cream of tartar
6	tablespoons sugar

1 In a large saucepan, combine the sugar, cornstarch and salt. Stir in milk until smooth. Cook and stir over medium-high heat until thickened and bubbly. Reduce heat; cook and stir for 2 minutes. Remove from the heat. Stir a small amount of hot filling into egg yolks; return all to the pan. Bring to a gentle boil; cook and stir for 2 minutes. Stir in butter and vanilla until butter is melted; keep warm. Slice bananas into the pastry shell.

2 In a large bowl, beat the egg whites and cream of tartar on medium speed until soft peaks form. Gradually beat in sugar, 1 tablespoon at a time, on high until stiff glossy peaks form and the sugar is dissolved.

3 Pour hot filling over bananas. Spread meringue evenly over filling, sealing edges to crust. Bake at 350° for 15 minutes or until the meringue is golden brown. Cool on a wire rack for 1 hour.

4 Refrigerate for at least 3 hours before serving. Store leftovers in the refrigerator. **Yield:** 6-8 servings.

Pretzel Dessert

This recipe makes a big batch of the sweet and salty, creamy and crunchy treat. That's fine with us because any dessert that's left over is super the next day, too.

—Rita Winterberger, Huson, Montana

2	cups crushed pretzels
3/4	cup sugar
3/4	cup butter
2	envelopes whipped topping mix
1	cup cold milk
1	teaspoon vanilla extract
1	package (8 ounces) cream cheese, softened
1	cup confectioners' sugar
1	can (21 ounces) cherry pie filling

1 In a large bowl, combine the pretzels, sugar and butter; set aside 1/2 cup for topping. Press the remaining mixture into an ungreased 13-in. x 9-in. x 2-in. dish.

2 In a large bowl, beat the whipped topping mix, milk and vanilla on high speed for 4 minutes or until soft peaks form. Add the cream cheese and confectioners' sugar; beat until smooth.

3 Spread half over crust. Top with pie filling and remaining cream cheese mixture. Sprinkle with reserved pretzel mixture. Refrigerate overnight. **Yield:** 16 servings.

Blueberry Pear Cobbler

Mom used her home-canned pears in this warm dessert, but the store-bought variety works just as well. People are amazed something that comes together in a cinch tastes this wonderful.

—**Susan Pumphrey, Hot Springs, Arizona**

- 2 cans (15-1/4 ounces *each*) sliced pears
- 1 package (7 ounces) blueberry muffin mix
- 3 tablespoons butter

1 Drain pears, reserving 3/4 cup juice (discard remaining juice or save for another use). Pour pears and reserved juice into a greased 2-qt. baking dish. Sprinkle with muffin mix; dot with butter.

2 Bake, uncovered, at 400° for 20-25 minutes or until bubbly and the top is lightly browned. **Yield:** 8 servings.

Warm Apple Slices

Cherry soda adds fun flavor to these tender apples. You can serve them as a two-ingredient side dish, or add a dollop of whipped topping and cinnamon for a no-fuss dessert.

—**Helen Turner, Upland, Indiana**

- 3 large tart apples, peeled and sliced
- 1 can (12 ounces) cherry soda

Whipped topping and ground cinnamon, optional

1 Layer apple slices in an 11-in. x 7-in. x 2-in. microwave-safe dish. Pour soda over the apples. Microwave, uncovered, on high for 5-9 minutes or until apples are tender. Serve warm with whipped topping and cinnamon if desired. **Yield:** 8 servings.

EDITOR'S NOTE: This recipe was tested in a 1,100-watt microwave.

Spiced Cocoa Cupcakes

These cupcakes remind me of a heavenly cup of spiced cocoa. The drizzled desserts are a budget-friendly finish for any meal.

—**Shirley Glaab, Hattiesburg, Mississippi**

- 1-1/2 cups all-purpose flour
- 3/4 cup sugar
- 1/4 cup baking cocoa
- 3/4 teaspoon baking soda
- 1/4 teaspoon salt
- 1/4 teaspoon ground cinnamon
- 1/4 teaspoon ground nutmeg
- 1 egg
- 3/4 cup applesauce
- 1/4 cup butter, melted
- 1/2 cup dried cranberries
- 1 cup confectioners' sugar
- 4-1/2 teaspoons milk

1 In a bowl, combine the first seven ingredients. In another bowl, whisk the egg, applesauce and butter; stir into dry ingredients just until combined. Fold in the cranberries.

2 Fill greased or paper-lined muffin cups two-thirds full. Bake at 350° for 18-20 minutes or until a toothpick comes out clean. Cool cupcakes for 5 minutes before removing from pan to a wire rack to cool completely.

3 In a small bowl, combine the confectioners' sugar and milk until smooth. Drizzle over cupcakes. **Yield:** 1 dozen.

Frosty Lemon-Strawberry Dessert

This fun, frosty treat came from a very dear elderly friend who was a great cook. I think of her whenever I make it. It's so simple, cool and refreshing on a hot summer day. For a patriotic showstopper, you can also add fresh blueberries!

—**Gail Marshall, Fort Lauderdale, Florida**

- 1 quart fresh strawberries, hulled
- 1/2 gallon vanilla ice cream, softened
- 1 can (12 ounces) frozen lemonade concentrate, thawed
- 2 teaspoons grated lemon peel

1 Place strawberries in a food processor; cover and process until pureed. Transfer to a large mixing bowl; add the ice cream, lemonade concentrate and lemon peel. Beat until blended.

2 Pour into an ungreased 13-in. x 9-in. x 2-in. dish. Cover and freeze overnight. Remove from the freezer 15 minutes before serving. **Yield:** 12 servings.

Fluffy Orange Gelatin Pie

For an exceptionally light citrus dessert that practically melts in your mouth, try this pie. It's so easy that kids can help prepare it.

—**Frann Clark, DeRidder, Louisiana**

- 1 can (15 ounces) mandarin oranges
- 1 package (3 ounces) orange gelatin
- 1 can (5 ounces) evaporated milk, chilled
- 1 reduced-fat graham cracker crust (8 inches)
- 1 medium navel orange, sliced

1 Drain liquid from oranges into a measuring cup. Add enough water to measure 1 cup; set oranges aside. Pour liquid into a saucepan; bring to a boil. Stir in gelatin until dissolved.

2 Transfer to a large bowl; place mixer beaters in bowl. Cover and refrigerate until mixture forms syrupy consistency.

3 Add milk. Beat on high speed until nearly doubled. Fold in mandarin oranges. Pour into crust. Refrigerate for 2-3 hours or until set. Garnish with orange slices. **Yield:** 8 servings.

Chewy Peanut Butter Bars

These yummy peanut butter bars have been a favorite in our family for years. One pan never lasts long around our house.

—Deb DeChant, Milan, Ohio

- 1/2 cup butter, cubed
- 1/2 cup creamy peanut butter
- 1-1/2 cups sugar
- 1 cup all-purpose flour
- 2 eggs, lightly beaten
- 1 teaspoon vanilla extract

1 In a large saucepan, melt the butter and peanut butter. Remove from the heat; gradually add sugar and flour and mix well. Stir in the eggs and vanilla.

2 Spread into a greased 13-in. x 9-in. x 2-in. baking pan. Bake at 350° for 28-32 minutes or until lightly browned and edges start to pull away from sides of pan. Cool on a wire rack. Cut into bars.
Yield: 2 dozen.

EDITOR'S NOTE: Reduced-fat or generic brands of peanut butter are not recommended for this recipe.

Chocolate Cream Dessert

I bake a tender cake from a mix, then layer it with a cream cheese blend, chocolate pudding and whipped topping. This is a cool and delicious finale on a warm summer day.

—Pam Reddell, Linden, Wisconsin

- 3/4 cup cold butter, cubed
- 1 package (18-1/4 ounces) chocolate cake mix
- 1 egg, lightly beaten
- 1 package (8 ounces) cream cheese, softened
- 1 cup confectioners' sugar
- 4 cups whipped topping, *divided*
- 3 cups cold milk
- 2 packages (3.9 ounces *each*) instant chocolate pudding mix
- 2 tablespoons chocolate curls

1 In a bowl, cut butter into cake mix until crumbly. Add egg and mix well. Press into a greased 13-in. x 9-in. x 2-in. baking dish. Bake at 350° for 15-18 minutes or until set. Cool completely on a wire rack.

2 In a small bowl, beat the cream cheese and confectioners' sugar until smooth. Fold in 1 cup of whipped topping. Carefully spread over the crust; refrigerate.

3 In a large bowl, whisk the milk and pudding mix for 2 minutes; let stand for 2 minutes or until soft-set. Spread over the cream cheese layer. Top with the remaining whipped topping. Refrigerate for 2 hours before cutting. Garnish with chocolate curls. Refrigerate leftovers. **Yield:** 12 servings.

Oatmeal Raisin Bars

These tender bars have a sweet raisin filling tucked between a golden oat crust and topping. The old-fashioned treats are perfect for potlucks.

—Rita Christianson, Glenburn, North Dakota

- 1 cup sugar
- 2 tablespoons plus 1-1/2 teaspoons cornstarch
- 1 teaspoon ground cinnamon
- 1-1/2 cups (12 ounces) sour cream
- 3 eggs, lightly beaten
- 2 cups raisins

CRUMB MIXTURE:
- 1-3/4 cups all-purpose flour
- 1-3/4 cups quick-cooking oats
- 1 cup packed brown sugar
- 1 teaspoon baking soda
- 1/2 teaspoon salt
- 1 cup cold butter, cubed

1 In a large saucepan, combine the sugar, cornstarch and cinnamon. Stir in sour cream until smooth. Cook and stir over medium-high heat until thickened and bubbly. Reduce heat; cook and stir 2 minutes longer. Remove from the heat. Stir a small amount of hot filling into eggs; return all to pan, stirring constantly. Bring to a gentle boil; cook and stir 2 minutes longer. Remove from the heat. Gently stir in raisins. Cool to room temperature without stirring.

2 Meanwhile, in a large bowl, combine the flour, oats, brown sugar, baking soda and salt. Cut in butter until crumbly.

3 Firmly press 3-1/2 cups of crumb mixture into a greased 13-in. x 9-in. x 2-in. baking pan. Spread with the raisin filling. Sprinkle with the remaining crumb mixture.

4 Bake at 350° for 25-30 minutes or until golden brown. Cool on a wire rack. Cut into bars. Refrigerate leftovers. **Yield:** about 3 dozen.

Stovetop Rice Pudding

This is my mom's recipe, which she called creamy steamed rice. Although many people would eat it for dessert, it was one of my favorite things for breakfast when I was growing up.

—Mandy Barnhart, Pensacola, Florida

- 1-1/2 cups water
- 3/4 cup uncooked long grain rice
- 1/2 teaspoon salt
- 4 cups milk
- 1/2 cup sugar
- 2 tablespoons butter
- 1/2 teaspoon ground cinnamon
- Cinnamon sticks and fresh fruit, optional

1 In a large heavy saucepan, bring water to a boil over medium-high heat; stir in rice and salt. Reduce heat; cover and simmer for 15 minutes or until the water is absorbed.

2 Stir in the milk and sugar. Cook, uncovered, over medium heat for 30-40 minutes or until thickened, stirring frequently. Remove from the heat; stir in butter.

3 Serve warm or chilled. Sprinkle with cinnamon. Garnish with cinnamon sticks and fruit if desired. **Yield:** 4-6 servings.

Creamy Strawberry Pie

I like to end a nice company meal with this make-ahead dessert. The eye-catching pie has a big strawberry flavor and extra richness from ice cream.

—Dixie Terry, Marion, Illinois

- 1 package (10 ounces) frozen sweetened sliced strawberries, thawed
- 1 package (3 ounces) strawberry gelatin
- 2 cups vanilla ice cream
- 1 pastry shell (9 inches), baked

Sliced fresh strawberries, optional

1 Drain strawberries into a 1-cup measuring cup and reserve juice; set berries aside. Add enough water to juice to measure 1 cup; pour into a large saucepan. Bring to a boil over medium heat. Remove from the heat; stir in gelatin until dissolved. Add ice cream; stir until blended. Refrigerate for 5-10 minutes or just until thickened (watch carefully).

2 Fold in reserved strawberries. Pour into pastry shell. Refrigerate until firm, about 1 hour. Garnish with fresh strawberries if desired. Refrigerate leftovers. **Yield:** 6 servings.

Apple Spice Snack Cake

Nothing could be simpler or more delicious than this moist apple cake. It's easy to create the four-ingredient treat with a spice cake mix...and even easier on your grocery budget.

—Reba Savoie, Roswell, New Mexico

- 1 package (18-1/4 ounces) spice cake mix
- 1 can (21 ounces) apple pie filling
- 2 eggs
- 2 tablespoons vegetable oil

1 In a large bowl, combine all the ingredients; beat on low speed for 30 seconds. Beat on medium for 2 minutes.

2 Pour into a greased 13-in. x 9-in. x 2-in. baking dish. Bake at 350° for 30-35 minutes or until a toothpick inserted near the center comes out clean. Cool on a wire rack. **Yield:** 15 servings.

Orange Sponge Cake Roll

People will think you spent hours working on this pretty, melt-in-your-mouth sponge cake.

—**Michelle Smith, Sykesville, Maryland**

- 7 egg whites
- 4 egg yolks
- 3/4 cup sugar
- 1 tablespoon grated orange peel
- 1 tablespoon lemon juice
- 1/2 teaspoon vanilla extract
- 1 cup cake flour
- 1/8 teaspoon salt
- 2 tablespoons confectioners' sugar, *divided*
- 1-1/4 cups orange marmalade *or* apricot spreadable fruit

Orange peel strips (1 to 3 inches), optional

1 Place egg whites in a large bowl; let stand at room temperature for 30 minutes. Line a greased 15-in. x 10-in. x 1-in. baking pan with waxed paper; coat the paper with cooking spray and set aside.

2 In a large bowl, beat egg yolks on high speed for 5 minutes or until thick and lemon-colored. Gradually beat in sugar. Stir in the orange peel, lemon juice and vanilla. Sift flour and salt together twice; gradually add to yolk mixture and mix well (batter will be very thick).

3 In a large bowl with clean beaters, beat egg whites on medium speed until stiff peaks form. Gradually fold into batter. Spread evenly into prepared pan.

4 Bake at 350° for 12-15 minutes or until cake springs back when lightly touched in center. Cool in pan on a wire rack for 5 minutes.

5 Invert cake onto a kitchen towel dusted with 1 tablespoon confectioners' sugar. Gently peel off waxed paper. Roll up cake in the towel jelly-roll style, starting with a short side. Cool completely on a wire rack.

6 Unroll cake; spread marmalade evenly over cake to within 1/2 in. of edges. Roll up again. Place seam side down on a serving platter. Cover and refrigerate for 1 hour. Dust with remaining confectioners' sugar. Garnish with orange peel strips if desired. **Yield:** 8 servings.

Frosty Peach Pie Supreme

This impressive dessert is just peachy! With only four ingredients, it's so simple to make.

—**June Formanek, Belle Plaine, Iowa**

- 1 cup sliced fresh *or* frozen peaches, *divided*
- 2 cups (16 ounces) fat-free reduced-sugar peach yogurt
- 1 carton (8 ounces) frozen reduced-fat whipped topping, thawed
- 1 reduced-fat graham cracker crust (8 inches)

1 Finely chop half of the peaches; place in a bowl. Stir in the yogurt. Fold in whipped topping. Spoon into the crust. Cover and freeze for 4 hours or until firm. Refrigerate for 45 minutes before slicing. Top with remaining peaches. **Yield:** 8 servings.

Pear Gingerbread Cake

With canned pears and a cake mix, you can create this classic cake all year long. I use fresh ripe pears when they're in season.

—Cindy Reams, Philipsburg, Pennsylvania

- 1/4 cup butter, melted
- 2 cans (15-1/4 ounces each) sliced pears, drained and patted dry
- 1/3 cup sugar
- 1 package (14-1/2 ounces) gingerbread cake mix

1 Spread the butter in a 9-in. square baking dish. Arrange pear slices in rows over the butter. Sprinkle with sugar. Prepare cake mix batter according to package directions. Carefully pour over the pears.

2 Bake at 350° for 30-35 minutes or until a toothpick inserted near the center comes out clean. Cool on a wire rack for 10 minutes before inverting onto a serving plate. **Yield:** 9 servings.

Flaky Fruit Dessert

Craving an old-fashioned crisp? Cornflakes easily create the yummy topping on this quick and comforting dessert.

—Clara Honeyager, Mukwonago, Wisconsin

- 1 can (21 ounces) fruit pie filling of your choice
- 1 teaspoon lemon juice
- 1/4 cup packed brown sugar
- 2 tablespoons butter, softened
- 1 teaspoon ground cinnamon
- 2 cups cornflakes

1 In a bowl, combine pie filling and lemon juice. Transfer to a lightly greased 1-qt. baking dish. In another bowl, combine brown sugar, butter and cinnamon; add cornflakes. Spread over filling. Bake at 350° for 15-20 minutes or until heated through. Serve warm. **Yield:** 6 servings.

Chocolate Ribbon Bars

No one will be able to eat just one of these bars, which are full of butterscotch, peanut butter and chocolate flavor. Unlike similar crispy cereal treats, these aren't sticky! Over the years I've accumulated quite a few recipes from my coworkers, and this one is easy to prepare.

—Gail Wiese, Athens, Wisconsin

1	package (10 to 11 ounces) butterscotch chips
1	cup peanut butter
8	cups crisp rice cereal
2	cups (12 ounces) semisweet chocolate chips
1/4	cup butter, cubed
2	tablespoons water
3/4	cup confectioners' sugar

1 In a large microwave-safe bowl, melt butterscotch chips and peanut butter; stir until smooth. Gradually stir in cereal until well coated. Press half of the mixture into a greased 13-in. x 9-in. x 2-in. pan; set remaining mixture aside.

2 In another large microwave-safe bowl, melt semisweet chocolate chips and butter. Stir in water until blended. Gradually add the confectioners' sugar, stirring until smooth.

3 Spread over cereal layer. Cover and refrigerate for 10 minutes or until chocolate layer is set. Spread remaining cereal mixture over the top. Chill before cutting. **Yield:** 2 dozen.

EDITOR'S NOTE: Reduced-fat or generic brands of peanut butter are not recommended for this recipe.

Chocolate Oatmeal Cake

This cake is a real treat—it's so moist and topped with a scrumptious coffee frosting.

—Deborah Sheehan, East Orland, Maine

1-1/2	cups boiling water
1	cup quick-cooking oats
1	cup (6 ounces) semisweet chocolate chips
1/2	cup butter, softened
3/4	cup sugar
3/4	cup packed brown sugar
2	eggs
1-1/2	cups all-purpose flour
1	teaspoon baking soda
1	teaspoon salt

COFFEE FROSTING:

2	teaspoons instant coffee granules
1/4	cup half-and-half cream, warmed
1/2	cup butter, softened
1	teaspoon vanilla extract
1/8	teaspoon salt
4	cups confectioners' sugar

1 In a bowl, combine the water and oats. Sprinkle with chocolate chips (do not stir); let stand for 20 minutes. In a large bowl, cream butter and sugars. Add eggs, one at a time, beating well after each addition. Beat in oat mixture. Combine the flour, baking soda and salt; add to the creamed mixture and mix well. Pour into a greased 13-in. x 9-in. x 2-in. baking pan.

2 Bake at 350° for 35-40 minutes or until a toothpick inserted near the center comes out clean. Cool on a wire rack.

3 For frosting, dissolve coffee granules in cream; set aside. In a small bowl, cream butter; add vanilla and salt. Gradually beat in sugar. Beat in enough of the coffee mixture to achieve spreading consistency. Frost the cake. **Yield:** 12 servings.

Vanilla Chip Cherry Cookies

Chopped maraschino cherries and vanilla chips make a great color and flavor combination in these sweets. They're a nice change from chocolate chip cookies.

—Margaret Wilson, Hemet, California

1	cup butter, softened
3/4	cup sugar
3/4	cup packed brown sugar
2	eggs
1/4	teaspoon almond extract
2-1/4	cups all-purpose flour
1	teaspoon baking soda
1/2	teaspoon salt
1	package (16 ounces) vanilla *or* white chips
1	jar (10 ounces) maraschino cherries, drained and chopped

1 In a large bowl, cream butter and sugars until light and fluffy. Add eggs, one at a time, beating well after each addition. Beat in almond extract. Combine the flour, baking soda and salt; gradually add to the creamed mixture and mix well. Stir in chips and cherries.

2 Drop by rounded tablespoonfuls 2 in. apart onto ungreased baking sheets. Bake at 350° for 10-12 minutes or until lightly browned. Remove to wire racks to cool. **Yield:** 4-1/2 dozen.

Honey Lemon Cookies

Grated lemon peel in the batter and on the icing of these soft, cake-like cookies gives them their fresh citrus flavor.

—Betty Thompson, La Porte, Texas

7	tablespoons butter, softened
1/2	cup sugar
1	egg
1-3/4	cups all-purpose flour
1	teaspoon baking powder
1/2	teaspoon salt
1/3	cup honey
1/4	cup plain yogurt
2	teaspoons grated lemon peel
1/2	teaspoon lemon extract

ICING:

1	cup confectioners' sugar
2	tablespoons lemon juice
2	teaspoons grated lemon peel

1 In a small bowl, cream butter and sugar. Beat in egg. Combine flour, baking powder and salt. Combine honey, yogurt, lemon peel and lemon extract. Add dry ingredients to creamed mixture alternately with honey mixture.

2 Drop by tablespoonfuls 2 in. apart onto greased baking sheets. Bake at 350° for 10-12 minutes or until golden brown. Remove to wire racks.

3 In a small bowl, combine the confectioners' sugar and lemon juice until smooth. Brush over the warm cookies; sprinkle with the lemon peel. **Yield:** about 3 dozen.

TIP . . . .
Save Your Citrus

Don't let lemons and limes go to waste. Squeeze out all of the juice. Grate the zest from the entire peel. Measure what you need for your recipe. Freeze extra juice in 1 tablespoon portions in ice cube trays. Store the extra zest in a resealable plastic bag in the freezer.

Cinnamon-Sugar Crisps

These sweet and spicy refrigerator cookies go great with a cup of coffee or a glass of milk. You won't be able to eat just one!

—Kim Marie Van Rheenen, Mendota, Illinois

3/4	cup butter, softened
1/3	cup sugar
1/3	cup packed brown sugar
1	egg
1	teaspoon vanilla extract
1-3/4	cups all-purpose flour
1	teaspoon ground cinnamon
1/4	teaspoon salt
2	tablespoons colored sprinkles

1 In a large bowl, cream butter and sugars until light and fluffy. Beat in egg and vanilla. Combine the flour, cinnamon and salt; gradually add to creamed mixture and mix well. Shape into a 12-in. roll; wrap in plastic wrap. Refrigerate for 2 hours or until firm.

2 Unwrap rolls of dough and cut into 1/2-in. slices. Place 2 in. apart on ungreased baking sheets. Decorate with sprinkles.

3 Bake at 350° for 10-12 minutes or until lightly browned. Remove to wire racks to cool. **Yield:** 3-1/2 dozen.

Chewy Almond Cookies

These old-fashioned cookies are often requested by my children and grandchildren. The unbaked cookie dough can be frozen, well wrapped, for up to 1 year. When ready to bake, remove from the freezer and let stand at room temperature for 15-30 minutes. Then just slice and bake.

—Betty Speth, Vincennes, Indiana

3	tablespoons butter
1	cup packed brown sugar
1	egg
1/4	teaspoon vanilla extract
1/4	teaspoon almond extract
1-1/2	cups all-purpose flour
1/4	teaspoon baking soda
1/4	teaspoon ground cinnamon
1/2	cup sliced almonds

1 In a large bowl, beat the butter and brown sugar until crumbly. Beat in the egg and extracts. Combine the flour, baking soda and cinnamon; gradually add to the butter mixture and mix well. Shape into two 6-in. rolls; wrap each roll in plastic wrap. Refrigerate overnight.

2 Unwrap; cut into 1/4-in. slices. Place 2 in. apart onto greased baking sheets. Sprinkle with almonds.

3 Bake at 350° for 7-10 minutes or until lightly browned. Cool for 2-3 minutes before removing to wire racks. **Yield:** 4-1/2 dozen.

Peanut Butter Brownie Cups

Because these treats are made in muffin cups, they're especially convenient to take along on picnics. The peanut butter and chocolate combination can't be beat.

—Joyce Gibson, Rhinelander, Wisconsin

1/2	cup peanut butter
1/4	cup packed brown sugar
2	tablespoons plus 1-1/2 cups all-purpose flour, *divided*
3	squares (1 ounce *each*) unsweetened chocolate
1/2	cup butter, cubed
3	eggs
1-1/2	cups sugar
2	tablespoons water
1	teaspoon vanilla extract
1	teaspoon baking powder

1 In a small bowl, beat the peanut butter, brown sugar and 2 tablespoons flour until blended; set aside.

2 In a microwave-safe bowl, melt the chocolate and butter; stir until smooth. Cool slightly. In a large bowl, beat the eggs, sugar and water; stir in chocolate mixture and vanilla. Combine baking powder and remaining flour; gradually add to chocolate mixture.

3 Fill paper-lined muffin cups one-fourth full. Top each with about 1 teaspoon of peanut butter mixture. Spoon remaining batter over the top. Bake at 350° for 13-15 minutes or until centers are set (do not overbake). Cool for 5 minutes before removing from pans to wire racks. **Yield:** 2 dozen.

EDITOR'S NOTE: Reduced-fat or generic brands of peanut butter are not recommended for this recipe.

TIP
Measuring Peanut Butter

Before putting peanut butter in a measuring cup, lightly coat the inside with cooking spray. The peanut butter will simply slide right out without scraping.

Vanilla Wafer Cookies

These cookies are chewy and irresistible. They're an inexpensive way to round out a meal.

—Edith MacBeath, Gaines, Pennsylvania

- 1/2 cup butter, softened
- 1 cup sugar
- 1 egg
- 1 tablespoon vanilla extract
- 1-1/3 cups all-purpose flour
- 3/4 teaspoon baking powder
- 1/4 teaspoon salt

1 In a large bowl, cream butter and sugar until light and fluffy. Beat in egg and vanilla. Combine dry ingredients; add to creamed mixture and mix well.

2 Drop by teaspoonfuls 2 in. apart onto ungreased baking sheets. Bake at 350° for 12-15 minutes or until edges are golden brown. Remove to wire racks to cool. **Yield:** about 3-1/2 dozen.

Soft Chewy Caramels

My first experience with large-scale cooking was helping my mother make these sweet candies for Christmas. We'd make eight to 12 batches a year!

—Robert Sprenkle, Hurst, Texas

- 1 tablespoon plus 1 cup butter, *divided*
- 2-1/4 cups packed brown sugar
- 1 can (14 ounces) sweetened condensed milk
- 1 cup dark corn syrup

1 Line a 15-in. x 10-in. x 1-in. baking pan with foil; grease the foil with 1 tablespoon butter. In a heavy saucepan over medium heat, melt remaining butter. Add brown sugar, milk and corn syrup. Cook and stir until candy thermometer reads 250° (hard-ball stage). Pour into prepared pan (do not scrape saucepan). Cool completely before cutting **Yield:** about 2-1/2 pounds.

EDITOR'S NOTE: We recommend that you test your candy thermometer before each use by bringing water to a boil; the thermometer should read 212°. Adjust your recipe temperature up or down based on your test.

Banana Custard Pudding

This tasty banana pudding is easy to stir up anytime. It's a cool, creamy ending to any meal, especially in summer.

—Hazel Fritchie, Palestine, Illinois

- 1/2 cup sugar
- 1 tablespoon cornstarch
- 1/8 teaspoon salt
- 1-1/2 cups milk
- 3 egg yolks, lightly beaten
- 1 teaspoon vanilla extract
- 1 medium firm banana, sliced

Fresh mint, optional

1 In a small saucepan, combine sugar, cornstarch and salt. Stir in milk until smooth. Cook and stir over medium-high heat until thickened and bubbly. Reduce heat to low; cook and stir 2 minutes longer. Remove from the heat. Stir a small amount of hot filling into the egg yolks; return all to the pan, stirring constantly. Bring to a gentle boil; cook and stir for 2 minutes. Remove from the heat; gently stir in the vanilla.

2 Cover and chill for 1 hour. Just before serving, fold in the banana slices. Garnish with mint if desired. **Yield:** 4 servings.

Chewy Fudge Drop Cookies

Chocolate lovers won't be able to eat just one of these chewy treats. The delectable fudge drops are loaded with chocolate flavor and attractively topped with a sprinkling of confectioners' sugar.

—Taste of Home Test Kitchen

1	cup (6 ounces) semisweet chocolate chips, *divided*
3	tablespoons vegetable oil
1	cup packed brown sugar
3	egg whites
2	tablespoons plus 1-1/2 teaspoons light corn syrup
1	tablespoon water
2-1/2	teaspoons vanilla extract
1-3/4	cups all-purpose flour
2/3	cup plus 1 tablespoon confectioners' sugar, *divided*
1/3	cup baking cocoa
2-1/4	teaspoons baking powder
1/8	teaspoon salt

1 In a microwave, melt 3/4 cup chocolate chips and oil; stir until smooth. Pour into a large bowl; cool for 5 minutes.

2 Stir in brown sugar. Add egg whites, corn syrup, water and vanilla until smooth. Combine the flour, 2/3 cup confectioners' sugar, cocoa, baking powder and salt; gradually add to chocolate mixture until combined. Stir in the remaining chocolate chips (dough will be very stiff).

3 Drop by tablespoonfuls 2 in. apart onto baking sheets coated with cooking spray. Bake at 350° for 8-10 minutes or until puffed and set. Cool for 2 minutes before removing to wire racks. Sprinkle cooled cookies with remaining confectioners' sugar. **Yield:** 4 dozen.

Glazed Lemon Cake

My mother baked this light, moist treat when I was a child. I loved it as much then as my children do now. Boxed cake and pudding mixes make this delightful dessert simple.

—Missy Andrews, Rice, Washington

- 1 package (18-1/4 ounces) white cake mix
- 1 package (3.4 ounces) instant lemon pudding mix
- 3/4 cup vegetable oil
- 3 eggs
- 1 cup lemon-lime soda
- 1 cup confectioners' sugar
- 2 tablespoons lemon juice

1 In a large bowl, combine the cake mix, pudding mix, oil and eggs; beat on low speed or 30 seconds. Beat on medium for 2 minutes. Gradually beat in soda just until blended.

2 Pour into a greased 13-in. x 9-in. x 2-in. baking dish. Bake at 350° for 40-45 minutes or until a toothpick comes out clean.

3 In a small bowl, combine the confectioners' sugar and lemon juice until smooth; carefully spread over warm cake. Cool on a wire rack. **Yield:** 12 servings.

Lime Sherbet

This frozen treat is just as refreshing when it's made with orange or raspberry gelatin. My family really enjoys it in the summer.

—Julie Benkenstein, Arcola, Indiana

- 1 package (3 ounces) lime gelatin or flavor of your choice
- 1 cup sugar
- 1 cup boiling water
- 2 tablespoons lemon juice
- 1-1/2 teaspoons grated lemon peel
- 4 cups cold milk

1 In a large bowl, dissolve the gelatin and sugar in boiling water. Add lemon juice and peel. Whisk in milk. Pour into an ungreased 9-in. square pan. Cover and freeze for 2 hours.

2 Transfer to a large bowl; beat for 2 minutes. Return to pan. Cover and freeze for 1 hour; stir.

3 Freeze 1 hour longer or until firm. Let stand for 10 minutes before serving. **Yield:** 8 servings.

Ice Cream Tortilla Cups

It takes just minutes to make these individual ice cream cups. I make this special treat when my local supermarket has a good sale on ice cream.

—Kelly Olson, Moab, Utah

- 1/4 cup butter, melted
- 6 flour tortillas (6 inches), warmed
- 6 tablespoons sugar
- 1/2 teaspoon ground cinnamon

Strawberry ice cream or flavor of your choice

1 Brush butter on one side of each tortilla. Combine the sugar and cinnamon; sprinkle evenly over tortillas. Press each tortilla, sugar side up, into a greased muffin cup.

2 Bake at 400° for 6-8 minutes or until lightly browned. Cool for 5 minutes. Remove tortilla cups from pan, gently separating edges. Place a scoop of ice cream in each tortilla. **Yield:** 6 servings.

Gingersnap Dip

This easy-to-fix dip is a fun way to dress up a package of gingersnaps. It's great for fall gatherings and makes a sweet snack for the holidays.

—Tessie Hughes, Marion, Virginia

- 1 package (8 ounces) cream cheese, softened
- 1 cup confectioners' sugar
- 2 teaspoons pumpkin pie spice
- 1 carton (8 ounces) frozen whipped topping, thawed
- 1 package (16 ounces) gingersnaps

1 In a small bowl, beat the cream cheese, confectioners' sugar and pumpkin pie spice until fluffy. Beat in whipped topping until blended. Refrigerate until serving. Serve with gingersnaps. **Yield:** 3 cups.

Cola Floats

These thick, frosty floats add fun to any casual meal. Try substituting other soda-ice cream blends for the floats, such as root beer and caramel-swirl vanilla.

—Taste of Home Test Kitchen

- 4 cups cherry cola, chilled
- 1 teaspoon vanilla extract
- 8 scoops fudge ripple ice cream
Whipped cream in a can, optional
- 4 maraschino cherries

1 In a pitcher, combine cola and vanilla. Place two scoops of ice cream in each of four chilled glasses. Pour cola over ice cream; top with whipped cream if desired and cherries. **Yield:** 4 servings.

Fruity Tapioca

Folks who like tapioca will enjoy this fruity variation. Convenient canned peaches and mandarin oranges give refreshing flavor to this economical dessert.

—Louise Martin, Mohnton, Pennsylvania

    4   cups water
    1   cup sugar
  1/3   cup quick-cooking tapioca
    1   can (6 ounces) frozen orange juice concentrate, thawed
    1   can (29 ounces) sliced peaches, drained and diced
    1   can (11 ounces) mandarin oranges, drained

1 In a large saucepan, combine the water, sugar and tapioca; let stand for 5 minutes. Bring to a full rolling boil. Remove from the heat; stir in orange juice concentrate. Cool for 20 minutes. Stir in the peaches and oranges. Transfer to a serving bowl. Cover and refrigerate until serving. **Yield:** 10 servings.

Pineapple Sour Cream Pie

A luscious alternative to lemon meringue pie, this dessert is one of our favorites. The meringue is so creamy and the pineapple filling so refreshing that your family will request it again and again.

—P. Lauren Fay-Neri, Syracuse, New York

  1/2   cup sugar
    2   tablespoons all-purpose flour
    1   can (20 ounces) crushed pineapple, undrained
    1   cup (8 ounces) sour cream
    3   egg yolks, lightly beaten
    1   pastry shell (9 inches), baked

MERINGUE:
    3   egg whites
  1/2   teaspoon vanilla extract
  1/4   teaspoon cream of tartar
    6   tablespoons sugar

1 In a large saucepan, combine the sugar and flour. Stir in the pineapple and sour cream until combined. Cook and stir over medium-high heat until thickened and bubbly. Reduce heat; cook and stir 2 minutes longer.

2 Remove from the heat. Stir a small amount of hot filling into egg yolks; return all to the pan, stirring constantly. Bring to a gentle boil; cook and stir 2 minutes longer. Remove from the heat. Pour into pastry shell.

3 In a small bowl, beat the egg whites, vanilla and cream of tartar on medium speed until soft peaks form. Gradually beat in sugar, 1 tablespoon at a time, on high until stiff, glossy peaks form and sugar is dissolved. Spread evenly over hot filling, sealing edges to crust.

4 Bake at 350° for 15-18 minutes or until meringue is golden brown. Cool on a wire rack for 1 hour. Refrigerate for at least 3 hours before serving. Refrigerate leftovers. **Yield:** 8 servings.

Crispy Caramel Treats

Kids love these triple-decker treats during the holidays—or any time at all. I always make several batches because my neighbors can't seem to get enough of them.

—Marlis Asprey, West Sacto, California

1/2	cup plus 10 tablespoons butter, *divided*
8	cups miniature marshmallows, *divided*
8	cups crisp rice cereal, *divided*
1	package (14 ounces) caramels
1	can (14 ounces) sweetened condensed milk

1 In a large saucepan, melt 1/4 cup butter and 4 cups marshmallows; stir until smooth. Stir in 4 cups cereal. Pat into a greased 13-in. x 9-in. x 2-in. pan; set aside.

2 For caramel filling, place the caramels and 10 tablespoons butter in another saucepan; cook and stir over low heat until melted. Stir in the milk until smooth. Cool for 10 minutes; pour over cereal layer. Refrigerate for about 30 minutes or until firm.

3 In a large saucepan, melt the remaining butter and marshmallows. Stir in remaining cereal. Spread over caramel layer. Cover and refrigerate for 30 minutes or until firm. Cut into bars. Store in the refrigerator. **Yield:** 2-1/2 dozen.

EDITOR'S NOTE: This recipe was tested with Hershey caramels.

Chocolate Chip Cake

A delightful chocolate and cinnamon filling is sandwiched between tender white cake layers in this recipe. It's the perfect size for a smaller group.

—Sue Reichenbach, Langhorne, Pennsylvania

1/2	cup butter, softened
1-1/2	cups sugar, *divided*
2	eggs
1	teaspoon vanilla extract
2	cups all-purpose flour
1	teaspoon baking powder
1/2	teaspoon baking soda
1	cup (8 ounces) sour cream
3/4	cup semisweet chocolate chips
1	teaspoon ground cinnamon

1 In a large bowl, cream butter and 1 cup sugar until light and fluffy. Add eggs, one at a time, beating well after each addition. Beat in vanilla. Combine the flour, baking powder and baking soda; add to the creamed mixture alternately with sour cream, beating well after each addition.

2 Spread half of the batter into a greased 9-in. square baking pan. Sprinkle with the chocolate chips. Combine cinnamon and remaining sugar; sprinkle over chips. Spread with remaining batter.

3 Bake at 350° for 45-50 minutes or until a toothpick inserted near the center comes out clean. Cool on a wire rack. **Yield:** 8 servings.

Strawberry Graham Dessert

My mother passed the recipe for this luscious dessert on to me...and my family has enjoyed it for years. These days, I often make this for my granddaughter.

—Audrey Huckell, Wabigoon, Ontario

- 1 cup graham cracker crumbs (about 16 squares)
- 2 tablespoons butter, melted
- 1 package (3 ounces) strawberry gelatin
- 1 cup boiling water
- 1 package (16 ounces) frozen sweetened sliced strawberries, thawed
- 1 tablespoon lemon juice
- 4 ounces cream cheese, softened
- 1/2 cup confectioners' sugar
- 1 teaspoon vanilla extract

Dash salt

- 1 cup heavy whipping cream, whipped

Fresh strawberries and mint, optional

1 In a small bowl, combine cracker crumbs and butter; set aside 1 tablespoon for topping. Press the remaining crumb mixture onto the bottom of a greased 8-in. square baking dish. Bake at 325° for 10-14 minutes or until golden brown. Cool on a wire rack.

2 In a large bowl, dissolve gelatin in boiling water; stir in strawberries and lemon juice. Refrigerate until partially set, about 1-1/2 hours.

3 In a small mixing bowl, beat the cream cheese, sugar, vanilla and salt until smooth. Fold in whipped cream. Spread half over cooled crust. Cover and refrigerate remaining cream mixture.

4 Pour gelatin mixture over filling; refrigerate until firm. Top with remaining cream mixture. Sprinkle with reserved crumb mixture. Refrigerate overnight. Garnish with fresh berries and mint if desired. **Yield:** 9 servings.

Alphabetical Index

Refer to this index for a complete alphabetical listing of all recipes in this book.

General Index

This handy index lists every recipe by food category, major ingredient and/or cooking method, so you can easily locate recipes to suit your needs.

NUTS
Bulgur with Pine Nuts, 168
Chewy Almond Cookies, 239
Chocolate Ribbon Bars, 236
Walnut Romaine Salad, 206

OATS
Chocolate Oatmeal Cake, 237
Honey-Oat Casserole Bread, 219
Oatmeal Raisin Bars, 232
Oatmeal Wheat Bread, 218
Peanut Butter Banana Oatmeal, 14
Toasted Granola, 14

ONIONS
Baked Onion Rings, 191
Beans 'n' Caramelized Onions, 176
Cauliflower Puree with Onions, 172
Flavorful Onion Burgers, 42
Fried Apples and Onions, 162
Onion Barley Casserole, 164
Onion Crescent Rolls, 220
Onion French Bread, 215
Onion Soup with Sausage, 200
Soft Onion Breadsticks, 219

ORANGE
Breaded Chicken with Orange Sauce, 71
Fluffy Orange Gelatin Pie, 230
Orange Chicken, 73
Orange French Toast, 123
Orange Ginger Scones, 216
Orange-Mustard Grilled Chicken, 78
Orange Slush, 13
Orange Sponge Cake Roll, 234
Savory Orange Dressing, 178
Sunny Carrot Sticks, 180
Yogurt Breakfast Drink, 18

OVEN ENTREES (also see Casseroles; Meat Pies; Pizzas)
Beef and Ground Beef
Baked Salisbury Steak, 28
Double Meat Loaf, 142
Flavorful Meat Loaf, 46
Garlic Swiss Steak, 33
Green Pepper Meat Loaf, 128
Herbed Sirloin Tip, 34
Mom's Meatballs, 103
Peppery Roast Beef, 45
Pizza Meat Loaf Cups, 147
Savory Beef Stew, 35
Steak over Potatoes, 46
Swiss Pot Roast, 41
Traditional Meat Loaf, 45
Veggie Beef Bundles, 47
Chicken
Chili Chicken 'n' Rice, 73
Country Roasted Chicken, 68
Creamy Baked Chicken, 83
Garlic Clove Chicken, 82
Honey Barbecued Chicken, 84

Italian Chicken Roll-Ups, 145
Orange Chicken, 73
Oregano-Lemon Chicken, 69
Oven-Fried Chicken, 78
Roasted Chicken, 120
Wild Rice Mushroom Chicken, 155
Fish
Cajun-Style Catfish, 87
Dijon-Crusted Fish, 90
Easy Fish Fillets, 88
Fish Fillets Italiano, 93
Garden Fish Packets, 99
Lemony Salmon Patties, 94
Oven-Fried Fish Nuggets, 94
Meatless
Black Bean Nacho Bake, 89
Pork and Ham
Double Meat Loaf, 142
Ham with Cherry Sauce, 108
Hearty Ham Loaves, 158
Herbed Pork Roast, 138
Pineapple Ham Loaf, 61
Plum-Glazed Country Ribs, 59
Pork and Cabbage Rolls, 62
Pork with Apricot Sauce, 127
Savory Pork Roast, 131
Turkey
Cranberry Turkey Loaf, 80
Garlic Rosemary Turkey, 74
Teriyaki Turkey Breast, 115
Turkey Enchiladas, 69

PANCAKES
Sausage Pancakes, 13
Zucchini Pancakes, 22

PASTA & NOODLES
Amish Chicken Corn Soup, 210
Asian Oven Omelet, 16
Bean Counter Chowder, 211
Cabbage Chicken Salad, 205
Cajun Macaroni, 42
Chicken and Bows, 150
Chicken Noodle Soup, 194
Chicken Tetrazzini, 156
Chili Manicotti, 100
Chili Spaghetti, 35
Classic Macaroni Salad, 195
Con Queso Spirals, 183
Easy Chicken and Noodles, 80
Easy Lasagna, 107
Fettuccine with Black Bean Sauce, 91
Garden-Fresh Spaghetti, 132
Garlic Angel Hair Pasta, 188
Garlic Salmon Linguine, 89
Hamburger Hot Dish, 37
Hamburger Stroganoff, 159
Hay and Straw, 56
Italian Sausage Spaghetti, 111
Italian Vegetable Soup, 212
Lemon Dill Couscous, 185
Linguine in Clam Sauce, 96
Meat Sauce for Pasta, 148

Meatball Lasagna, 103
Meatball Minestrone, 103
Minestrone Macaroni, 206
Noodle Rice Pilaf, 191
Noodles Florentine, 171
Orzo with Zucchini and Feta, 171
Parmesan Bow Ties, 190
Pasta Primavera, 95
Penne with Cannellini Beans, 168
Pepper Steak Fettuccine, 26
Pizza Pasta Casserole, 159
Pork Noodle Casserole, 138
Pork Pasta Bake, 55
Pretty Ham Primavera, 108
Ranch Turkey Pasta Dinner, 81
Ravioli Primavera, 90
Sausage Broccoli Manicotti, 132
Sausage Macaroni Bake, 57
Sausage Vermicelli, 66
Spaghetti Casserole, 141
Supreme Spaghetti Salad, 202
Szechuan Chicken Noodle Toss, 79
Taco-Filled Pasta Shells, 155
Three-Cheese Kielbasa Bake, 144
Three-Meat Sauce, 106
Tomato Spinach Spirals, 181
Tuna Mushroom Casserole, 93
Tuna Pasta Salad, 210
Turkey Macaroni Bake, 115
Turkey Tetrazzini, 82

PEACHES
Barbecued Ham 'n' Peaches, 59
Frosty Peach Pie Supreme, 234

PEANUT BUTTER
Chewy Peanut Butter Bars, 231
Peanut Butter Banana Oatmeal, 14
Peanut Butter Brownie Cups, 240

PEARS
Blueberry Pear Cobbler, 229
Pear Cranberry Sauce, 165
Pear Gingerbread Cake, 235

PEAS
Hay and Straw, 56
Pleasing Peas and Asparagus, 192
Snappy Pea Pods, 175

PEPPERS
Green Pepper Meat Loaf, 128
Pepper Steak Fettuccine, 26
Pepper Steak Sandwiches, 116

PIES
Creamy Strawberry Pie, 233
Fluffy Orange Gelatin Pie, 230
Frosty Peach Pie Supreme, 234
Hoosier Cream Pie, 228
Pineapple Sour Cream Pie, 245
Sweet Potato Custard Pie, 225

PINEAPPLE
Frosty Pineapple Salad, 205
Pineapple Beef Stir-Fry, 32